MOST
DANGEROUS
WOMEN

ANNE WILTSHER

■ **Anne Wiltsher** is a freelance writer and sub-editor. She has written for the *Guardian*, the *Observer* and for a wide variety of magazines. This is her first book. She is 34 and lives in London.

Cover design by Marion Dalley.

PANDORA PRESS HISTORY

MOST
DANGEROUS
WOMEN

FEMINIST PEACE CAMPAIGNERS OF THE GREAT WAR

ANNE WILTSHER

PANDORA

LONDON, BOSTON AND HENLEY

First published in 1985
by Pandora Press plc
(Routledge & Kegan Paul plc)
14 Leicester Square, London WC2H 7PH, England

9 Park Street, Boston, Mass. 02108, USA and

Broadway House, Newtown Road,
Henley on Thames, Oxon RG9 1EN, England

Set in Sabon
by Columns of Reading
and printed in Great Britain
by The Guernsey Press Co. Ltd
Guernsey, Channel Islands

Library of Congress Cataloging in Publication Data

Wiltsher, Anne.
Most dangerous women.
Bibliography: p.
Includes index.
1. World War, 1914–1918 – Women. 2. Pacifists.
3. World War, 1939–1945 – Protest movements.
4. Women and peace. I. Title.
D639.W7W55 1985   940.3'162   85–9522

ISBN 0–86358–010–6

To Greenham women everywhere

CONTENTS

ILLUSTRATIONS

America. Loved by many, she literally made others more
peaceful in her presence. However, Carrie Chapman Catt
called her 'slippery Jane' and Rosika Schwimmer said Hull
House reminded her of her convent school. p. 156

8 At the 1919 Zurich Congress: from left to right: Anita
Augspurg, Charlotte Despard, Lida Gustava Heymann, Rosa
Genoni, Frau Kulka, Alice Hamilton. 'Only in freedom is
permanent peace possible,' Catherine Marshall told the
Congress, and they adopted the name Women's International
League for Peace and Freedom. By a majority of one, they
also voted to support only peaceful methods of change.
p. 203

PREFACE

THE IDEA for this book came when I was commissioned to write an article for a women's magazine on 'women in the peace movement'. During the research someone gave me a leaflet outlining the history of a group called the Women's International League for Peace and Freedom. My article was never published but I became fascinated with the origins of WILPF, which was founded in 1915. Greenham Common Women's Peace Camp had just been set up and I was excited to learn that this was not the first time the feminist and peace movements had been linked so closely.

Visiting the Fawcett Library of women's history, I realised that it wasn't just feminist peace campaigns about which I was abysmally ignorant but also how my own sex had fought for its freedom in the past. I learnt that the Votes for Women campaign was, in fact, made up of not just suffra*gettes* but suffra*gists*. The first term was a derogatory nickname coined by the *Daily Mail* in 1906. The militant section of the movement led by Emmeline Pankhurst and her daughter Christabel, who formed the Women's Social and Political Union, adopted it enthusiastically. A suffra*gist*, on the other hand, meant someone who did not believe in illegal tactics and opposed all forms of violence to get the vote. They probably belonged to the National Union of Women's Suffrage Societies, which was the largest non-militant group, led by Millicent Garrett Fawcett. Another eye-opening discovery was that the women's suffrage movement had been international. Women weren't just demanding to be politically represented in Britain but in Germany, Holland, France, Sweden, Hungary, Russia, America and so on. The International Woman Suffrage Alliance had member sections in twenty-six countries. All this is elementary feminist history – not one word of which I had been taught at my all girls' school.

I must stress that this book is not the official history of the Women's International League for Peace and Freedom; that is very ably provided by Margaret Tims and Gertrude Bussey in *Pioneers for Peace*. Rather, it makes a start – and it is only a start – at assessing how the women's suffrage movement responded to the First World War, concentrating on those feminists who worked for peace. The reader should know, too, that the meaning of the word 'pacifist' has changed over the past seventy years. Today it tends to mean someone who believes it to be wrong to kill anyone, under any circumstances, even if under threat of death oneself. In 1914, it was used to include anyone who doubted the war and did not wish to 'fight on until the last man'. It's with this latter, broader meaning that I have used the word, for many of the suffragists and suffragettes who opposed the First World War were not absolute pacifists.

People always ask what they can learn from history. I personally have learnt two things from writing this book. The first is that war cannot be conducted rationally and the second is not to trust too much in 'progress'. In 1912, Jane Addams, an American suffragist, believed that men would refuse to fight if they were ever asked again. Society was much more civilised, she reasoned, nationalities mixed together in immigrant communities, poverty was being eliminated through the new social conscience – besides, there hadn't been a war for over forty years. Politicians were arguing that this forty-year peace was a result of the 'balance of power' of armaments in Europe. Echoes from today sound down the ages.

Newspapers appear to have changed very little. Feminism is bad enough but when the silly women want peace as well, it's anathema. One imagines that tabloid editors, should they ever visit Room 101, would scream, 'Not a woman for peace, no no *anything* but that!' British suffragist Helena Swanwick once said that propaganda was the essence of war. And after travelling around Europe in 1915, Jane Addams felt that the newspapers in all countries played such a key role in sustaining narrow nationalism that she believed 'something would have to be done' about their future management and ethos. In the meantime, and until 'Argie' and 'Hun' are replaced by something more grown-up, feminist peace campaigners should never expect favourable press coverage.

On this theme of progress, whilst sitting at a conference of European feminists, struggling with the French translation through my earphones, I wondered whether Hungarian suffragist Rosika Schwimmer, who had so passionately wanted a federated Europe (and world), would consider that the world had progressed, were her spirit to return and survey the scene. Well, she might say, it's a pity about the East-West divide and the prospect of nuclear winter but at least there's not much likelihood of a war with Germany. She might not like the food mountains and the expense accounts but the EEC countries were at least working together. And feminists from half of Europe (the other half being behind the Iron Curtain) were still meeting, talking and planning, just like the old international suffrage movement. I could see her in Strasbourg, making a speech on behalf of the women's caucus in the European Parliament. This is when knowing feminist history is so wonderful, it makes us feel less lonely and keeps us going.

Had I been alive in 1914, like the women in this book, I am sure I would have been a pacifist in the First World War. Like many of them, I would probably have renounced my beliefs in 1939 because of the horrors of fascism. I like to think that were *they* alive *today*, they would be visiting Greenham Common to save what was fought for in their time from destruction by nuclear holocaust.

ACKNOWLEDGMENTS

MANY PEOPLE have helped me with this book but there are two in particular whom I must thank; without them the book would have taken a great deal longer to complete and would have been a lot less fun to write. The first is Edith Wynner, who used to work as Rosika Schwimmer's assistant and is now consultant to the Schwimmer/Lloyd papers in New York: when I arrived in that city in February 1983 and accidentally came across this huge collection (an incorrect reference book stated there were 'six boxes'), she took me under her wing, gave me copious advice, suggested books for background reading, showed me her research notes (hopefully her biography of Rosika Schwimmer will be out soon), fed me delicious noodle soup and generally talked all the while about Schwimmer's life and times. Six months later she sent a further package of xeroxed material to my London address. It's obvious that her help was invaluable.

The second person I must especially thank is David Doughan, assistant librarian at the Fawcett Library in London. His great enthusiasm and wealth of knowledge about the books in this wonderful library, and about feminist history in general, particularly helped and inspired me in the early days.

Other people I must thank are Jill Liddington, for passing on information on sources and for reading and commenting on the manuscript – this was especially useful after the first six chapters, when I hit a low ebb and despaired of ever finishing; Jo Vellacott, for telling me about Catherine Marshall and for commenting on my chapter on the NUWSS split; Jo Eglin for helping with sources and reading (along with David Doughan) an awfully tatty first draft; Sybil Oldfield for her information on Mary Sheepshanks and others; Mrs Edwards for her help with German translation and research; Margot Miller and Margaret Tims of the Women's International League for Peace and Freedom and Lesley Merryfinch for first telling me about the existence of the above organisation and giving me an inkling that the modern women's peace movement had a history. Photographs are courtesy of WILPF, Carlisle Record Office and the Schwimmer/Lloyd Collection. I must thank Pippa Brewster at Pandora Press for taking a chance on a first time author and giving me the opportunity to write the book. Finally I cannot forget Pete, who has lived with this project for as long as I have – and my cat, who in the latter days provided welcome breaks from the interminable task of footnote writing, by periodically sitting on the typewriter.

INTRODUCTION

THE WORLD has heard plenty about what women did for the war effort during the traumatic four years of the First World War. Everyone knows about the suffragettes who handed out white feathers; about Lloyd George's munition workers and the 'Land Girls', who dug fields to feed the home front and shocked rural Britain by wearing breeches. Mrs Pankhurst and her daughter Christabel, then the scourge of respectable society, urged their followers to abandon arson and the struggle for political freedom and help save the Empire instead. As a result, they were accepted into the British establishment. These are some of the most memorable incidents and resilient images of the Edwardian era.

However, that's not the whole story. Half the leading women in the British suffrage movement *opposed* the war. They thought the death of thousands of young men was insane. Despairing at the slaughter, they linked up with other women in the international suffrage movement from all over Europe and America and tried to push the men in power towards a negotiated peace.

By November 1915, just one year into the war, they had organised themselves into peace groups in eleven European countries, seven of which were at war. Women in Austria, Belgium, Britain, Germany, Italy, France and Hungary, where war propaganda and national sentiment were fierce, pressed their governments to stop fighting. They were vilified by the press and sometimes imprisoned for their pains. In America, which remained neutral until 1917, suffragists urged President Wilson to act as a mediator between the warring nations across the Atlantic. In Scandinavia, which managed to stay out of the entire war, they also put pressure on their governments to mediate.

In all the countries, these women had a vision. Very few of them had the vote – that tool of democracy which so many of us take for granted today. They wanted to have a voice in public affairs, for society to be governed by consent, for everyone to have a say. And if that seemed such a good idea within a nation, then why not between nations too? Wasn't it time that disputes between countries were settled in an international forum, with women playing an equal part, they asked? They wanted to link together:

> . . . the Women's Movement and the Pacifist Movement. The first has been recognised as one of the greatest of world movements towards liberation; it is time the second should be recognised as another. Only free women can build up the peace which is to be, themselves understanding the eternal strife engendered by domination, and, by their teaching, liberating the minds of their sons for active, creative, beneficient co-operation.[1]

Helena Swanwick, Margaret Ashton, Catherine Marshall, M· ude Royden, Kathleen Courtney and Chrystal Macmillan were some of the British women who opposed the war. They were all ex-executive members of the National Union of Women's Suffrage Societies, led by Millicent Garrett Fawcett. It was the largest non-militant suffrage organisation in the country, with 600 societies and 100,000 affiliated suffragists before the war – and until August 4th, 1914, growing rapidly with 800 new members a month.

They were all strong, able women as their personal histories testify. Helena Swanwick was someone who wrote superb descriptive prose about others but was seldom its subject. Half Dane and half English, she had been born in Bavaria, the daughter of Herr Oswald Sickert, a musician and artist. After an unhappy childhood she became a writer and journalist for the *Manchester Guardian*. In 1914, she was 50 years old. Here is a rare pen portrait of her written just after the war:

> She is slender and fair, with a delightful boyish mop of pale gold hair which curls up at the ends, and sky blue eyes. She is a person of quite extraordinary intellectual power . . . [who] finds it extremely difficult to obey the scriptural

injunction to 'suffer fools gladly'. She is apt to take strong prejudices against people, which is annoying to herself, since it is inconsistent with her own standard of intellect and the conduct she demands of other people . . . but . . . I should not be surprised to discover that in her prejudices she is generally right. . . .

She is very delicate and yet contrives to do the work of three people . . . she staked everything except her self-respect when she took a public stand against the ignorant hatreds of the war. She is full of artistic appreciation, hates cant and humbug, and is devoted to practical things and persons. She is a very consistent and intrepid feminist. . . .'[2]

Margaret Ashton was another of Mrs Fawcett's fierce rebels. She too was middle-aged by the time the war came, having been Manchester's first woman councillor, and Chair of Manchester Suffrage Society from 1906, the year after Christabel Pankhurst first spat on a policeman outside a Liberal Party public meeting and 'militancy' was born. Ashton remained with the constitutionalists, nicknamed the 'Polites' by their militant sisters, only to go on and attract just as much, if not more, abuse and hostility by her public pacifist stand against the war than any pro-war suffragette had ever suffered by demanding votes for women. In 1926, on her 70th birthday, when she was partially blind – and despite her immense service to the city – Manchester city art gallery refused to hang her portrait because of her past pacifist activities.

Home Office files have her on record as early in the war as July 1915, for urging 'the movement of Socialism for the immediate cessation of hostilities', and she was still being investigated by Special Branch three years later, when she was telling people that if they bought War Bonds, they would be subsidising the death of yet more men.

One of nine children, the daughter of a well-to-do cotton manufacturer (who refused to let her into the family business because she was a girl), Margaret Ashton's first ambition was to train as a nurse, a profession which Florence Nightingale had just made respectable, but she soon became more and more absorbed in public affairs. 'Devastatingly honest', 'abrupt in manner' and 'often giving offence without meaning to', she could never be very bothered to play the traditional female role of putting on an act to please men. 'I hate dress in every form,'

she once confessed to a friend, 'and manage to get through
sufficiently to please my people with as little worry to myself as
I can.'[3]

Before the war, Catherine Marshall was one of the most
successful suffragists in winning politicians over to her point of
view. Now 34, she had spent her twenties campaigning for the
vote, first in Cumbria, then in London. Up until 1915, she was
Parliamentary Secretary of the NUWSS; David Lloyd George,
Chancellor of the Exchequer since 1908, and Sir Edward Grey,
Foreign Secretary, were just two of the leading politicians with
whom she was in contact. At that time Herbert Henry Asquith
was Prime Minister and the Liberals had been in power from
1906, since when they had embarked on an unparalleled
programme of social reform. Marshall was also in charge of the
Election Fighting Fund, the most active section of the NUWSS,
which didn't just collect money but was responsible for
galvinising trade union support for women's suffrage and
building up local organisations to fight for Labour candidates
in by-elections. Support for women's suffrage had not been
easily won from labour representatives but Labour was the
only party to make such a promise.

From an intellectual family, who had been life-long supporters of the Liberal Party, Marshall's whole life was suffrage
politics. Her father was a retired housemaster from the boy's
public school, Harrow. Her mother, Caroline, an extrovert
character, was an active suffragist too, and their large house
'Hawes End', built in an idyllic spot on the edge of
Derwentwater in the Lake District, often acted as a sanctuary
for exhausted political activists. Unusually tall, Marshall's
friends remembered that she always looked smart and had a
penchant for blue velvet dresses.[4]

Maude Royden was the daughter of a Conservative MP for
Liverpool who had 'shipping interests'. Disabled from birth,
she had studied at Oxford, where women's collegs were opened
for the first time in the late nineteenth century. She joined the
NUWSS in 1908, when she was 32, and, like Helena
Swanwick, had a spell editing the Union's journal, *The
Common Cause*. A devout Christian, she was not normally
permitted to preach from an Anglican pulpit because of her sex
but she managed to become assistant preacher at the City
Temple in London in 1917, where she proceeded to give highly
controversial 'political' sermons on the evils of war. Her

magnetic public speaking was renowned.[5]

Kathleen Courtney was another one who had managed to 'kick over the traces' of family custom and code. In her case, father was an army man, who fought in the Zulu War. After 1914, at the age of 37, Courtney spent most of her life working for various organisations which opposed nationalism and imperialism, with the aim of developing a co-operative world community. Catherine Marshall laid much of the 'progressive work' of the NUWSS in the few years before the war at Courtney's feet, but later seemed to regret that Courtney was not more interested in matters of political philosophy. In later years, she was well known for her clear-headed ability to cut through verbiage to the main point at issue, but, as we shall see, to non-Anglo-Saxons she sometimes seemed a little cool. In looks, she was small, slight and dark, with tiny facial features.[6]

Chrystal Macmillan, as we shall see later, played a particularly significant role in the women's peace movement of the First World War. A 42-year-old Scot from Edinburgh, she was the only daughter in a wealthy family of eight sons. She rejected her scholarship to Girton College (the first Cambridge college open to women) and entered Edinburgh University on October 5th, 1892, the first day women were admitted to Scottish universities. A brilliant mathematician, she had shocked her staid tutors by devoting all her energies to the women's movement, taking the case for suffrage for women graduates through the Scottish courts and finally to the House of Lords, where she conducted her own case. A hard-working lawyer and highly proficient at logical argument, she was a woman of few words. She had a 'keen sense of Scottish humour' and photographs show her as a tall, handsome woman with a kind face and a 'knowing' look.[7]

Other women who vigorously opposed the war were suffragettes Emmeline Pethick-Lawrence, Helen Crawfurd, Sylvia Pankhurst and Charlotte Despard. Together with her husband Frederick, Pethick-Lawrence had worked for the Women's Social and Political Union until they fell out with Emmeline and Christabel Pankhurst in 1912. From the West Country, she was the second eldest of a family of thirteen and described by suffrage colleagues as 'good-humoured', 'vivacious, eloquent and warm'. She cut a dash in any crowd by wearing what a friend described as 'lush clothing'.[8]

Helen Crawfurd was from the Gorbals, a Jewish working-class district of Glasgow. The fourth child in a baker's family of seven and married to a clergyman, she had been active in the WSPU in Scotland. On one occasion she acted as part of Emmeline Pankhurst's bodyguard protecting her from arrest at St Andrew's Hall, Glasgow; another time she smashed windows at the Ministry of Education down in London. A fiery character, she had a passionate hatred of injustice and became a socialist when she saw the filthy conditions in which the shipbuilders of Glasgow lived. She was 37 at the outbreak of war.[9]

Sylvia Pankhurst was the pacifist of the family, along with her less well known sister Adela. In 1914 she was 32, two years younger than Christabel and had given up her work as an artist to serve the suffrage cause. Her mother despaired at her scruffy dress but like Margaret Ashton, she could never be very bothered. 'Why not a mask for one's face?' she was once tempted to retort when a somewhat old-fashioned acquaintance asked why she didn't wear gloves whilst working in the East End of London. Like the Pethick-Lawrences, she had broken with her sister and mother before the war and ran her own independent suffrage organisation, the East London Federation of Suffragettes. A melodramatic maverick, she was gutsy, well loved and dedicated to fighting poverty and deprivation.[10]

Charlotte Despard was nicknamed 'the grandmother of the revolution'. Half Irish and half Scottish, she was a tall, thin, striking woman who possessed a 'quick imagination and a warm heart'. Before the outbreak of war she had done welfare work in Battersea for twenty-five years and at 71 she was still the very active President of the Women's Freedom League, a militant suffrage group. She always wore loose, black gowns and sandals on her feet with her white hair pinned up into a bun, under a black Spanish lace mantilla. Dress reform, along with vegetarianism, was one of her passions. Her brother stood at the opposite end of the political spectrum to her and was no less than Field Marshall Sir John French, Commander of the British Expeditionary Forces in France. Her sister, Catherine Harley, an NUWSS executive member, died in France in 1917, whilst working as an administrator for a Scottish women's hospital.[11]

These are just some of the women who opposed the Great War. Throughout the four years, but especially after the start of 1917, they organised demonstrations, spoke from public platforms, wrote pamphlets, helped conscientious objectors, monitored and issued statements on government foreign policy. Above all, they thought deeply about how they could prevent such a catastrophe from happening again. Their sisters in Europe and America were doing the same. But that is still not the whole story. For all this happened after an historic exercise in unofficial diplomacy with the top statesmen of Europe, which is one of the greatest things that women ever achieved. It all began the week before Britain declared war on Germany, in that hot summer seventy years ago. . . .

CHAPTER 1

A Hungarian in London

ON JULY 27th, 1914, three women workers sitting in the London headquarters of the International Woman Suffrage Alliance were feeling despondent. It was Monday, the beginning of a new working week, and they were having a publicity meeting. The subject for debate was the fact that their great international women's organisation, with members in twenty-six countries, hardly ever got a mention in the newspapers, whereas incidents like the breaking of a window by two militant suffragettes,[1] which they felt were disastrous for the votes for women campaign, were regularly reported on the front page of *The Times*. It was one of the hottest summers for years and as they tried to bear up to the heat, they discussed how they could counter the activities of the Pankhursts and their followers – and stop men all over Europe who were opposed to female suffrage from having the excuse that women were unfit for political rights because of their violence.

One of the women participating in the debate was a Hungarian feminist in her mid-thirties called Rosika Schwimmer.[2] She had recently been asked to take up the job of International Press Secretary at the Alliance headquarters by Carrie Chapman Catt, the American leader of the organisation. Schwimmer had all the right qualifications for the job: she was familiar with European suffrage affairs, having travelled widely on lecture tours, she had nine languages, and she knew what newspaper editors liked to print, having worked as a journalist. She also had the kind of wit, eloquence and extrovert personality needed to make an effective publicist. Her instructions were to get news of women's international fight for suffrage and equal rights into the press, so that the public

Rosika Schwimmer in September 1914. No one was neutral about her.
A human dynamo with a forceful personality, she was somebody you
either loved or hated – frequently people did both at different times.
(Photographer: Harris & Ewing, Washington DC)

would concentrate on the issues, rather than broken windows and burnt cricket pavilions.

No one was neutral about Rosika Schwimmer. A human dynamo with a forceful personality and tireless energy, she was somebody you either loved or hated – frequently people did both at different times. Known as the 'comedienne' of the European women's movement who provoked 'shouts of laughter'[3] from female audiences for her pungent attacks on the male sex, she was much in demand as a speaker and could make men laugh their way into agreeing with women's suffrage by her clever use of satire, driven home by dramatic hand gestures.

She must have stood out from some of the women at the National Union of Women's Suffrage Societies (NUWSS). This was the organisation which made up the official British 'wing' of the IWSA, and while there were a number of leading radical suffragists within its ranks, it still generally retained its aura of Victorian middle-class respectability. By the standards of the day, Schwimmer, who called herself a 'very, very radical feminist',[4] did not always behave in a way which women were expected to at that time. She smoked and liked the odd glass of wine, when this was quite rare for women. Traditionalists did not take to her bright, loose-fitting dresses, 'more suggestive of the boudoir than the public platform',[5] which, being a follower of the dress reform movement, she wore without a corset or brassiere. Her stocky build – thick, black, frizzy hair, already tinged with grey and worn in a bun at the nape of her neck or on top of her head, her round face, narrow nose and very dark eyes and brows, as well as her aristocratic gold pince-nez, gave her a striking appearance. She had been married in 1911 and divorced two years later but this was a fact, given the social codes of the time, which she kept a life-long secret. She had no children.

Born in Budapest, into an upper-middle-class Jewish family Schwimmer was the eldest of three children. Her father was an experimental farmer dealing in highly prized seed corn, whose business failures meant that she had had to seek work as a book-keeper at the age of 18, in order to help support the family. Her father was an agnostic; her mother a 'free-thinker'. Her uncle, Leopold Katscher, founded the Hungarian Peace Society and helped the famous Baroness Bertha von Suttner organise the pre-war European peace movement. Yet another uncle, Major Edler von Lederer, although of high rank in the Austro-Hungarian army, was an outspoken opponent of bellicose militarism.

So reform was in Schwimmer's blood when at the age of 20, in 1897, she began to work for the National Association of Women Office Workers (Nötisztviselök Országos Egyesúlete) in Budapest, eventually becoming its President. She founded the first Hungarian Association of Working Women in 1903. In 1904, at the age of 27, after attending the inaugural conference of the International Woman Suffrage Alliance in Berlin as a reporter, she was inspired to fight for the vote for Hungarian women.

Returning home after the conference, she began the Hungarian Feminist Association (Feministák Egyesülete) with her teacher friend Vilma Glücklich, which won the vote for women in one of the shortest campaigns in women's suffrage history – a mere sixteen years. The Association also fought for equal education and employment opportunities for women, birth control, reform of marriage laws, reform of women's dress and centralised housekeeping to free women from domestic servitude. It was concerned with the problems of prostitution and wanted the abolition of child labour. And when peasant women began to join, it became involved in land reform and the establishment of small-scale localised industries. Like many other suffrage groups, this was no mono-causal organisation but one with far-reaching ideas, some of which women are still fighting for today – eighty years later.

By 1913 Schwimmer was a well-known figure in the international suffrage movement, and that year she played the leading role in organising the Seventh Congress of the IWSA which was the most lavish there had ever been. There were 3,000 participants from all over the world, 800 of whom travelled the last stage of their journey from Vienna to Budapest down the Danube by steamer.[6]

But now Schwimmer was in London and landed with probably the most difficult public relations job in the world. Catherine Marshall and Emily Leaf, Parliamentary and Press Secretary of the NUWSS, were the other two women in the IWSA office that hot, sunny morning. They had come to see Schwimmer to discuss publicity ideas. We already know that Catherine Marshall, from the Lake District, was one of the ablest organisers in the suffrage movement. Emily Leaf hadn't been involved with suffrage campaigning so long. She joined up in 1912 and was Honorary Secretary of Oxon, Berks and Bucks Suffrage Federation before coming to work in the press office at the London NUWSS headquarters. Before that she had gone to Oxford, done social work in Stratford as a sub-warden of St Helen's House Settlement and travelled to Canada, where she lived for four years, earning her living by doing, in her words, 'manual work'. In 1914, she was 36.

After work, Schwimmer and Marshall returned to the home they shared with another suffragist of about the same age, called Mary Sheepshanks. Mary leased a narrow, eighteenth-century, ivy-covered red brick house in a small road close to Westminster Abbey, called Barton Street. From the top window of the house you could see the Houses of Parliament over the roofs. Each woman had a bedroom and a study but they shared the dining-room and backyard. The house was in an ideal situation for their work, being around the corner from the NUWSS offices in Great Smith Street and a pleasant walk up Victoria Embankment by the Thames to the IWSA office in Adam Street, off the Strand. It was also, of course, ideal as a base from which the women could lobby politicians.

Mary Sheepshanks ran the IWSA office and edited *Jus Suffragii*, the IWSA journal. The Latin title meant 'the right of voting', and the journal, published in English and French, cost either 4 pence, 4 marks or 4 francs. Schwimmer described Sheepshanks as the 'rebellious daughter of a Bishop', which indeed she was. The eldest of seventeen children, she had escaped the experiences of an unhappy childhood in an austere vicarage in Liverpool by immersing herself in the intellectually stimulating life of Newnham Women's College at Cambridge. Here she was a much sought-after dinner guest, guaranteed to provide entertainment. Her father thoroughly disapproved of these new influences in her life, especially when she embarrassed him by handing out atheist tracts outside a royal garden party given by the Bishop of Norwich.

By 1914, she was 42, a tall, upright woman who wore glasses and hated having her photograph taken. Like Emily Leaf, when she left university she worked in a 'settlement' in Southwark. Settlements were pre-welfare-state prototypes of the social services. Then came fourteen years at Morley College, where she started as a voluntary teacher and ended up Principal. By 1913, she was such a recognised suffrage activist that she was asked to go on a speaking tour through Europe promoting votes for women. Her father, incidentally, was in favour of this new interest because he thought outdoor speaking was good for the health! Of all the nationalities she met on her trip, she found German men the most exasperating.[7]

That Monday evening, Mary and Rosika Schwimmer wandered through the hot and humid West End streets to try and find an outdoor restaurant. The weather was oppressive and Mary complained that she couldn't wait to get away to the sea, like thousands of other holidaymakers all over Europe. The two women began discussing the internal politics of the Alliance. There had just been an executive meeting in London with representatives from all the member countries. Visits to other suffrage organisations – militant and non-militant – had been arranged and there had been tea with sympathetic members of Parliament on the House of Commons terrace. There was plenty to talk about.

But although good times seemed to be ahead, Schwimmer knew in the back of her mind that international catastrophe could be imminent. She was widely travelled and well informed about politics, especially Eastern European affairs. In 1909, she had been the first foreign woman invited to address the House of Commons' Foreign Affairs Committee.[8] She knew that a month earlier on June 28th, the heir to the Austro-Hungarian Empire,[9] Archduke Franz Ferdinand, had been killed at Sarajevo in Bosnia, an eastern province of Austria- Hungary. He had been shot by a 19-year-old boy, backed by freedom fighters from neighbouring Serbia. They wanted Bosnia to be given independence from Austria-Hungary, like Serbia. There had been power struggles between the Slavs and Teutons in this part of Europe for years.

On July 9th, Schwimmer had had breakfast with Lloyd George[10] at 11 Downing Street (this was not one of the Welsh politician's amorous liaisons: he was wont to have business meetings early in the morning) and told him that the British government were not giving enough attention to the assassination of the Archduke Franz Ferdinand, which had provoked a storm of protest throughout the Austro-Hungarian Empire such as she had never seen before. She told the Chancellor that unless something was done immediately to appease the resentment, she believed it would result in war with Serbia, with the very high risk that other European countries could be dragged in. Russia was bound to back Serbia, she said, Germany to back Austria-Hungary, and Germany and France were long-time enemies. Lloyd George, however, thought this was alarmist and could not be substantiated by the official reports he was receiving. He was convinced that because Germany and Britain were equals in armament – Germany had its army and Britain had its navy – war would be prevented between them. Indeed, the Cabinet did not even discuss the issue before July 24th.

On Tuesday, July 28th, the day after the publicity meeting, Schwimmer was up early to see Carrie Chapman Catt off at King's Cross station. Catt was boarding a ship at Liverpool to return to New York. Marshall and another NUWSS worker, Kathleen Courtney, came too. Saying goodbye on the platform, Catt hugged Schwimmer and urged her to come over for the New York State Suffrage Campaign. Every time they got a boatload of German immigrants, she said, the campaign was set back several years and they needed the Hungarian's persuasive oratory to win them over. She was one of the few suffragists who could speak their language fluently.

Walking back to the office, grabbing a newspaper on the way, Schwimmer arrived to find a queue of reporters outside the door. The first poster which the IWSA had ever published had been banned from the London Underground. Publicity at last! Designed by the Hungarian artist, Willy Pogány, the poster featured a woman dressed in flowing robes and carrying a baby: underneath her were statistics showing that in countries where women had the vote, there was less infant mortality. It was the naked baby which London Transport did not like. 'The extent of British prudery is unbelievable,' thought Schwimmer but both she and Mary duly answered questions from newspaper reporters all morning.

Back for lunch at Barton Street, however, any euphoria the Hungarian might have felt at getting the IWSA into the press soon disappeared. She spread open her newspaper to find that her home country had declared war on Serbia. No longer could she pretend to ignore what was happening in Europe. She must have felt the fear and loneliness that comes from having some ominous knowledge, about which everyone else is blissfully unaware.

That afternoon, Catherine Marshall and Emily Leaf discussed with Schwimmer the likelihood of Britain being drawn into the hostilities. Obligations to the rival alliances of the Triple Alliance, comprising Germany, Austria-Hungary and Italy, and the Triple Entente, comprising Russia, France and Britain, made this a possibility. Shocked and apprehensive, Marshall suggested that they organise a public rally to urge the British government not only to remain neutral but also to mediate between Austria-Hungary and Serbia. They decided, too, to present mediation appeals to the Foreign Secretary, Sir Edward Grey and all the relevant Ambassadors in London.

The events of the following week were to prove fatal for Europe. We can imagine the suffragists' horror as they faced the possibility of war. Jolted out of the world of suffrage politics, where they at last seemed to be moving towards success in a round of exciting events, the immediate future must have seemed extremely frightening.

At the IWSA meeting the next day, the drafts of the mediation appeals were discussed and the method of delivery decided upon.[11] Schwimmer felt it was vital to talk to the Ambassadors personally in order to have any effect, otherwise, she thought, the letters would just end up in the wastepaper basket. Millicent Fawcett, the Vice-President of the IWSA, however, could not see the point of sending personal envoys when 'a penny stamp would suffice'. Finally Fawcett was outvoted, and she, Schwimmer and Macmillan hailed a motor-cab and drove to the Foreign Office with the aim of seeing Sir Edward Grey – or so the younger suffragists thought. However, when they arrived, Fawcett got out of the taxi, told the others to wait inside and handed over the letter to a footman. One by one they visited all the embassies and repeated this performance until finally Fawcett dismissed the cab, requested that they split the seven shillings and three pence fare between them and travel home by public transport. Schwimmer and Macmillan could not believe it. The Hungarian was particularly furious with the 'stubborn old woman' as she called her.

It is important to relate this incident because later on, during the war, Schwimmer was accused of both extravagance and arrogance for her part in initiating peace initiatives. But much as she admired the earlier generation of suffrage leaders and lived at a time when respect for one's elders was expected, from that time on, she vowed that she would not let economy, misplaced respectability or expediency prevent her from following her gut reaction and doing what she believed to be right: to try and stop the most widespread war in the world's history up to that time. As Schwimmer wrote later, 'I was too distressed about the lack of understanding for the immense tasks before us to appreciate the beauty of saving seven and threepence for the treasury of a world organisation of women',[12] and from then on she called Mrs Fawcett 'Mrs Seven and Threepence'.

This incident can also give us an insight into the very different character of Millicent Fawcett. She was the President of the NUWSS and had effectively been leader of the non-militant suffragists since 1890. Her elder sister, Elizabeth Garrett, had opened the way for women to become doctors and Elizabeth Garrett's close friend, Emily Davies, founded Girton College in 1873 after an arduous campaign to allow women into universities. With such models, it is little wonder that Fawcett took up the battle for the vote. But it was duty which drove her, not rebellion. Married to Henry Fawcett (Postmaster-General in Gladstone's 1880 government) for seventeen years, she was solidly upper-middle-class and an admirer of the British establishment. She looked every inch the respectable Victorian lady; a tiny, plump-faced woman, in her late sixties, who wore neat, dark silk dresses with white lace collars. She was, she wrote, a 'worshipper at the inner shrine, the holy of holies, all that England stands for to her children, and to the world'.[13]

By the time the IWSA suffragists had delivered the appeals, other women's organisations like the Women's Labour League and the Women's Co-operative Guild had also thought of mobilising for a women's peace rally and they approached both the IWSA and the NUWSS to ask if they could co-ordinate it. This was agreed and a date was set for the following Tuesday, August 4th.[14] Volunteers were brought in to help the paid workers. Leaflets had to be written and printed. A hall booked. Speakers invited.

Debates during the planning meetings can give us further insight into suffrage politics. A believer in broad-based campaigns, Schwimmer caused a stir by wanting to ask all the different suffrage societies to unite in opposition to the war. More than that, she wanted to ask anti-suffrage women to join them too. Warring governments would be appealing to their peoples to drop class, religious and race differences in the name of war, she argued, and women must do the same for peace. It would be a good idea to invite to the rally the Pankhursts and other militant leaders – and women like Mrs Humphrey Ward and Violet Markham, who had opposed votes for women. The room fell silent. Mrs Fawcett looked horrified.

Surely, Schwimmer went on, it would be difficult for the Pankhursts to protest against the war – against 'national militancy' – as they would be accused of hypocrisy in doing so. Asking them to the rally would give them 'a way out'. As for the anti-suffragists, she wanted them only if they admitted that women's suffrage and peace were linked; that a world run solely by men made war more likely. Maybe they would see that now.

Marshall and some of the others came to agree with her, and she almost convinced Fawcett at one point but eventually she was outvoted. The splits in the suffrage movement went too deep. It would have been a powerful protest had these invitations been issued and accepted but Fawcett was probably right when she said that the WSPU and the anti-suffragists would refuse to join them – although possibly the non-Pankhurst militant suffrage organisations might have accepted.

Yet another point of conflict arose over Schwimmer's inclusion of Olive Schreiner and Emily Hobhouse on the invitations list. Schreiner was the brilliant South African author whose well-read books included *The Story of an African Farm* about an unmarried mother (shocking for its time), and *Women and Labour*, the bible of the pre-war women's movement, which had been published in 1911. She had been placed under house arrest in South Africa for criticising the British army during the Boer War of 1899-1902. Emily Hobhouse had also criticised the British army during this time. She was a British woman who travelled to South Africa to see for herself the conditions in the British prisoner-of-war camps. Unable to beat the guerilla tactics of the rural Boers, the British army had adopted a policy of farm burning. After first ransacking and then destroying homes, they would herd Boer women and children into filthy makeshift camps. Needless to say, when she publicised her critical report to a British public high on a wave of jingoism, it caused a storm of controversy.[15]

We can imagine that at a time of great political sensitivity, the last people Millicent Fawcett, given her imperialist views, wanted to be seen sharing a platform with were women who had been called 'traitors' when Britain was last at war. Furthermore, it was she who had led a Committee of Women, set up by the ruling Conservative government of the time, to investigate Hobhouse's complaints. Predictably, Millicent Fawcett threw up her hands in horror at the idea of Schreiner and Hobhouse being invited. However, this time she was outvoted and the invitations went out.

Meanwhile, events in Europe were daily growing more alarming.[16] The Austro-Hungarian government had not only declared war on Serbia but ordered a general mobilisation to show that it could take on Russia as well, if necessary. Far from being frightened off by Austria-Hungary's action, Russia ordered a general mobilisation from its own troops on Thursday, July 30th. All the European countries had built up huge armies of conscripts and believed that attack – or the threat of attack – was the best method of defence.

The German government, which was already pledged to back Austria-Hungary, knew that if it came to it, it could not fight both France and Russia at the same time. Since 1892, it had had a military plan to attack France first before the lumbering Russian war machine could roll into action. With the Russian decision to mobilise, the Germans knew they would lose any advantage of greater speed if they did not initiate the action. They sent an ultimatum to Russia demanding that it demobilise within twelve hours, or they would declare war. Russia refused. Germany declared war on Russia on Saturday, August 1st, and on August 3rd declared war on France.

In Britain, August 1st was the start of August Bank Holiday but news of Germany's threats dampened the holiday spirit. There was panic food buying and customers queued up outside the Bank of England to get gold. On Sunday, when the news of Germany's Luxemburg invasion reached the news-stands, people picnicking in the hot sun in their gardens, in the public parks and on crowded beaches began to feel the increasing tension and pondered on Britain's likelihood of becoming involved. In London, the Cabinet had been in session since early morning.

On Sunday afternoon, the Labour Party organised a mass demonstration against the war in Trafalgar Square. Keir Hardie, under a dark sky and in the midst of a fierce downpour, condemned the prospect of a British alliance with Tsarist Russia to a sea of black umbrellas. The miners' leader,

Robert Smillie, said that if a strike of European workers could stop the war, the miners would be part of it.[17] Like many thousands of others, Schwimmer and her friends attended the rally, which was a welcome break from the frantic search to find a printer for their own leaflets and posters for the Women's Peace Meeting on Tuesday. 'England is civilised,' thought Schwimmer, who was a great Anglophile, 'we won't be dragged into the war. Britain is the European champion of the cause of civilising Russia – she won't fight on the side of Russian Tsarism!'[18]

Indeed, opposition to Britain being dragged into the war came from the Liberal camp as well as Labour, and from influential sections of the City. On August 1st, the *Daily News*, the most important London Liberal paper, stated, 'If we crush Germany in the dust and make Russia the dictator of Europe and Asia, it will be the greatest disaster that has ever befallen Western culture and civilisation.'[19]

The *Manchester Guardian* took a similar line and probably half the members of the Liberal government shared this view.

On Monday, the suffragists heard news that Germany had demanded the right to move its troops through Belgium. The Schlieffen Plan (named after the Chief of the German General Staff) had long been the German contingency plan for attacking France and involved crossing Belgium to invade northern France and encircle Paris – which was much easier than trying to attack the heavily fortified narrow French/German border. Belgium refused entry and appealed to Britain for help. Catherine Marshall returned from the House of Commons to the IWSA office, to report that there was a growing likelihood of Britain entering the conflict because under the Treaty of London of 1839, Britain was guarantor of Belgium's neutrality. In a speech in the Commons, Sir Edward Grey, the Foreign Secretary, had secured the agreement of all but a few members of Parliament to the delivery of an ultimatum to Germany, demanding the withdrawal of its troops by midnight the following day. Public opinion rapidly changed: small, neutral Belgium was being invaded by Germany; tiny Serbia by the Austro-Hungarian Empire; small nations must be protected, how could Great Britain honourably stand by and do nothing? Outgoing trains from London were full of Europeans recalled to their own countries, while crowds of people in holiday clothes began to fill Whitehall and street traders did a roaring trade in Union Jacks.

In the days which led up to the start of the First World War, the strength of the international women's movement was shown by German, French, Italian, Dutch, Hungarian and Canadian women living in or passing through London, who called at the IWSA headquarters and asked the Alliance to take action. Letters came from all over Europe hoping that Carrie Chapman Catt was still in Britain and asking her *to do something*.

Frida Perlen, the leader of the German wing of the Suffrage Alliance, telegraphed from Stuttgart on July 30th, two days before Germany declared war on Russia: 'Is it possible the Alliance arranges immediately manifestations for peace?'[20]

Elna Munch, one of the most active women in the international suffrage movement, wrote from Copenhagen the same day, saying how Danish women had expected to get the vote in September but that now with the war, they supposed it would be postponed: 'Do you know Mr Wilson personally?' she asked Catt. 'Would it not be possible to get him to intervene in the quarrels here in Europe?' The United States, she said, with its federal states united in a democratic republic, and with pacifist leaders preaching peace on platforms that no European politician could dream of mounting, was the only country that could mediate.[21]

'It is a terrible thing to let all this be done without women interfering,' wrote Madame de Witt Schlumberger, the President of the French section, from Paris on August 2nd.

> Certainly, I am afraid it is too late, and we French women cannot take the lead in anything. But if you are still in London, do you think it possible for you as an American and as President of the Alliance to make a sort of appeal against war, a sort of manifesto, *in the name of the Alliance*. It is a very difficult thing to word, for in the name of women one must not seem *afraid* of anything, and there must be no mistake about this. It must be applicable to the women of all nations, and if done it should be sent to all the governments and widely spread. Is it possible? Is it feasible?[22]

'Do help your European sisters,' wrote Anita Dobelli Zampetti, an Italian suffragist from Rome.

> I beg you most fervently – I do not see now the division of

nations: but just one great division, the home destroyers on one side, the homekeepers — the women, the children on the other. Why will only the first have always the prevalence when *our* cause is best?[23]

Carrie Chapman Catt was the one hope '. . . for hundreds of thousands of women all over the world who had learned to believe in her as a courageous, fearless leader, with the vision of a world made better by women, unspoiled by the traditions that fettered men,' wrote Schwimmer later.[24] But Catt was half-way across the Atlantic, oblivious to the cries for help. Unlike so many other ships, the one on which she was travelling was not called back upon the declaration of war.

CHAPTER 2

Enemy alien

HOURS before the Women's Peace Meeting was due to start at 8 o'clock on the evening of August 4th, crowds had gathered outside the Kingsway Hall in London. By the time the meeting began, two thousand women were crammed inside and hundreds more had to be turned away. That morning it had become clear that Britain's supposed neutral stand, which the demonstration had originally been called to support, was an illusion and that the government would declare war against Germany in the next few hours. The organisers had been overtaken by events but they decided the rally should go on.

It was a sad meeting. The audience, who were at first excited and enthusiastic, quickly became subdued as they listened to speech after speech from women, most of whom stated that no matter how much they personally disagreed with government policy, there wasn't much anyone could do about it – least of all women without a voice in Parliament.

The great majority of 'organised' women were represented, with the notable exception of the Pankhursts' WSPU. Mary Macarthur, a pioneer in women's trade unionism, represented the National Federation of Women Workers, Marion Phillips came from the Women's Labour League and Eleanor Barton from the Women's Co-operative Guild. German, French, Russian, Finnish and Hungarian feminists represented the IWSA. Helena Swanwick represented the NUWSS. Charlotte Despard, President of the Women's Freedom League, and Olive Schreiner were on the platform.[1]

Millicent Fawcett, who was presiding over the meeting, made her attitude quite clear: was was 'insensate devilry', she said, and as women were voteless they could not be responsible for the political events which led up to it. But she concluded that 'the highest and most precious of national and international aspirations and hopes' would have to be put aside 'as we as citizens have now our duty to perform'.[2]

Two resolutions were passed unanimously: one urging mediation by the countries not yet involved in the war, the other urging women's organisations to 'offer their services to their country'. But a sense of frustration prevailed. What could women do? "Down tools!" came a shout, but most of those present must have known that in view of the national enthusiasm which had pervaded the country, there would be little support for a general strike that night in 1914.

At 10 o'clock, the women emerged from the crowded hall into the hot summer night, to hear boys calling out news of that evening's speeches in Parliament. A deputation took the Women's Peace Meeting resolutions to 10 Downing Street, where the Cabinet was waiting for an answer to the British ultimatum that German troops leave Belgium. As the delegates posted their envelope through the Prime Minister's door, King George V was sanctioning a declaration of war with Germany, if an answer to the ultimatum was not received by 12 midnight, Berlin time. Crowds had gathered in Whitehall. There was no talk for or against the war, just a nervous apprehension, with people whispering to each other.

When Big Ben struck 11 o'clock and it was midnight in Berlin, a wave of sound surged through the throng and people began to shout 'War is declared! War is declared!' over and over again. It was then that Sir Edward Grey, looking out of his window at the Foreign Office, made his famous comment, 'The lamps are going out all over Europe; we shall not see them lit again in our lifetime.'

Millicent Fawcett, who had joined the milling crowd, along with Rosika Schwimmer, Chrystal Macmillan and other women from the meeting, walked silently home, believing her life's work was destroyed. She wrote later,

> The day on which we knew that we were actually at war with the greatest military nation on earth was the most miserable day of my life. I do not think I ever doubted that in the end we should win. The idea that Great Britain should ever really be crushed by the iron heel of German militarism never found a place in my mind; but so ill did I read the

future that I thought the hope of women's freedom was indefinitely postponed, and that this was the supreme sacrifice asked of us at this stupendous moment. Black indeed the outlook seemed.[3]

Schwimmer and Macmillan had difficulty trying to push their way against the weight of the crowd, which had become a sea of stunned faces, gasping and chattering and endlessly repeating 'War is declared!' Cars appeared, containing young men and women, who were yelling hysterically and hooting car horns. Suddenly the street seemed to be filled with a shrieking mob, joyously celebrating a night on the town, with the same war fever which had afflicted Berlin and Paris a few days before.

'Mafficking,' murmured Macmillan, explaining to Schwimmer, whose English wasn't perfect, that the word meant 'to rejoice with hysterical boisterousness'. The Hungarian feminist felt a sudden affection for her companion, who was better known in suffrage circles for her highly efficient, reserved nature than for expressing her emotions to colleagues. She was to remember the comfort that Macmillan's company had given her, during the first few days of the war, when news of her family was scarce. On the night of August 4th, the Scotswoman refused to leave Schwimmer alone in Whitehall, because she was afraid someone would recognise her as a foreigner and turn nasty.

The two of them finally got back to Barton Street at 2 o'clock in the morning, where they met Catherine Marshall, who was about to leave the house to post some letters. The three of them sat in the front room for a few minutes. 'I don't understand how Sir Edward Grey could be party to England's alliance with Russia!' said Marshall, incredulously. 'There must be a mistake somewhere. How could he, of all our statesmen, enter the war?' she asked the others.

Later in the night, her mind racing and unable to sleep, Schwimmer left her bedroom and went down to her study on the lower floor. Unbearable heat hung over the house and the shrill sound of a bugle call from a nearby barracks rang out, followed by the sound of horses' hooves and heavy artillery wagons on the cobbled street. As dawn broke, Schwimmer sat at her desk by an open window and composed a four-page 'Open Letter' addressed to 'All Men, Women and Organisations who want to stop the international massacre at the earliest possible moment'.[4] It began:

The war has anyway to be terminated by mediation, therefore do not let us wait, but let us urge it now. President Wilson hastened to offer mediation at once, at the outbreak of war, and added to his offer 'but if you do not wish it now, do let me know when you are ready for it.' This means that one or other of the combating nations is expected *to call* President Wilson. . . .

As all the combating nations are resolved 'to conquer or be killed to the last man' waiting for the call for mediation is equal to waiting until the absolute destruction of one or other of the belligerent nations is accomplished.

There are those who are saying that we must wait for the *psychological* moment, others call it the *right* moment. This is the time honoured plan used in ordinary wars between two or a few more nations. But what is going on today is not merely a war, but the breakdown of a world – the earthquake of civilisation.

She suggested that Wilson or his Secretary of State, William Jennings Bryan, should come immediately to Europe and call together government representatives from the neutral countries – Switzerland, the Netherlands, Sweden, Denmark, Norway and Spain. This International Watching Committee should sit in Norway (The Hague was too near the battlefield) and send offers to mediate to the warring governments every single day, she wrote.

The Committee must not be offended if the combatant Governments refuse their offer in a rude or purposely offensive tone, or if they don't answer at all. The incessant renewal of this offer is the only means of hastening 'the right moment' for mediation, because it allows any of the combatant nations to climb down any moment before they are absolutely exhausted, whether they are victorious or defeated. . . .

The repeated offers would make it possible *to accept instead of to ask for* mediation.

This would take away the stigma of humiliation which is dreaded more than anything else by the nations. They prefer to sacrifice any further number of their people because of false pride.

The vision of such glorious common sense and understanding

of the human psyche being part of international diplomacy is heart-warming even today.

Schwimmer leant out of her window and looked at the street below. There was no one about except for the policemen standing outside two local Cabinet ministers' houses. They stood guard night and day against possible militant suffragette attacks. The bugle sounded a second time and more wagons rolled by. She sat down again, and added sections to her 'Open Letter' about the need for a new international organisation in Europe and how the political will could be brought about to achieve it. Then she asked readers to contact her if they supported the scheme, signed her name and put down her pen. 'Women must come of age politically to make this a human world,' she thought. 'It's the only hope left.'[5]

After the trauma of the last few days and so many sleepless nights, she wondered how it could be that her head felt as cool and clear as it did during holidays in the Alps.

When Schwimmer went down to breakfast the next morning, she was surprised to find the atmosphere of the house had changed. Catherine Marshall had already left. The maid was in a nervous panic about the declaration of war; the cook had gone on holiday and Mary Sheepshanks seemed irritable. A stiff conversation followed about the work that should be done in the IWSA office that day. Mary Sheepshanks said that she intended to draft an appeal to English women asking them not to hoard gold and to economise on food. Hurt by her colleague's attitude and bemused by her intentions, Schwimmer asked if such an appeal was appropriate for the work of an international organisation. Sheepshanks said she didn't care if it was or not – she would do it anyway.

Rightly or wrongly, the Hungarian began to suspect that her nationality would now be an embarrassment to her co-workers. She had already decided that from now on she would concentrate all her energies on urging collective mediation in the war by neutral governments. Would she be able to do this from the IWSA offices? She interpreted Mary's words as evidence that the English woman was finding it difficult to resist official propaganda and national enthusiasm. Would her other colleagues be the same? She wrote to Millicent Fawcett on August 5th,

After very careful, earnest and calm consideration I have come to the conclusion to resign my post as paid organising and press secretary of the IWSA. . . .

A conversation I had this morning with Miss Sheepshanks revealed to me the fact that my working under the present conditions may lead many of you, as it has led already some – to misunderstand my motives and ways of work.

This is not the time for explanations of personal matters, as all our strength and force has to be devoted to concentrated work connected with the horrible state of the whole of Europe. . . .

At the same time when I beg you to relieve me of the paid post I offer my unpaid services to do the international work which, in my opinion, has at this moment greater importance than ever. There is no other spot in Europe where work can be done which will enable all our European affiliates to continue their work, as if it had not been interrupted but in England. And though I long to be near all those who are dearest to me I feel that I could nowhere be more useful to them, as well as to the cause to which I have given my life, than here, where I can *work*. I wish therefore to remain here as long as I may be legally allowed to stay.

I beg you to accept my *offer* to continue the work as well as my *resignation* of the paid post.[6]

Meanwhile, members of the NUWSS executive were sorting through 200 letters they had received from branches in response to a circular sent out asking what the Union should do if war was declared. The majority of replies stated that it should suspend suffrage campaigning and devote its energies to war relief work.[7] Within hours, this became official policy and a week later the editorial of the NUWSS journal, *The Common Cause*, written by Millicent Fawcett, stated,

Women, your country needs you. As long as there was any hope for peace most members of the National Union probably sought for peace, and endeavoured to support those who were trying to maintain it. But we have another duty now. . . . LET US SHOW OURSELVES WORTHY OF CITIZENSHIP, WHETHER OUR CLAIM TO IT BE RECOGNISED OR NOT.[8]

The great organising machine of the NUWSS launched itself into solving the problems which the declaration of war had created. The disruption of banking and overseas trade meant business collapse and sudden unemployment – and in the time-honoured tradition, women were the first to lose their jobs. Non-essential trades like millinery, dressmaking, art dealing and the hotel trade were particularly affected, but factories closed as well. The NUWSS national office, the office of the London Society for Women's Suffrage and a new office for the union's Active Service League were used as emergency centres. The union set up an employment agency and told women where they could get retrained. It provided two workrooms with sewing work for the most destitute until they could find jobs. The centres also acted as contact points between 'enemy aliens' – as well as Belgian refugees – and the English who were prepared to give them accommodation. Two thousand women visited these offices for help during the first four weeks of the war.

In the provinces, the suffragists helped organise facilities for the new army barracks, providing voluntary staff for canteen running and the repair of army garments. They worked with the Red Cross, the newly formed Citizens Committee and the Women's Co-operative Guild, which continued its work of setting up maternity clinics. The Soldiers and Sailors Families Association also needed help, as many women were left destitute by male breadwinners who had gone off to fight, although this problem was less widespread in Britain at this early stage in the war than in Germany and France, where there was universal conscription.[9] During the first few months of the war the 'mopping up' work which women's suffrage organisations did must have saved much human misery but it was not until the following year that the government specifically made a plea for women's help in the war effort. Up until then the official attitude was often more akin to 'keep quiet and don't interfere'. However, by March 1915, when the Board of Trade issued an appeal for women to register for 'paid employment of any kind', and later that year, when they were ushered into munitions work by Lloyd George's newly created Minister of Munitions, the men who were running the war had begun to realise that women could be useful to them and the revolutionary mass takeover of men's jobs by women began to take place.

Catherine Marshall, Chrystal Macmillan and Emily Leaf soon spent most of their waking hours immersed in relief work but it would be wrong to interpret this as whole-hearted support for the war, either amongst them or the other executive members of the NUWSS. As early as October 1914, Helena Swanwick suggested a meeting with suffrage society representatives to discuss NUWSS policy with regard to future terms of peace. She had joined the Union of Democratic Control[10] in August, which was a group of predominantly male intellectuals and politicians against the war — Bertrand Russell and Ramsey MacDonald were members. Two other executive members, Maude Royden, a lecturer in English at Oxford, and Isabella Ford, a Quaker from Leeds, opposed the war on religious grounds. Margaret Ashton, from the Manchester and District Federation of suffragists, was anxious that her branch should take a lead in discussing how peace negotiations could begin. So a considerable proportion of the executive were already trying to think of wider issues, despite the immediate heavy demands put upon them.

Meanwhile, Schwimmer — uncompromising as usual — had no wish whatsoever to get involved with relief work because she believed it 'narcotises so many good people to believe everything is done if we care for victims, while we don't care to prevent the making of new ones' [sic].[11]

She was visiting British pacifist societies, or anyone she thought would be sympathetic to the ideas in her 'Open Letter'. An item in the *Pall Mall Gazette* caught her eye and she wrote to the editor,

> I see in some papers an appeal from a gentleman who wants
> to form a Foreign Legion to give foreign *men*, who are not
> obliged to fight, a chance of taking part in the foreign
> slaughter. I wish to appeal to all foreign *women* living in
> England to form a Foreign Legion, which shall support any
> serious effort organised to urge mediation on the part of the
> States not yet involved in war. I appeal therefore to the
> foreign women at present living in England who wish to help
> secure a speedy settlement to join the proposed Women's
> Foreign Legion.[12]

Catherine Marshall thought this a splendid idea but when Schwimmer showed her letter to Sheepshanks, her 'landlady' attempted to tear it up, and shouted, 'You can't use my address for this!' From then on, there was little hope of spreading the plan for a negotiated peace from 1 Barton Street.[13]

Schwimmer did not like to use the IWSA offices either. When there was finally time to discuss her resignation, Millicent Fawcett persuaded Schwimmer to accept three months' salary and leave immediately: 'May we again express the hope . . .

that you should at once offer your services by cable as a . . . lecturer to the United States and go there as soon as you can secure a passage . . . the work would help you through this terrible time,' wrote Fawcett to her on August 9th.[14]

The declaration of war between Britain and Austria-Hungary the next day struck Schwimmer another blow. Of course, intellectually she knew it was inevitable because her home country was allied with Germany, but emotionally she couldn't come to terms with these facts. Now she was officially an alien, which she pronounced something like 'a lyon'. And an 'enemy alien', too. She had left Hungary nine months ago, determined to live in Britain because she loved everything about it, its institutions, its literature, its people. She had planned to earn her living as a journalist based in London – to her joy she had been accepted as the first woman member of the Foreign Correspondents Club – and now she was an 'enemy alien'.

She began to be interrogated by officials and was no longer so free to travel around. She wrote later,

> The dull performance of answering endless questions about oneself and one's ancestors generations back was then a novel torture. It grew during the war to one of the rites to be performed every blessed time one wanted to move three steps from one's [door] . . . at the first registration – when I mentioned how it hurt to be labelled 'alien enemy', the officer said kindly, 'It certainly is too bad. And we don't feel really hostile. Especially not to the Austrians and Hungarians. You know, madam,' he added, lowering his voice, 'you Austrians and Hungarians are more lady-like and gentleman-like, not like the Germans.' It meant to be a compliment [sic].[15]

Xenophobia was now rife in both Britain and Germany. Even naturalised Germans who were resident in Britain faced compulsory registration and many were interned at once. Shopkeepers with German sounding names were hounded, their shops smashed up. There was an hysterical spy mania, and even long-serving German nannies were suspect. So it is no wonder that Schwimmer was overcome by the hostility. The paranoia grew to such an extent that flickering lights, especially on the coast, were denounced as signals to the enemy, and dachshunds, the German breed of dog, presumably considered a security risk, were destroyed. Things were no better in Germany, where Englishmen in particular were threatened in the street ('England' was *the* enemy, and it was 'England', in those days, not 'Britain'). In Germany the elimination of all foreign names and words was official policy, so that the Café Piccadilly became Café Vaterland, and the Hotel Westminster the Lindenhof. But perhaps the most potent symptom of the hate fever was the plethora of 'atrocity stories', which were rampant in both countries because of the lack of any real news as to how the war was progressing. The British heard rumours of German soldiers raping Belgian nuns and cutting the hands off children; while the common belief in Germany was that heartless Belgian women systematically gouged out the eyes of innocent German prisoners-of-war.[16]

Schwimmer soon realised that she could not stay in London, no matter how much she desired to, but she was determined to continue trying to get a delegation of prominent Englishmen over to President Wilson with a mediation plan, and also to collect support from international women's organisations to put pressure on the American government. As for herself, she supposed that she would join some peace movement in the United States.

The next two weeks were spent energetically organising travel arrangements as well as pursuing the peace plan. A boat ticket for her Atlantic passage was secured from the Savoy Hotel, where a group of Americans had set up a committee to help tourists; some wanted to take the first ship home and others wanted to postpone the return journey and sell their tickets because the war was a sightseeing extra not to be missed! Then Schwimmer wrote to Carrie Chapman Catt (somewhat reluctantly as she felt she was imposing on her) and asked if she could stay at her home on arrival. She reserved enough money for her survival for a week in New York, so that she could get to see President Wilson. Next there was the printing of the 'Open Letter' and its translation into German, French, Italian and Swedish. No pacifist organisation would back it so there was no alternative but to draw up a list of likely sympathisers, and publish and circulate it herself. She communicated (mainly by telegram as time was so short) to anyone she could think of who might join her in pushing the prospect of mediation by neutral governments – including all the IWSA national sections all over the world.

Not surprisingly, money soon became short and Schwimmer had to sell her jewellery and typewriter to remain solvent. She even tried to sell her clothes in order to be able to telegraph more contacts in European countries. At first a Yorkshire friend, Mrs Illingworth from Bradford, seemed to come to the rescue by offering a £50 loan but it turned out that she was only prepared to release this in £10 sums. She sent £15, £5 of which was to replace what Schwimmer had so 'recklessly' spent on telegrams![17] (Since a cab fare was 7s 3d – about 35p in new British currency – we can estimate that the £50 loan would be worth about £500 in today's terms.) In the end, Schwimmer refused her loan because Mrs Illingworth was restricting what she could spend it on.

Financially insecure, hurt by what she saw as the coolness of many of her colleagues, worn down by tedious police interrogation, horrified by the prospect of world war and worried about her family in Hungary, life must have seemed pretty impossible to Schwimmer.

'YOUR KING AND COUNTRY NEEDS YOU!' declared the moustachioed Field Marshall Lord Kitchener from posters all over town, his finger pointing menacingly. 'SAVE FOOD', 'DON'T HOARD GOLD', 'BUSINESS AS USUAL' went others. 'How could it be business as usual,' Schwimmer thought, as she watched young boys drilling with wooden rifles in Dean's Yard, next to Westminster Cathedral. In her country, men hated conscription but here lads were crowding to enlist at recruitment stations, excited and giggling, seduced by 'Holy War' propaganda. Newspapers, posters and songs told of the glory of war. 'We must not let them die,' thought Schwimmer as she walked the streets, visiting one pacifist organisation after another. 'We must not let them kill each other, destroy civilisation, we must not let them. . . .'[18]

There was little sign that the international organisations she visited would take action. She wrote despairingly to Mrs Illingworth,

> 'When the belligerent part of the world will be at peace, the pacifists will begin to fight each other. They do not recognise even yet, that lack of unity, lack of a broad based plan has brought forward their failure, and they want to remain in the same disorganisation each cherishing a special plan, sometimes quite a clever one, sometimes very ridiculous ones, but in one single thing they all agree – sit and wait. Wait. Wait.[19]

Keir Hardie seemed to be right when he warned her that 'the so-called Peace people are the most helpless and inefficient crowd on the face of the earth'.[20]

'The war will have to be ended by mediation so why not do so now?' argued Schwimmer to one such leading pacifist. 'What is needed is to get all the neutral countries together – because no single mediator will be acceptable to both sides.' 'Why not?' came the answer. She despaired at the lack of imagination but struggled on. 'Eight countries are already involved. Don't you see that some would suspect a single mediator of being partial to their adversaries?'

Over and over again people could not understand what seems, in retrospect, such an obvious, commonsense proposal.

> They were encrusted with the conventional passive pacifists attitude, revelling in abstractions and paralyzed by the need for action. They issued tons of literature telling the world how sorry they were about the war; good-will expressions oozed from the lifeless pages. That was all the ever anaemic old-time pacifist movement offered to counteract the carnage.[21]

Even thinking people who were not normally swayed by popular opinion were bowled over by the wave of nationalism. Bertrand Russell wrote later that he was 'tortured by patriotism . . . but felt that for the honour of human nature those who were not swept off their feet should show that they stood firm.'[22]

Five members of the Liberal government resigned in protest at Britain's entry into the war, and Ramsay MacDonald stood down as the Labour leader because his views conflicted with those of the party's national executive (political truce was agreed) but these men were very much a minority, and despite their resignations they were still ambivalent about the war in many ways. Only the small Independent Labour Party opposed the war from the start in its newspaper the *Labour Leader*, edited by the young Fenner Brockway. But even the ILP shied away from an open, public peace campaign; branch members felt powerless to change the national mood and merely aimed to keep the organisation strong so that it could have future influence.

The war fever was the same all over Europe. The tiny Russian and Serbian socialist parties were the only others in the warring countries to express opposition to the war.[23] In Germany, the Social Democratic Party, the biggest party in the German parliament, had almost unanimously voted for war credits (funding for the war) despite initial mass protests against Austria-Hungary's 'brutal' ultimatum to Serbia. Only a few brave left-wingers, notably Rosa Luxemburg, Clara Zetkin and Karl Liebknecht, continued to oppose the war – and they soon ended up in prison.

In the circumstances, it is surprising that Schwimmer even got the support (mainly from women) which she did. She received positive answers to her telegrams from the IWSA representatives in France, Germany, Hungary, Holland, Sweden and Norway. In London, it was her individual suffrage friends who gave her most encouragement; 70-year-old Isabella Ford, upon whom Schwimmer looked as a 'favourite aunt', Catherine Marshall, Emily Leaf, Kathleen Courtney and a few other women met up regularly at 'good old Isabella's' London pied-à-terre and let off steam about 'fish-blooded' pacifists.

On August 22nd, three days before Schwimmer left from Liverpool for Boston on the steamer *Arabic*, she wrote to Emily Hobhouse, the woman who had criticised British army policy in the Boer War. Schwimmer had been trying hard to gain Hobhouse's support. She told her that the appeal she planned to present to President Wilson, to try to get him to initiate mediation with the other neutral governments, would be signed entirely by women now. The men had been too slow to respond, she explained. And in another letter, to Catherine Marshall, Schwimmer developed her plan and declared that if the American President refused to take action to solve the European war, she would rally the women of America to force him to do so.

On August 31st, the following report was published in the *Daily Express*, under the heading 'OUR GERMAN FRIENDS – SYMPATHY FOR THE ENEMY':

> A *Daily Express* reader sends us a circular which he has received from some 'brotherly love' faddists, who hope to create a peace agitation in Britain, though they admit it would be hopeless to expect anything of the kind in Germany. The handwriting on the envelope is decidedly German and the name of Rosika Schwimmer of New York, who seems to be the moving spirit, seems to have a Teutonic sound. The envelope was originally the property of the Cunard Company and apparently the circulars were addressed on board ship.

As the circular would have been bound to have explained the mediation plan, it seems that the journalists on the *Daily Express* were unable to grasp an imaginative international concept for stopping a war which was to wipe out the best part of a generation in Britain, France and Germany alone, with a total of ten million dead and another twenty million injured. Internationalism was obviously beyond serious consideration in an organ of the infant popular press, created to meet the needs of a new generation of literate readers.

WHILE the British non-militant suffragists and their European counterparts prepared for the peace rally in London, Christabel Pankhurst packed her suitcases and left her apartment in Paris, where she had lived in self-imposed exile since March 1912. For over two years she had directed the Women's Social and Political Union from across the Channel in order to avoid arrest. It was a period during which the militant campaign became increasingly violent with the use of arson on a large scale, although care was always taken to choose buildings in which there were no people or animals which could be hurt by fire. From November 1912, the WSPU tactics were to aim to make the British public so angry that they would force Parliament to grant female suffrage. After all, women *had* been asking for the vote for nearly fifty years. Christabel had been assured by French officials that she would not be extradited.

Now the French President Poincaré had proclaimed a state of seige throughout France and Algeria in response to Germany's ultimatum, and as Christabel climbed aboard a train bound for St Malo in Britanny, where her mother was on holiday, she wondered what the two of them should do now that war had broken out. All the hard work and sacrifice of the WSPU over the past eleven years must not be lost. The war was a particularly bitter blow for suffragettes, thought Christabel, because she believed they were on the point of victory. Should they give up the campaign? Paris was empty when she left, the buildings had their shutters down for the summer and she had been unable to share her thoughts with anyone, except to say a few words to her maid and the shopkeepers. After two years in its capital, France felt like her second home – and now it was under threat of invasion. Both she and her mother were ardent Francophiles.

Emmeline Pankhurst had also come to France to escape British law. She was in a state of utter exhaustion after her continuous imprisonments and hunger strikes since 1908 – five of which had been in the past eight months. Under the Prisoners' Temporary Discharge for Ill-Health Act introduced because of suffrage agitation in 1913, prisoners who damaged their health by hunger striking were temporarily released to recover and then re-imprisoned. Having received a three-year sentence in April 1913 for inciting women to commit crimes to property, Emmeline Pankhurst courageously began the debilitating routine of hunger striking, being released, carrying on the campaign and being arrested again. No wonder the 1913 legislation soon became popularly known as the 'Cat and Mouse Act'.

By the time the order for French mobilisation came on August 2nd, Christabel was in St Malo with her mother. There were few enthusiastic farewells amongst country people for the young men marching off to war, more an irritation at the loss of labour to help with the harvest. In Paris, the whole city suddenly seemed to be queuing outside food shops and banks, or accompanying reservists to the Gare de l'Est, which was the main railway station for trains to the front. Later, the marching troops were to be pelted with flowers as they left factories, offices and the public services unmanned.

Once in Britanny, and able to talk to each other, the two WSPU leaders seemed to have had little difficulty in deciding what they should do. 'War was the only course for our own country to take,' wrote Christabel later. 'This was national militancy. As Suffragettes we could not be pacifists at any price.'[24] And yet only in June, Christabel had been writing,

> Warfare as developed by men had become a horror unspeakable . . . a mechanical and souless massacre of multitudes of soldiers. . . . The soldier, like the civilian, is a human being and a citizen. Why should we be so willing for him to suffer, merely because he enlisted, it may be very young, and not really knowing what the terrors of modern warfare are. . . .
>
> Not only soldiers though: non-combatants die, too, some by enemy attack – others from famine and disease, the result of war – war is bad enough now. Men are making it worse. Aviation, which should be a link between nations, is to be used to make war more dreadful . . . any 'defended' place, however thickly populated, may have bombs rained down upon it . . . [this] is the tragic result of the unnatural system of government by men only.[25]

Her initial reactions to the European war, which she recorded some time before she left Paris and which appeared as the editorial of *The Suffragette* on August 7th, also had a different emphasis from what she was to preach only a month later.

Under the headline 'WORSE THAN *WOMEN'S* MILITANCY' and accompanied by a cover depicting fighting soldiers, she wrote,

> A dreadful war-cloud seems about to burst and deluge the peoples of Europe with fire, slaughter, ruin – this then is the World as men have made it, life as men have ordered it. . . .
>
> A civilisation made by men only is a civilisation which defies the law of nature. . . .
>
> Had women been equal partners with men from the beginning human civilisation would have been wholly different from what it is. The whole march of humanity would have been to a point other than we have reached at this moment of horrible calamity.[26]

The next issue of *The Suffragette*, dated August 14th, was printed but never distributed. In it, Emmeline Pankhurst showed that her immediate concern was the WSPU members in prison and she wrote that no Red Cross nursing or similar work should be undertaken while suffragettes remained in jail. But she concluded:

> That disputes between free and equal nations shall be settled in peace and harmony is the ideal which the WSPU holds and which it believes the enfranchisement of women will succeed in realizing. But if and when fighting has to be done for the sake of protecting another nation whose existence is precious to the world then no Suffragette will hesitate to say 'Let us fight!' It is not by timidity or slothfulness nor from holding back from fighting at the eleventh hour that peace can be advanced. The cure for warfare will come when women have the power to rebuild civilisation and to reframe statesmanship on new principles – principles according to which peace and honour will come to mean one and the same thing.[27]

In other words, unlike some of the non-militant suffragists, Emmeline Pankhurst believed that no form of international diplomacy could stop the war once it had started. Peace was to be postponed until a time when women had the vote and the world was a different place. The government must have been relieved at the support of the 'Pankhurst menace', for as Christabel acknowledged later, if the militant suffragettes had continued their campaign during the war others with a grievance might have followed suit.[28]

Worries about imprisoned WSPU members proved unfounded because the Home Secretary, Reginald McKenna, released them all unconditionally on August 10th as part of new wartime conditions, along with people convicted for offences in connection with strikes. In response, the Pankhursts sent out a circular to all WSPU members advising them that the activities of the Union were temporarily suspended. This would not only save the organisation much money, Emmeline Pankhurst wrote, but give the opportunity

> to those individual members who have been in the fighting
> line to recuperate after the tremendous strain and suffering of
> the past two years. With the patriotism which had nerved
> women to endure endless torture in prison cells for the
> national good, we ardently desire that our country shall be
> victorious – this because we hold that the existence of all
> small nationalities is at stake and that the status of France and
> Great Britain is involved.[29]

The arson stopped and the militant campaign was over.

The initial reaction from the Union's rank and file seems to have been to accept the Pankhursts' truce with the government with little apparent dissent. Some were anxious not to seem unpatriotic or disloyal at this time. Others were exhausted and probably received the outbreak of war almost with relief. But as time went on there was much dissatisfaction with and withdrawal from the WSPU by members who were angry at its adoption of war propaganda. There were two breakaway groups, the Suffragettes of the WSPU and the Independent WSPU who wished to 'entirely disassociate themselves from the line Mrs Pankhurst has taken up since the outbreak of war'.[30]

Annie Bell, formerly a Pankhurst favourite, asked Emmeline Pankhurst to apologise publicly for calling suffragettes who did not agree with Christabel's views pro-German and was banned from the WSPU meetings. When she dodged the stewards and made another protest, she was charged with obstruction and sentenced to one month's imprisonment, but she went on hunger strike and was released after a few days. In 1915, two meetings were held by WSPU dissidents asking for a statement of the organisation's funds and protesting against non-suffrage work,[31] but overall it is difficult to judge just how many former suffragettes wanted to distance themselves from the Pankhursts.

Christabel made her first public appearance in Britain at the

London Opera House on September 8th – billed to speak on 'THE GREAT NEED OF VIGOROUS NATIONAL DEFENCE AGAINST THE GERMAN PERIL'. The Opera House was decked with flags of the Allies and a women's band played the national anthem. She stood alone, spotlit on the stage, which was hung with dark green velvet drapes, and her fans, excited by her homecoming, placed wreaths at her feet.

'Votes for Women!' cried out Victor Duval, from the Men's Political Union for Women's Enfranchisement, but Christabel Pankhurst answered him impatiently, 'We cannot discuss that now.'[32] She declared that

> 'In the English-speaking countries under the British flag and the Stars and Stripes, women's influence is higher. She has a greater political radius, her political rights are far more extended than in any other part of the world. . . . I agree with the Prime Minister that we cannot stand by and see brutality triumph over freedom.'[33]

At this, some members of the audience started to laugh. Was this the woman who had led such a long and bitter campaign against Asquith and his Liberal government?!

Emmeline Pankhurst told the *Daily Sketch* that as the 'Downing Street of the women's movement'[34] the WSPU would not nurse soldiers or knit socks but would continue to work on national lines, and soon they began to stomp the country with colleagues Flora Drummond, Annie Kenney, Grace Roe and Mrs Dacre Fox, on an army recruiting campaign.

As the war progressed, the Pankhursts (excluding Sylvia and Adela Pankhurst, who we will hear more about later) became increasingly chauvinistic. Publication of *The Suffragette* was resumed on April 16th, 1915 but was devoted to war propaganda and renamed *Britannia* in October 1915. The same year, Emmeline was reported to believe that the stewards at Liberal meetings, who had roughly ejected heckling suffragettes in pre-war years, had been 'Huns'. And in 1916, Christabel Pankhurst was writing that German spirits were influencing Sir Edward Grey towards pro-German pacifism. In 1917, they vigorously denounced 'Bolshevik agitators and traitorous pacifists'.[35]

It is perhaps not surprising that, given the emotional nationalism that existed in late 1914, the Pankhursts should have adopted the stance they did. After all, Belgium had been invaded and it probably appeared to them that Germany was issuing military threats on all sides for no apparent reason. There had been a steady stream of articles about Germany's aggressive intentions towards the Great British Empire's colonies in the years leading up to the war, which Emmeline, at least, believed. It was 'absolutely clear to everyone who had studied what had been going on in Germany for years past that the German plan was first to crush France and then to invade England,' she told the *Sussex Herald* on September 22nd, 1914.

In the circumstances, to want to rally the maximum national effort from both men and women seems an understandable way of wanting to shorten the war, reduce the cost in lives and ensure victory. But what is less understandable is why the two suffrage leaders continued to repudiate any suggestion of a negotiated peace once it was obvious to all that 'the boys weren't going to be home by Christmas' as had originally been thought; why they were so fantastically 'anti-Hun' and why after four years of killing they still wanted to continue the war. Unlike Millicent Fawcett, neither of them had a record of imperialist sympathies. They had both spoken out against the Boer War and supported Dr Richard Pankhurst's unswerving life-long advocacy of peace and internationalism.

One reason may be that having been 'the most hated woman in Britain' during the last two pre-war years, Emmeline Pankhurst was anxious to show that even militant suffragettes were good English patriots. The WSPU could come in from the cold, and it would surely have been a relief to have been at one with public opinion after so long. It could also be argued that both women were excited by conflict – by the 'joy of battle' – and it seems likely that they would have found it hard to resist 'national militancy', as they called it. Certainly they had used military parallels for the WSPU for years past. They described it as 'a fighting body and as such must have autocratic control if it is to wage wars more successfully'. 'When going into battle,' Emmeline Pankhurst had said, 'a general does not take a vote of his soldiers to see they approve his plans. They are there to obey his orders. That is how the WSPU has been run and that is how it will continue to run.'[36]

They talked of the European war as if it was an extension of the moral crusade which Christabel Pankhurst had launched in *The Suffragette* in 1913, with a series of articles entitled *The Great Scourge and How To End It*, about the miseries of prostitution and venereal disease for women, brought about by a completely one-sided sexual morality. They drew international parallels with the result of this cruel patriarchy: Germany was a 'male' nation, they argued, brutal and tyrannical, which had raped gentle, democratic 'female' Belgium and France.[37] Only by the good 'feminine' forces banding together could the forces of evil be destroyed.

It was probably accurate that Germany was a more overt patriarchy but the Pankhursts showed little recognition of the starvation and bereavement which their German sisters and other women 'enemy aliens' faced because of the war. After all, German women had not made the decision to invade Belgium. And Christabel Pankhurst seemed to have forgotten her editorial on war being 'a mechanical and souless massacre' of innocent young soldiers when she shouted from recruiting platforms and scorned conscientious objectors. More importantly, perhaps, the WSPU leaders do not appear to have given any critical thought as to how such widespread warfare could be prevented from happening again – except for saying that it would be, when women got the vote.

On the night of Christabel Pankhurst's first public appearance back in Britain, another member of the family was in the audience. She was Sylvia Pankhurst, who had not seen her sister or her mother since January that year – when she had travelled to Paris to be told by Christabel that she thought it would be better if they did not work together any more.

Since 1912, Sylvia Pankhurst had been working with the women in the East End of London for the suffrage campaign, and had founded the East London Federation of Suffragettes, a more or less autonomous organisation but still officially under the banner of the WSPU. The ELF was composed mainly of working-class women and included socialism and pacifism in its programme. There were increasing strains between the two sisters: Sylvia wanted to retain the early links the women's suffrage campaign had had with the labour movement, whereas Christabel wanted it to be a women-only campaign; the former rejected the use of arson as a tactic (though not violent protest as such) whereas the latter was the very architect of the arson policy.

Disagreements came to a head when Sylvia appeared on the same platform as labour leaders in protest against a lockout of Dublin workers and the imprisonment of James Larkin, an Irish trade unionist, in November 1913. An invitation had already been refused by Christabel because she didn't think the protest relevant to women's suffrage but, as second choice, Sylvia had accepted because she saw a chance to speak to an audience of 10,000, at a time when the WSPU had been forced underground. However, there could only be one arbiter of WSPU policy, hence the visit to Paris which marked the end of the working relationship.

When war had broken out Sylvia had been in Ireland investigating a story for the Federation's newspaper *The Woman's Dreadnought* about soldiers firing on an unarmed crowd. Keir Hardie, who was a close friend and lover, had warned her that war was likely but she had not believed him. Returning to England by boat, she watched while crying women said goodbye to their men and supposed that the same scene would be happening all over Europe. She was dismayed when she heard Christabel's speech, which seemed to her to completely ignore the huge cost in human suffering the war was bound to bring, and in response she resolved that she would write and speak more urgently for peace herself. Backstage, her sister and mother virtually ignored her, while outside the rival cries for 'Christabel!' and 'Sylvia!' irritated and embarrassed her profoundly.[38]

The 1914-18 war was to split the Pankhurst family even further apart. Emmeline Pankhurst denounced her pacifist daughter publicly and wrote to her saying she was 'ashamed to know' where she and her less well known younger sister, Adela,[39] stood. Sylvia wept with rage when she heard of her mother's army recruitment campaign and she could not forget or forgive it when Emmeline Pankhurst announced that she wished her dead son – Sylvia's beloved brother, who had died earlier that year – could be one of those marching to the front.

CHAPTER 3

American incredulity

WHEN Rosika Schwimmer reached the other side of the Atlantic, she stayed with suffrage leader Carrie Chapman Catt in New York, before going with her to see both President Woodrow Wilson and the American Secretary of State, William Jennings Bryan. She explained her concept of a conference of neutral nations to the politicians and presented her international women's petition. Afterwards, she boldly told the *New York Times*, 'The President told me he was thinking day and night about the possibility of peace in Europe. He seemed to be deeply interested in the movement and said that he would lose no opportunity of taking practical steps to end the war.'[1]

Schwimmer's personal notes state that women representing suffrage societies in Australia, Canada, Denmark, France, Great Britain, Holland, Hungary, Italy, Norway, Russia, Sweden, Germany and the United States had written or wired to London in support of her open letter. Individual women who had added their names to the petition were Elna Munch, whose husband was the Danish Minister of War, Madam Randi Blehr, whose husband was the Norwegian Minister of the Interior, and Dr Anna Howard Shaw, President of the American National Women's Suffrage Association.

America in 1914 was a country as eager for change and social reform as Britain. The war had shocked public opinion and Schwimmer found plenty of support for her viewpoint. Peace seemed as natural a part of progressive change as the increasing independence of women and the hankering after industrial reform. Americans thought of their country as modern: the women's suffrage movement, which stalwart feminist pioneers like Lucretia Mott, Elizabeth Cady Stanton and Susan B. Anthony had been pushing since the middle of the nineteenth century, was gaining strength. It had taken thirty years for four out of the then forty-five American states to give women the vote but between 1910 and 1914, seven more had been won. In 1912, the suffrage parade up New York's Fifth Avenue saw 15,000 marchers, cheered by a crowd of half a million; three years later it had grown to 40,000 women.

There was greater freedom for American women in general: they disregarded the restricting corsetry of the early 1900s, threw away ornate hats and wore shorter skirts. Increasing numbers demanded birth control information and went out to work as typists, shop assistants and telephonists. Women smoked cigarettes and drank alcohol for the first time – and the middle classes were driving Henry Ford's revolutionary 'universal car' in increasing numbers.

Although economic growth continued, about a third to a half of American workers still worked anything up to twelve hours daily, sometimes seven days a week. Increasing labour unrest at the inequality of wealth was met with violence from company guards and often local police and state militia. One seven-month strike of 9,000 Colorado coal miners in 1914 ended with the death of twenty-one men and a hundred wounded, when company guards opened fire on them. Not surprisingly, the most radical union, the Industrial Workers of the World (commonly known as the 'Wobblies'), was growing in strength and demanding the overthrow of capitalism. There was pressure for more progressive education; for the end of often brutal racism towards Jews and black people, and for prohibition.

When war broke out all over Europe, Americans saw it as a horrifying anachronism. The majority of people were from either German or British descendants and despaired at the bloodshed. War did not seem of their age, of their time – all about them was the clamour for social reform. The last time Europe had seen war was in the 1870s; the Americans had had their own Civil War in the 1860s. American women, in particular, had become increasingly concerned with rendering warfare obsolete. In 1872, a woman called Julia Ward Howe had been converted to pacifism by the Franco-Prussian war, which had caused mass starvation in Paris. She went to Europe to try and organise an international women's peace congress but failed to do so because too many women thought it wasn't their business to interfere. Since then more and more American women had become stirred by her conscience, and by 1914 most women's organisations, whatever their base, had adopted resolutions committing them to peace and arbitration. Charlotte Perkins Gilman's book *The Man-Made World*, published in 1911, had also been widely read. She took as her premise a theory already propounded in some scientific circles, which was that in racial evolution women had originally been dominant and that therefore man was congenitally inferior to women in characteristics making for social progress. 'In warfare, per se, we find maleness in its absurdest extremes,' wrote Gilman in her chapter on 'War'. 'Here is to be studied the whole gamut of basic masculinity, from the initial instinct of combat, through every form of glorious ostentation, with the loudest possible accompaniment of noise.'[2]

So when Rosika Schwimmer arrived in America, the ground was ripe for peace agitation, and particularly ripe amongst women. Opposition to the European war was almost unanimous throughout the country. A cartoon in the *Philadelphia North American* showed, on a background marked EUROPE, a mass of men in deadly combat whilst Emmeline Pankhurst looked on with an inscrutable expression on her face. There was universal press approval when a prominent suffragist, Fanny Garrison Villard, 'her hair whitened in the cause of peace and Woman Suffrage', led a procession of 3,000 women down New York's Fifth Avenue on August 29th against the war. The main banner declared, 'We demand a mobilisation of the Hague Conference'. The women wore black and marched to the beat of muffled drums, with the flags of the fighting nations carried in a cluster. The city, which was usually deserted at this time of year, was thronged with onlookers. Harriet Stanton Blanch, leader of the Women's Political Union, the daughter of suffrage pioneer Elizabeth Cady Stanton and one of the organising committee of 100 declared beforehand,

> We wish to have a meeting of the Hague Peace Conference called. It can be done, and we want it to be done. If you are bleeding to death you do not consider the means by which you stop the flow of blood. . . . We want a Peace Conference that is a perpetual thing – not something that is called from time to time.
> We want to disarm the individual countries, and have an

international army and navy. We want to send out word to the women of every organisation, little and big, the world over. . . . We do not call this demonstration a protest, but a march for civilisation. We want Suffragists and Anti-Suffragists in it; the women's trade unions are interested, the settlements, women of all kinds.[3]

True to her promise to Catherine Marshall, Schwimmer set out on a speaking tour to try and rouse the American people – and especially the American women – to press their government to mediate in the war in Europe. For the first few weeks, her platform was officially a suffrage one (she was being paid by the National American Woman Suffrage Alliance), and she began her crusade in Ohio, which was in the throes of a statewide campaign for votes for women. But later she employed Katherine Leckie, a former newspaper reporter who ran a feminist lecture bureau and literary agency in New York, as her booking agent. Speaking three to six times a day, not only in public halls but on street corners and at factory gates, by December 1914 Schwimmer had been heard in no less than sixty of America's largest cities, scattered over twenty-two states. The tour was exhausting; on one occasion Schwimmer had to lie down on the stone floor of a cloakroom for five minutes in order to recover between talks. But the news she was receiving from Belgium, through smuggled letters, of rapes and suicides of women, only made her more convinced of the desperate need for action and drove her on with a ferocious sense of urgency.

She adopted a more formal oratorial style as it was quicker to get her point across in this way. People who had known her before the war found that her humour and irreverent statements had gone: 'It was as if the pain that millions . . . now endure had suddenly acquired a voice and through her spoke its own desperate language,'[4] one such acquaintance said.

She can't have known full details of what was happening but her despair was certainly justified: by the end of the year each side had one million casualties after five months of fighting. A war of movement had become a static war bound in muddy, rat-infested trenches which stretched from the North Sea to Switzerland, with opponents facing each other across a No Man's Land of between 200 and 800 metres. The German

Schlieffen Plan had failed. Having come within sight of the Eiffel Tower in early September, the German troops had been beaten off by the French and British regular armies, together with a makeshift Parisian fighting force which had left the city in long queues of buses and taxis, to fight what became known as the Battle of the Marne. In the East, the Russians, ill-equipped and incompetently led, had suffered terrible losses at Tannenberg and the Masurian Lakes near the Baltic coast, where thousands of men had been driven into huge lakes or swamps to drown.

At the end of every speech to her American audiences, Rosika Schwimmer begged them all to send a resolution – a copy of which was on every seat – to the American President insisting that he demand immediate cessation of hostilities (later she learnt that there was a special room in the White House where the American administration filed peace resolutions and petitions). And she publicly criticised American peace organisations for talking theory as those in Britain had done[5] instead of taking action. Such was the passion and intensity of her campaigning that she must have realised that the sooner international mediation machinery was erected, the more likely it would be to succeed. Winston Churchill, already a member of the British government at the time, wrote later that before December 1914, 'the terrific affair was still not unmanageable' but that after that, 'the rhythm of the tragedy'[6] had been set. Schwimmer had easily as much, if not more foresight than most politicians, so it is little wonder that she was in such a hurry.

Chicago became a particular centre for peace activity. When Schwimmer spoke in that city, she sometimes visited Jane Addams at the famous Hull House Settlement to try and get her to launch a women's peace organisation. Addams, now in her fifties, was probably the most respected woman in America. At the age of 29, after many years of misery with an 'empty middle-class woman's existence', she had found a purpose for herself in life. With her friend, Ellen Starr, she set about building a community centre in the slums of Chicago, to which Italian, German, Polish, Austrian, Hungarian, Irish and Greek immigrants had come from their countries to start a new life. From the beginning, the aim of the centre was not only to provide practical help and education for disadvantaged immigrants but also to help heal the frustration and sense of uselessness amongst the first generation of American college women, for whom few careers were open. Hull House was not a charitable mission in the old sense; it soon became involved in radical politics and trade union activity. In 1893 Addams was appointed secretary of an Industrial Arbitration Committee. Besides offering practical help and education, the settlement workers made reports on, and campaigned for, improvements in local conditions. By 1911, 400 similar settlements had sprung up as a result and Addams spent much of her time writing articles and books and giving lectures around the country.

It is very rare to find anything derogatory written about Jane Addams; she became a legend in her own time. Many suffragists in different countries greatly admired her. She seems to have had a certain presence, which literally made others more peaceful in her company. Her looks were homely, with her hair scraped back in a bun, and she always wore a rather sad, world weary expression. In later years, because of her reputation, she was sought out to provide leadership for progressive causes but she was not a true radical, and we will see that on at least two occasions she compromised her principles. The few who criticised her resented the Mother Earth image which they said hid a manipulative tendency. She appears to have liked being liked and assiduously collected flattering newspaper cuttings about herself.[7]

Schwimmer, whose many talents did not include Addams's genius for compromise and conciliation, had played hostess to the social reformer at the Budapest Suffrage Conference in 1913, where they had met for the first time. Naturally, she was anxious to get Addams's support for her peace campaign and had written to her before leaving London. Schwimmer's persuasive powers would not have fallen on deaf ears, for as one of a group of social reformers, Jane Addams had been amongst the first to make a statement against the European war. The statement was called *Towards the Peace That Shall Last* and was published in September 1914.

Jane Addams was not new to the peace movement either, having been a principal speaker at the convention of National Peace Societies held in Boston in 1904 and the National Peace Congress in 1907. She had written a book called *Newer Ideals of Peace*, which emphasised that it was the new social conscience, symbolised in the co-operation of international immigrants, child welfare and municipal reform, which paved the way for peace, more than the activities of any pacifist organisation. More civilised ways of settling international disputes would grow out of these new social impulses, she argued, and war would be eliminated through the national process of evolution. By the early part of 1914, she had believed for several years that working- class men all over the world would refuse to fight, if they were ever asked again, and that this resolve would be backed up by the 'nurturing instinct' in women, for whom warfare would be repugnant.

No wonder she greeted the First World War with such incredulity: 'It is impossible now to reproduce that basic sense of desolation, of suicide, of anachronism, which that first news of the war brought to thousands of men and women who had come to consider war as a throwback in the scientific sense,' she wrote later.[8]

While Rosika Schwimmer was on her campaign trail in the Mid-West, British militant suffragette Emmeline Pethick-Lawrence arrived in New York on October 27th. 'If we are going to accept war as inevitable, women might just as well give up living at once, for under these circumstances it is not worthwhile to continue the race,'[9] she declared in an interview the next day.

At the outbreak of war Emmeline Pethick-Lawrence had joined the Women's Emergency Corps Committee to help with the care of Belgian refugees. Like many other women she was swept up in the immediacy of relief work, fully absorbed and even proud that ex-militant suffragettes, like Dr Elizabeth Garrett Anderson and Dr Elsie Inglis, opened the way for women to be army doctors. But in the back of her mind remained the memory of women's international solidarity which had grown up around the campaigning for the vote. Had that all been just an illusion, she wondered? Could the women of the world remain silent while young men were offered up for sacrifice? Sacrifice for what?

In early October, she received a cable from New York asking her to speak at a public meeting in order to help initiate a new national American women's suffrage campaign. Quite who invited her is uncertain – it could have been Harriet Stanton Blatch, Alice Paul or some other American suffragist who had lived in London and been inspired by the Pankhursts and their organisations. Emmeline Pethick-Lawrence had been visited by Rosika Schwimmer before the latter left London.

Schwimmer had wanted help in obtaining a passage across the Atlantic and Pethick-Lawrence's support for the mediation campaign. Although the Englishwoman does not appear to have offered the Hungarian any immediate practical help, by the time the invitation from America arrived, she realised what a good opportunity it presented to get women campaigning for peace negotiations, and decided to go to New York. Her husband, Frederick, joined her.

Soon after her arrival, the British suffragette was given a welcome party by Lillian Wald, founder of the Henry Street Settlement in New York (in the mode of Hull House) and part of the Jane Addams social worker set, which had put out *Towards the Peace That Shall Last*. Pethick-Lawrence could not have had a more sympathetic contact; Wald had helped organise the peace march down Fifth Avenue. At the party Pethick-Lawrence met a radical lawyer called Madeleine Zabrisky Doty, who became enthusiastic about the idea of rallying the suffrage movement to the cause of a negotiated peace in Europe. Doty and Pethick-Lawrence immediately got on 'like a house on fire' and remained life-long friends. They both had charisma, dressed daringly with colour and style and loved to talk and debate more than anything else, particularly about Life and politics. Doty had written a series of controversial articles about New York prisons after having persuaded the authorities to pass her as an offender. She was part of the fashionable Greenwich Village feminist and radical set, which met every Saturday at a women's lunch club called Heterodoxy. Club members were in the vanguard of reforming campaigns: they helped organise strikes, occasionally went to prison and stood on street corners handing out birth control literature.

Doty invited Pethick-Lawrence to stay at her Greenwich Village apartment and meet her friends. One of these was Crystal Eastman, another progressive lawyer, who specialised in labour law and was a pioneer in the field of industrial health and safety. Her brother, Max Eastman, owned *The Masses*, a provocative, popular and witty radical magazine, which he had founded in the Village in 1911. The two of them were close and had together initiated various radical campaigns, but on the outbreak of war in Europe they dropped all other activities to campaign against American military involvement. Eastman saw the conflict as a war of colonial ambition, and militarism as an evil threat to freedom and social justice.[10]

So when Emmeline Pethick-Lawrence introduced the idea of a mediation conference for peace negotiations into her suffrage speech to Harriet Stanton Blatch's Women's Political Union, at a crowded Carnegie Hall on October 31st, many of the audience were already with her. It was time, the Englishwoman said, for the peace movement to become 'active and militant', for it to learn from the women's movement. In her dynamic way, Crystal Eastman wasted no time in taking up the idea and immediately set about forming the Woman's Peace Party of New York. Madeleine Doty, together with another feminist lawyer friend, Ida Rauh, arranged the press coverage, at which they were particularly successful, and within weeks, similar campaigning groups sprang up in Boston and Philadelphia.

For the next month, Emmeline Pethick-Lawrence spoke and wrote on women and war — its effects on women and the effect women might have on war, as well as expounding policies largely taken from the British Union of Democratic Control. What critics she had pointed to her militant past and said that her disclaimer of violence was insincere but at a time when the most popular song was 'I didn't raise my boy to be a soldier', she couldn't go far wrong.

Like many feminist peace campaigners in those days, she emphasised the good influence that the 'mothering instinct' would have on international politics. She wrote in *Harper's Weekly*,

> It is vital to the deepest interests of the human race that the mother half of humanity should now be admitted into the ranks of the articulate democracies of the world, in order to . . . enable them to combine the more effectively in their own defence against the deadly machinery of organised destruction, that threatens in the future to crush the white races and to overwhelm civilisation.

And in *The Survey*,

> I believe a great campaign for organising public opinion and bringing its pressure to bear upon the governments of the world could be initiated now by the women's movement in America. . . . A world-wide movement for constructive and creative peace such as the world has never seen, might even

51

now come into being – a movement which would influence the immediate development of humanity.[11]

Crystal Eastman urged Pethick-Lawrence to see Jane Addams, just as Rosika Schwimmer had been urged to see her. Like many others, Eastman believed that if a National Woman's Peace Party were to be formed and the social reformer to become its leader, it could have real influence on the world situation. However, Pethick-Lawrence had already accepted numerous speaking engagements on the East Coast and it wasn't until the end of November, when she was staying with a suffragist called Grace Hoffman White in Washington, that she reconsidered the idea. Grace Hoffman White was very anxious, she told the Englishwoman, to organise a conference in January at which a National Woman's Peace Party could be formed out of the numerous groups which Pethick-Lawrence's talks had inspired, and would she *please* go and ask Jane Addams if she would chair it?

Little did either of them know that the American nation's heroine had already received letters from all over the country urging her to call such a meeting but that she remained unconvinced of its advisability. A letter dated December 11th to Schwimmer, who was in New York at the time, sums up her initial attitude: 'The basis of constituency is very difficult. There is naturally much emotional reaction against the war, and people are eager to meet and talk about it, but I must say that I dread a large and ill assorted assembly and doubt if we could do anything about it.'[12]

From Washington, Emmeline Pethick-Lawrence went to Hull House in Chicago were, much to her surprise, she met up with Rosika Schwimmer. They hadn't seen each other since London and each seemed to have been largely unaware of the other's activities. Pethick-Lawrence was an admirer of Schwimmer, not because she thought that 'everything was best and wisest that she does' but because she 'always [got] the front page of newspapers for Peace'.[13] For her part, Schwimmer was worried by Pethick-Lawrence's propagation of UDC formulas for a post-war settlement, since she saw them as a diversion from taking action to stop the war.[14]

The two of them spoke together in Chicago. Pethick-Lawrence's speechmaking has been described as 'attracting young women to daring and sacrifice by methods that seemed

... hypnotic',[15] and Schwimmer's oratorial skill was legendary, so they must have made a powerful combination. At one meeting, a thousand people signed their petition to President Wilson.

In December, the Emergency Federation of Peace Forces was formed. This was also based in Chicago and peace, civic and professional organisations sent delegates to the inaugural meeting. Open to men and women, it was chaired by Jane Addams, and Louis Lochner, already Secretary of the Chicago Peace Society, became Secretary. However, both Pethick-Lawrence and Schwimmer refused to leave the country until there was at least the beginnings of a national *women's* peace organisation.

Whatever it was that finally prompted Carrie Chapman Catt (who had so far remained unmoved by the letters she was receiving from women around the country) to ask Addams to send out joint invitations to a great Woman's Peace Congress in the New Year, deserves a round of applause. No doubt she had been too preoccupied with the New York suffrage campaign, but now the idea which had been around so long, itching to be put into action, at last looked likely to come to fruition. The letter which the two women sent to all American women's organisations 'looked forward to the organization of women throughout the country into a peace movement.'

Jane Addams continued to have her doubts, particularly about it being women only, but she admitted that, compared to men, women seemed more anxious to take action and that the demand for places at the Woman's Peace Congress had been tremendously spontaneous and widespread. Bent under the weight of persuasion from all sides, she conceded that perhaps women could do something to stop the first world war there had ever been, and, as if with a sigh, set about doing her duty.

On January 10th, 1915, 3,000 women packed the Grand Ballroom of the New Willard Hotel in Washington, while hundreds had to be turned away. Eighty-six delegates, from a wide cross-section of women's organisations, represented further thousands. The two great suffrage societies – the National American Woman's Suffrage Association and the Federal Suffrage Association – were out in force, as well as the Women's Political Union and the Congressional Union and, of course, all the women's peace groups. Women's trade unions and professional associations were represented, as well as women of all political persuasions.

Sceptics as to why there should be a peace party for women only 'were shown that women held very few offices in the old societies and had some fresh methods of their own which they wanted to employ.' So wrote Lucia Ames Mead, a writer and lecturer on international issues, in a line of argument which has more than a little resonance today. 'Moreover, as women,' she continued,

> they felt that they had special work to perform in the interest of their suffering sisters beyond the sea and in influencing great organized bodies of women whom the older societies have not yet reached. While abhorring needless duplication of machinery, it seemed . . . that this new organisation need not duplicate any other, but might reach with new methods into new fields, not detracting from, but rather adding to, the influence of the older societies with which it sympathizes and is glad to co-operate.[16]

'Have we men big enough to do the work that would ensure the peace of the world?' asked Harriet Stanton Blatch, no doubt in quiet desperation, since it was nearly six months since she had marched down Fifth Avenue. 'If not, then we women are going to join internationally and try to do it. Practically every proposition that has been put out by men must wait until the end of the war to be put into operation!'[17]

More determined to present a united front of women in protest against the war than to argue over details, the conference quickly drew up a preliminary manifesto, agreeing to points from the platform often by a unanimous vote. A more detailed plan called 'Program For Constructive Peace' (see Appendix I) was developed next, and this was significant because it foreshadowed – more than any other programme from a peace organisation – President Wilson's Fourteen Points, which he issued to European governments later in the war as principles of future agreement. It called for a new world order to render warfare obsolete.

In her final speech, Carrie Chapman Catt said,

> The women of the country were lulled into inattention to the great military question of the war, by reading the many books put forth by great pacifists, who had studied the question deeply and who announced that there would never be another war. But when the great war came and the

women waited for the pacifists to move, and they heard nothing from them, they decided all too late to get together themselves and try to do something at this eleventh hour.[18]

However, an eleventh hour appeal by American women did not seem worth reporting in the newspapers. Despite the 3,000 delegates, many of whom were influential, the conference got almost no press coverage. Yet two months later, when the Emergency Federation of Peace Forces had their national conference, with only 300 men and women from a variety of socialist, commercial and trade organisations, it attracted considerable attention from journalists. As it happened, the Woman's Peace Party played a dominant role at that conference too: Jane Addams was in the chair and there was a majority of five women on the committee. It passed most of the Woman's Peace Party's manifesto, including the demand for women's suffrage.

In February 1915, two American senators, one from Wisconsin and the other from Nevada, introduced resolutions to Congress urging President Wilson to initiate a conference with the other neutral countries to mediate in the war. But despite efforts by the peace movement to make these resolutions rallying points for the campaign, they got little publicity. Both resolutions were sent to the Committee on Foreign Relations, and while gathering dust there were of little use, except to keep alive the flicker of hope which the peace movement had of government action.

Meanwhile, the Woman's Peace Party grew rapidly, recruiting members mainly on the Eastern seaboard but also in the states of Minnesota and California. 'The members scarcely realised', recalled Jane Addams later, 'that they were placing themselves on the side of an unpopular cause.'[19]

CHAPTER 4

Bitter divide

IF THEY thought about it at all in those first six months after August 14th, 1914, America must have seemed like a far-distant golden world to women suffragists in Germany, Austria-Hungary, Russia, France and Britain. It soon became apparent that it wasn't going to be a short war, and as the casualty lists grew longer, the harsh realities of modern armed conflict began to dawn on them.

Reports published in the international suffrage newspaper *Jus Suffragii* reveal a European women's movement plunged into war relief work but with the nagging desire, even if not completely expressed, to find a way to stop the killing. Mary Sheepshanks herself wrote an editorial slamming jingoism. It was not enough for women to do relief work, she warned, they must use their brains to urge peace along unvindictive lines, 'leaving no cause for resentment such as to lead to another war'.[1]

Suffragists in neutral countries were lucky enough not to have to choose between patriotism and humanity; not to feel the oppression of working against their own governments. Aletta Jacobs, President of the Dutch society, urged IWSA women to unite and 'make future wars impossible'.[2] The Italian suffragists, whose country would not enter the war until mid-1915, reported that they backed Rosika Schwimmer's plan, and Swedish feminists urged their government to mediate in the war.

As might be expected, the response from the warring countries was mixed. News was slow to come from France. In September, Paris had been turned into a city of women when all the able-bodied men had left to join the regular French army

56

against the Germans in the Battle of the Marne. The presence of enemy troops so close to the capital was traumatic, prompting memories of the Franco-Prussian war forty years earlier when there had been mass starvation in Paris. Many suffragists were in mourning or absorbed in vital war work.

In Germany, the suffrage leaders in the international women's movement were split. Anita Augspurg, Lida Gustava Heymann and others from the Hamburg-Altona Women's Suffrage Society were the first to 'stretch out sisterly hands'[3] to their official enemies through an open letter to Carrie Chapman Catt, whereas Marie Stritt, President of the German Union for Women's Suffrage in Dresden and also part of the IWSA German 'wing', felt that nationalism came first. Gertrude Baumer, another leading suffragist but not in the IWSA, was recruited by the German government to organise women for war work. Luise Zietz, representing socialist women, worked with her. By the end of September, well in advance of women in other warring countries, thousands of German women had been drafted into agricultural work and army equipment factories. As in Britain, unemployment at the outbreak of the war hit young German women the hardest and in Berlin cheap kitchens were set up to feed them. Even at this stage, the Germans were eating war bread.

By contrast, the Hungarian suffrage society, which had always included pacifism in its world-view since its formation ten years earlier, was devoting itself to direct peace propaganda. Bulgarian suffragists made an appeal for peace. And the Russian magazine *Women's Messenger* said that women must liberate themselves to put an end to war — as it was, many were following the men to the front.

In Britain, the war seemed less real, still at heart a Balkan affair. However, there was considerable disruption as 750,000 men volunteered in August and September alone, far exceeding Kitchener's request for 100,000. Sudden female unemployment caused considerable distress, especially in working-class districts. As in other countries, lights were dimmed in urban areas, theatres and newspapers were censored, entertaining was taboo and there were few cars on the road. Women's magazines focused on food economy rather than fashion. The presence of men in khaki, crowded recruiting stations and daily ambulances leaving Charing Cross station, greeted by flower women with bunches of violets in the courtyard shouting 'God bless you lads!',[4] were constant reminders, for Londoners at least, that men were dying. And if the majority of British people were as yet unmoved, the shelling of Hartlepool, Scarborough and Whitby in the middle of December, which caused 700 casualties, soon shocked them into believing the realities of modern warfare. Little did they know that this was the beginning of a trend towards the war strategy of full-scale air attack on civilians, which we fear so much today.

Officially, the British[5] wing of the IWSA wanted nothing more than for the Allies to beat Germany but as we know, several leading officials of the NUWSS did not give their government uncritical support. As an ardent nationalist, Millicent Garrett Fawcett was not among the dissenters and she lost no time in writing to *Jus Suffragii* to point out that Britain had been added to Schwimmer's international petition of women's suffrage societies in error. 'The only body in Great Britain which supported the petition was the Civil Union,' added Mary Sheepshanks in an editorial comment, 'a small body of men and women which has now ceased to exist.'[6]

There seems to have been an unfortunate misunderstanding over whether Schwimmer had been acting independently or on behalf of the IWSA when she had telegraphed to the various national suffrage leaders from London. Not only Fawcett but Madame de Witt Schlumberger from France and Elna Munch from Denmark[7] wrote to the suffrage newspaper to say that their societies did not support the petition to President Wilson. Signe Bergman, a Swedish suffragist, wrote a letter to Carrie Chapman Catt in October: 'In Sweden the position is this: when Rosika asked for the support of our organisation for her mission to President Wilson we cried 'Yes'. Sometime after we received her printed scheme . . . and decided to do nothing.'

However, the Swedes were prompted into action when they read that Schwimmer had succeeded in gaining an interview with the American President and consequently talked to their own Foreign Secretary, telling him that if the Swedish government decided to take the initiative on mediation they would rally the support of Swedish women. Afterwards Signe Bergman wrote to Elna Munch in Denmark and the Norwegian suffrage leader, Gina Krog, to ask them to do the same. 'What we all of us object to is that Rosika has used the name of our Associations for her printed scheme without asking us. There are many things in it of which we do not approve.'

The Swedish suffragists asked Catt to send out a circular outlining action that IWSA suffragists could take. Bergman concluded, 'It is a pity that a good thing should be spoilt because it did not emanate from the right quarters.'[8]

Bergman's criticism is understandable and bad wartime conditions did not help communications, but of course the point was that nothing *was* emanating from 'the right quarters'. Schwimmer took action because she wanted to stop the war and believed that mediation was the only way to do it. Rightly or wrongly, she was not the sort of person who waited until something could be done through official channels – especially when speed of action was so necessary and the disaster so catastrophic. She had already witnessed the failure of one IWSA attempt to talk to foreign ambassadors in London about mediation. And had not both Madame Schlumberger and Elna Munch written to the Alliance office begging Catt to take action? Back came Schwimmer's cable in response to Fawcett's disclaimer. It read, 'I never pretended support of National Union. Fifteen countries and Ireland united people [sic]. United States support plea enthusiastically – Schwimmer.'[9]

All in all, international sisterhood had taken a knock because of the war – but it wasn't broken. Whatever Mary Sheepshanks's reason for her apparent inflamed nationalism when dealing with Schwimmer in the first few days of the conflict, it did not last long and she maintained an admirable internationalist stance in *Jus* (as it was affectionately called) during the next four years. This international news was a great consolation and source of information to many in the face of the war propaganda and heavily censored news reports, found not only in newspapers like *John Bull*, the *Morning Post* and the *Daily Express* as might be expected but in almost the entire commercial press.[10] Letters of appreciation poured into the IWSA offices from the twenty-six countries with societies affiliated to the Alliance. There was some criticism that the newspaper had turned into a 'peace' instead of a 'suffrage' journal but as Mary Sheepshanks rightly pointed out, there was not very much suffrage work going on in Europe at the time. Distributed with the help of women in neutral Denmark and Switzerland, it seems that *Jus* always went out, despite the ban on mail between warring countries.

With little or nothing of regular IWSA work being possible, Chrystal Macmillan and Alena Stanton Coit, the treasurer and

a German woman married to an Englishman, started a relief
centre to help women stranded by the war. Two volunteers,
Elsie Rae and Geraldine Schafter, helped full-time. When
Antwerp finally surrendered to the Germans on October 10th,
a message came to the office that thousands of Belgian refugees
had swarmed into Holland. Chrystal Macmillan immediately
went to the Belgian Ambassador in London and, with credit
facilities guaranteed, she bought £200 worth of food – bread,
condensed milk, chocolate – from Lyons Headquarters and,
together with Mary Sheepshanks, went to Belgium by ship to
deliver it. At Flushing the two of them were shocked by the
tragic sight of hundreds of families sheltering from the damp
and bitterly cold in huge railway sheds lit up by harsh arc lights
and guarded by Dutch soldiers. Tarpaulins had also been set up
in the town square and on the river, women and children, many
without warm clothing and often clutching some useless
possession like a bird-cage, huddled together on barges. 'That
was the first wave of the tragic flood of refugees that has swept
across large tracts of the world ever since,' wrote Mary
Sheepshanks many years later, 'involving broken homes,
broken lives, desperate suffering and frustration.'[11] In retrospect, it's not surprising that it was Dutch suffragists, who saw
the full impact of the war even though they still lived under a
neutral government, who were the first to call for an
international conference of women.

In the forty years before 1914, over 400 religious, cultural,
professional, humanitarian and political international organisations had been formed on the continent. In 1910, representatives
from over a quarter of these groups had met in Brussels to
found the Union of International Associations, to act as a co-
ordinating body for what was becoming known as the new
'international movement'. And yet, as soon as war broke out,
not one of these international groups attempted to retain
contacts: clergymen were preaching the virtues of war from
pulpits all over Europe. Enemy culture – music, language,
food – was often prohibited and the great symbol of working-
class solidarity, the Socialist International, was in shreds.
Europe was fragmented; no one was meeting across the
European boundaries. It was in this context that a letter printed
in *Jus* on December 1st from Dutch suffragists was written:

In these dreadful times, in which so much hate has been

spread among the different nations, the women have to show that we at least retain our solidarity and that we are able to maintain mutual friendship.

Therefore it being impossible to hold the planned International Congress in Berlin next year, we suggest to organise an international business meeting of the Alliance in one of the neutral countries. We think Holland is one of the countries which can be reached easily by the different nations, and therefore we offer the arrangement of such a congress in Holland.

If the majority of the auxiliaries agree with us that we ought to come together, we propose to hold only a business congress, with no festivities. However, a lot of public meetings on which the women's point of view of the present situation of the world might be shown, could be held.

Inspired to act on the Dutch letter, and stressing that her suggestions were not those of either the IWSA or NUWSS committees, Chrystal Macmillan answered by circulating another letter on December 12th to all the twenty-six suffrage societies in the Alliance. She proposed that any meeting they should have, and she certainly thought they should have one, should be to 'discuss the principles on which peace should be made and, if so agreed, to act internationally'.

In her carefully considered letter, Macmillan suggested, with diplomacy, that there were three possible alternatives as to how such a meeting could be organised: '(a) the Alliance could have its regular convention with a business meeting afterwards; (b) the Alliance could *call* a convention attended by different women's organisations; (c) a conference could be summoned by individual women if (a) and (b) were opposed.'

She went on to suggest that the topics to be discussed should be similar to those dealt with by the various 'terms-of-peace' organisations which were forming in various countries:[12] international arbitration; democratic control of foreign policy; the criteria for transferring territory; disarmament; and the federation of states. It was also important, she emphasised, for women to take the initiative:

There are two proposals . . . in which it is specially important that women's suffrage should be kept to the front: (a) the suggestion that territory should not be transferred without the consent of the population of the country and (b) the suggestion that foreign policy should be open to discussion and democratic control. . . . It is essential to make it clear both nationally and internationally that women are included both in the population and in the democracy. This is an important reason why the Alliance should not let the organisation fall into other hands.[13]

There were plenty of women in the Alliance who wanted to meet. Emily Hobhouse, champion of the refugees in the Boer War, organised an open Christmas letter to the women of Germany and Austria-Hungary, which a hundred English-women signed. Hobhouse, who wanted to put the British Foreign Secretary, Sir Edward Grey, and the Kaiser each in a separate battleship and let them fight it out, felt more than ever that men were motivated by greed, fear and envy and were incapable of governing the world in a humane way.[14] The open Christmas letter, published in *Jus*, was delayed by wartime censorship and distribution problems but back came the answer in time to be printed in March: another open letter with warm greetings, signed by an equal number of German and Austrian women.[15]

However, it was the President of the Alliance, Carrie Chapman Catt in New York, who really had to decide, and she felt that she was 'too far away from the scene of difficulty to form a satisfactory opinion'. The decision on whether or not the IWSA should officially call a conference ought, she believed, 'to depend a great deal upon the votes of the women in the warring nations'. She wrote to Schwimmer,

I have sent the officers and presidents the enclosed non-committal letter and vote and have accompanied it by a personal letter in which I have said virtually the same thing as in the letters to the officers. These letters are to be mailed today.

Last night when I got home I found a cable from France, 'The French Committee refuses International Meeting'.

Of course if the French refuse it the Germans surely will and that makes an International Meeting impossible. The votes will go out just the same but personally I think it is already decided that there will be no such meeting. Lovingly yours. . . .[16]

Whether a more positive approach from Catt would have

swayed the national suffrage leaders we shall never know, but as predicted, the votes went against the Alliance calling a conference (see Appendix 2). Despite Schwimmer's perseverance and passion, as well as her close friendship with Catt, she had failed to convince the one person that really mattered of the necessity for women to take action internationally. But there was still Macmillan's third option that a gathering 'could be summoned by individual women', and Aletta Jacobs wasted no time in inviting the Scotswoman and a few others from nearby countries to come to Holland for an exploratory meeting in February 1915.

Kathleen Courtney, Catherine Marshall, Emily Leaf and a Quaker suffragist from Cumbria called Theodora Wilson-Wilson, who was a children's story writer, as well as Macmillan, made up the British contingent. From Germany came Dr Anita Augspurg, the first woman judge in her country, Lida Gustava Heymann, a pioneer feminist and trade union organiser, Helen Stöcker, a sexual reformer, and Frida Perlen, a suffrage worker. Five Belgian and several Dutch suffragists[17] joined them to plan a gathering which would make history.

Meanwhile, all this talk of internationalism was not having a good effect on NUWSS unity. Ever since war broke out, the storm had been gathering amongst executive members – a storm which was to split the largest British women's suffrage organisation into two.

As early as October 25th, 1914 Isabella Ford described the pressures on and divided loyalties of suffragists opposed to the war in a letter to Catherine Marshall: the dilemmas of whether to join with male peace activists or stay with suffrage; whether to do relief work, which would please the government and get them the vote, or do peace work which would not.

Don't think of resigning yet from the NU. I am recovering from the appalling horror which seemed to destroy everything in one at first – and am eager for work. . . . I consider we women must not combine with Morel & Co [E.D. Morel was the leading light of the Union of Democratic Control] yet. . . . But of course, as you know well, Mrs Fawcett is our stumbling block. She is not so bad quite, as I expected for she and Agnes were most unspeakable during the Boer War – till she went to the Camps. . . . I intend to take more definite action – I want to

63

visit branches and address them on 'Women's work in time
of War' – a most misleading title I assure you! . . . I shall
resign if Manchester and Newcastle resign, then we can
consider matters.

I am horribly tied up with C. Council work and Lord
Mayors' Committee, because for the sake of Woman with a
big W. & all that, I had to do it. Now, I am trying to find
tactful ways of shirking it for my whole mind and soul is
bent on Peace work. If our NU hangs back the cause of W.
Suff. will be irrevocably damaged in the future. Do you agree
with all this? My mind is absolutely firm. I've had 3 good
meetings, 2 ILP's & the very large Co-op meeting in
Leeds – & found them good. What an awful world it
is – Your loving Aunt Isabella.[18]

On October 15th, Helena Swanwick had suggested calling a
special Council meeting with representatives from each of the
NU affiliated societies to discuss future terms of peace: this had
been outvoted but a Provisional Council was scheduled for its
regular date in November. This gathering could not make
policy (that was up to the Annual Council which met every
year in February), but as a forum for discussion it was an
opportunity for all the many shades of opinion on the war to
be expressed.

At this early stage of the war, in 1914, before the desperate
time when it seemed the bloodshed would never stop, the
emphasis of the pro-internationalists was primarily to get
members of the Union to *talk* about the issue. Executive
member Alice Clark wrote to Catherine Marshall

we must encourage our members to form opinions as to the
methods which are needed to protect humanity against a
repetition of the horror of this war. I don't think it is our
place to prescribe the means, but I do think it is our duty to
encourage our members to think, just as I believed it was our
duty to encourage our members to think about the means of
preventing infant mortality & the abuses which the law
permits to be inflicted on married women.[19]

But even to talk in abstract terms of how war could be
avoided in the future was thought of as treason in some
quarters: 'The time to discuss proposals of peace is when peace
is nearer,' said executive member Lady Frances Balfour. 'We

can have no peace until Germany is beaten.' Several executive members were frightened of controversy should the Union publicly discuss peace issues. 'What would statecraft think of a body sitting in the middle of a war and affirming its belief in arbitration and conciliation as opposed to war?' asked Lady Balfour.[20]

However, the mood at the Provisional Council in November was considerably more liberal than Lady Balfour's views. A resolution proposed by Catherine Marshall in support of a speech made by the Prime Minister, Mr Asquith (see Appendix 3), on September 26th, 1914 in Dublin, in which he declared the need for 'a real European partnership' after the war, was carried by twenty-two votes to nine. Marshall wanted the Union's press organisation to build up public opinion on this issue and combat the spirit of revenge; the resolution committed the Union to do this. Another resolution, proposed by Manchester and amended by the North-Eastern Federation, was also carried. The resolution urged 'organised women of the world' to agitate for political freedom 'in the belief that the enfranchisement of women would facilitate ... the establishment of permanent peace'. And it was decided to throw open the Union journal *Common Cause* to all views on the causes of the war and how it could be prevented in future.[21]

What is very apparent is that, even at this stage, the internationalists realised that if the war really was 'the war to end all war', as was constantly being declared in the press, that if the terrible loss of life at the Battle of the Marne and Ypres and Tannenberg and the Masurian Lakes was to be avoided from ever happening again, then it was imperative that, firstly, the final peace terms were not made in a spirit of revenge, and secondly, that machinery be set up to replace war in deciding questions of international disagreement. Both these depended on sympathetic public opinion.

Britain was already committed not to make peace without the consent of France and Russia, said Catherine Marshall. It would be very difficult to find peace terms to which all three countries would agree and the extent to which the government could put pressure on France and Russia would depend on public opinion.[22] She wanted an 'educated and responsible public' when the time came for settlement, not an 'ignorant and prejudiced public which had taken its opinions ready-made from the party newspapers'.[23] It was useless to oppose all war,

Catherine Marshall in 1916. She once calculated that her work for conscientious objectors meant she was liable to 2,000 years' imprisonment. The *Labour Leader* called her 'the most able woman organiser in the land'.

she believed, until some better means than war had been established by which international disputes could be settled.

Linking work for peace with the women's movement was clear and obvious to the internationalists on the NUWSS executive, even though sometimes they didn't do their case much good by explaining it in rather confusing, high-flown philosophical phrases. To them, promoting peaceful co-existence between countries involved the same principle as fighting for women's equality with men; it was all a fight against oppression. To support the use of force between nations seemed to them to support the use of physical, economic and social force by men towards women. They wanted the recognition of equal rights and privilege both between the sexes and between the nations. They wanted 'right instead of might'.

They also believed that the development of representative democracy was a way of resolving conflicts in society, without resorting to the use of force, and that the extension of this principle to international affairs would prevent war. To illustrate just how novel a perception this was for the time, we need only to look at the arguments of pre-war anti-suffragists who said that women could not vote because they did not fight in armies, that government symbolised 'physical force' and that if women played a part in it it would become enfeebled.[24]

Ironically, Millicent Fawcett also believed that suffragists were committed to the extension of democracy. Her argument was that they should support the British government unequivocally in the war effort because 'the British Empire is fighting the battle of representative government and progressive democracy all over the world, and therefore . . . the aim of the National Union as part of the democratic movement is involved in it'.[25]

Both 'camps' within the NUWSS saw suffrage societies as part of a democratic movement; it was just that the internationalists had a broader, more far-seeing and imaginative definition of democracy. Meanwhile, Marshall noted somewhat bitterly that suffragists had never been so popular with the general public since they ceased to agitate for suffrage: 'Now you are doing something useful' people would say.[26]

Five executive members nearly resigned when it was decided not to have an emergency council but stayed on in the hope of getting the Union to act corporately on combating jingoism. Consideration for Fawcett may also have had something to do with it. Eleanor Rathbone, a suffragist in Liverpool, wrote,

> The more I think of it, the more aghast I feel at the idea of a
> possible exodus out of the Executive of yourself and the four
> others you mentioned. It would mean, I feel, the break up of
> the Union and also probably the break up of Mrs Fawcett. I
> don't believe younger people often realise what it means to
> older people to pull up old roots or to try to strike new ones.
> It is hard enough after 40. It is, I imagine, almost impossible
> after 60. Mrs Fawcett has always seemed to me a person
> whose roots probably go exceedingly deep.[27]

Not surprisingly, the tensions amongst executive members
increased and on November 28th, Marshall wrote a long,
angst-ridden letter to Fawcett, in a desperate effort to be
understood:

> I find it so hard to express myself in Committee or in
> conversation; & I feel that you have in some ways
> misunderstood what it is that I, & those who feel as I do,
> want the NU to do in this matter, & that the idea of what
> you *think* we want to do is causing you great worry and
> uneasiness. I believe there is really less difference than some
> of us have supposed between the 2 sections of opinion on the
> NU executive; and there is much ground for united action if
> only we can make up our minds to accept the fact that one
> group cannot admit that even *this* war was wholly justifiable
> & inevitable, whilst the other cannot understand how there
> can possibly be any difference of opinion on what seems to
> them an obvious case of right & duty.

Marshall told Fawcett that the only way to agreement was to
avoid discussion over what had occurred in the past and to stop
calling each other 'pro-German' on the one hand and 'pro-war'
on the other – 'two equally wounding forms of misrepresenta-
tion'.

> I would refrain from doing a good many things which as an
> individual, I should like to do, if only the union will take
> some corporate action. But I feel very deeply that we are
> responsible, both as individual women & Suffragists, & as a
> Union with an organisation which can do effective
> propaganda, for taking some part in forming public opinion
> in this grave crisis. If the Union cannot act, then I (& others,

I believe) will feel bound to free ourselves to act with some
other organisation. . . .[28]

The internationalists seem to have bent over backwards to
try and stay in the Union. This was partly for pragmatic
reasons because they knew they could influence public opinion
much more effectively from within it than as mere individuals
outside, but also because it was genuinely painful to give up on
an organisation which meant so much to them.

Millicent Fawcett must have known about Marshall's
strength of feeling but she seems to have been shocked when
she realised how widespread these views were on the executive.
On December 3rd, in response to the original Dutch invitation,
Chrystal Macmillan proposed to the committee that the
'National Union ask Mrs Catt to summon a business congress
in 1915'. The resolution was carried with only two members
opposed.[29] One of them was Millicent Fawcett. In a letter to
Carrie Chapman Catt, the NU President wrote that she was
very strongly opposed to calling any international convention,
mainly because women are 'as subject as men to *national*
prepossessions and susceptibilities', and it would hardly be
possible to bring together the women of belligerent countries
without violent bursts of anger and mutual recrimination.

> We should then run the risk of the scandal of a PEACE
> conference disturbed and perhaps broken up by violent
> quarrels. . . . It is true this often takes place at Socialist and
> other international meetings: but it is of less importance
> there: no one expects the general run of men to be anything
> but fighters. But a *Peace Congress of Women* dissolved by
> violent quarrels would be the laughing stock of the
> world. . . . I feel so strongly against the proposed convention
> that I would decline to attend it, and if necessary would
> resign my office in the IWSA if it were judged incumbent on
> me in that capacity to take part in the Convention.[30]

During the autumn months, Fawcett had been completely
preoccupied with the progress of the war and what efforts
women could make to support Britain's part in it. She knew, of
course, that some people, such as Quakers, were complete
pacifists and would have nothing to do with war, like her friend
Isabella Ford, and that there were others who were already
demanding a negotiated peace but they were, she thought, only

a tiny, mistaken and impractical minority, unworthy of serious consideration. She was horrified when she discovered that most of the chief officers of the Union, the editor of the Union newspaper and an actual majority of the executive committee members were not only part of this minority but believed it their positive duty as suffragists to discuss the war and attempt international action to stop it. She couldn't follow their arguments, they seemed abstract and visionary and hopelessly idealistic, yet she admired these women; she had worked closely with them, thinking them intelligent and very capable. Catherine Marshall's parliamentary and by-election work had considerably strengthened the National Union as a political force and Fawcett had trusted her judgment for years.[31]

As the February date for the NUWSS Annual Council Meeting drew near, Fawcett began to worry what would happen to the Union's good name if it spoke of peace and if women like Macmillan and Marshall, so respected by the members, carried the Council with them.

February 4th, 5th and 6th were the dates for the Council meeting, which took place in the same Kingsway Hall which had seen the sad Women's Peace Meeting six months before. Six hundred societies affiliated to the NUWSS were eligible to send 1,000 delegates between them and, despite the difficulties of wartime travelling and their time-consuming relief work, most of the delegates attended. The treasurer announced that £45,000 had been raised that year, despite the war.[32] A large number of resolutions[33] were discussed and, at the beginning, everything seemed to be going the internationalists way.

The Council supported the executive's invitation to Carrie Chapman Catt to call an IWSA Congress in a neutral country – although whether or not it wanted it to discuss the peace question was unclear. It also passed a resolution recommending the organisation of educational courses for the purpose of encouraging 'the study of the causes which lead to war, the consequences of war on the economic, intellectual, and moral aspects of life, and the consideration of what means can be taken to prevent war in the future'. Yet another called upon members to 'take every means open to them for promoting mutual understanding and goodwill between nations and for resisting any tendency towards a spirit of hatred and revenge'. Two of the resolutions passed dealt with the necessity for a new post-war international order. One of them 'urged the

Government to do its utmost to ensure that in the future International disputes shall be submitted to arbitration or conciliation before recourse is had to military force, and that the nations shall bind themselves to unite against any country which breaks the peace without observing these conditions.' Another confirmed the support for the Prime Minister's speech passed at the Provisional Council in which he advocated 'the substitution for force ... of a real International partnership, based on the recognition of equal right and established and enforced by a common will'.

But despite these international aspirations, the Council did not appear to have the courage of its own convictions and, after some confusing decisions from the Chair, threw out a clause committing the Union to work towards building public opinion on these principles. Marshall cynically described the attitude as 'Clap but don't vote'.[34] A resolution to 'sustain the vital forces of the nation' was also endorsed, so exactly what direction the work of the union should take was open to different interpretations.

Now these proposed policies were hardly 'peace at any price' ones but nevertheless, when Millicent Fawcett took the chair at a public meeting which had been arranged on the last day of the Council meeting, she was uneasy. The press were present and she could just imagine if the internationalists on the executive got carried away in their speeches, they would all be denounced as 'pro-Hun' and the Union might never recover its reputation. She believed that how women bore themselves in this war would have a profound effect, not only upon the outcome of the war itself but upon their future status in the country. What was more the NUWSS had invited Maria Vèrone to speak. She was a French lawyer, known as one of the most active internationalists before the war, who had made a brilliant, impassioned speech on 'La guerre contre la guerre' at the Budapest suffrage conference in the summer of 1913. Goodness knows what she was going to say now.

When it became time for Fawcett to make her speech she did so in her usual restrained manner. She emphasised the Union's decision to sustain the 'vital forces of the nation' and described in detail the relief work of the various societies. They agreed with the Prime Minister's principles for post-war organisation, she said, but speaking for herself, she considered the greatest national duty at present was to drive the German armies out of

France and Belgium. 'Until that is done,' she declared to the attentive audience and scribbling reporters, 'I believe it is akin to treason to talk of peace.'[35]

With the Council having just passed a resolution committing members 'to promote mutual understanding and goodwill between nations', Fawcett, as President of the Union, could not have said what she did without adding that it was a purely personal opinion. But that was of little odds to the Press, because as far as the general public was concerned, Millicent Garrett Fawcett *was* the National Union of Women's Suffrage Societies. Marshall and others sat in stunned dismay. Were they now to risk being called 'traitors' if they dared to debate ways of preventing future wars? Was it 'treason' to back the practical application of the Prime Minister's words?

As it happened, Maria Vèrone did not cause the embarrassment that Fawcett had anticipated, and the President must have been as surprised as everyone else when the Frenchwoman's forceful rhetoric contained almost exactly the same message as that of her own.

After the fateful Council, Marshall, Macmillan and Courtney left immediately for Holland and returned more convinced than ever of the value of organising an international women's congress. 'We are commissioned to form a Committee in this country to work for the . . . Congress which we have decided to hold at The Hague immediately after Easter – if Holland is still a neutral country. That will give us a good deal to do these next 8 weeks,'[36] wrote Marshall to a colleague. The cost would be £1,000 to be divided equally between the Dutch, German and British suffragists – and the women had issued invitations and draft resolutions from Holland.

The next NUWSS executive meeting on March 4th saw what was to be the beginning of a rush of resignations precipitated by the events in the previous six months. Kathleen Courtney's letter of resignation from the position of Honorary Secretary was read out. Maude Royden, the editor of *Common Cause*, had already given notice. Courtney wrote,

> I have for some months felt strongly that the most vital work
> at this moment is the building up of public opinion on lines
> likely to promote a permanent peace and I am also
> convinced that such work is entirely in accordance with the
> principles underlying the suffrage movement. I was therefore

anxious that it should be undertaken by the NUWSS and in the event of the Council deciding to undertake it, I was prepared to forego the expression of my own particular views for the sake of working with the NUWSS. . . .

The resolutions on the subject of war put on the Agenda . . . do not, of course, represent my own views; this, I neither expected or desired. They represent the minimum for which in my opinion a suffrage society should be prepared to work.

The Council, however, made it quite clear that they were not prepared to undertake work of this kind. They passed certain resolutions, it is true, but only on the understanding that they were not to be acted upon. . . . To my mind, this refusal on the part of the Council is not only a refusal to do the work which the moment demands, it is also a refusal to recognise one of the fundamental principles of the Suffrage Movement.[37]

Kathleen Courtney seems to have taken a gloomier view than the other internationalists over the strength of the reactionaries in the Union, as represented at the Council meeting. Catherine Marshall's mother Caroline, for example, who was also an active non-militant suffragist, working in Cumbria, was convinced that both Courtney and Marshall had got the wrong impression of the mood at the Council and accused them both of being 'the patient that did not want to live'. 'If you had had your say (& it was only the partiality of the *Chair* that prevented) you would have been compelled to alter your impression,' she concluded.[38]

For Catherine Marshall, the decision over whether or not to resign as Parliamentary Secretary of the NUWSS was an agonising one. She loved her work, especially the co-ordination of the Election Fighting Fund and her links with women in the labour movement. She saw this as sowing the seeds for a more egalitarian and democratic future, not only between women and men, but between poor and rich. Her status in the Union gave her 'the best means of serving the greatest cause in the world'.[39] Now, having experienced such opposition, she was stirred up, forced to think what it was that she really believed in. She sent a draft plan to Helena Swanwick dealing with the formation of a Women's Independent Party, 'an organisation that should stand for *real* democracy, *real* feminism, *real* internationalism, with a paper of its own, if possible a daily'.[40]

'I want a good progressive daily paper so dreadfully!' replied Swanwick. 'But I suppose a weekly is all we could ever dream of. . . .'

Swanwick preferred the name Democratic Party to Women's Independent Party and did not want to exclude men from joining. 'I would like to see a great humanist party rise, keen on equal suffrage, proportional representation, devolution, a reformed House of Commons & an abolished House of Lords, Free Trade & informed Diplomacy, & tremendous economic changes. . . .'[41]

For some reason, Marshall's letter of resignation, of which there were two copies, one for the Chairwoman of the committee, the other for Millicent Fawcett, did not arrive in time for Fawcett to read it before the executive meeting on March 4th. Mrs Rackham, who was in the Chair, handed the letter to the President minutes after the meeting had begun and it lay unopened while parts of the top copy were read aloud to the members:

> The spirit shown at the Council meeting . . . the refusal to pass the operative clause of the Asquith Resolution; Mrs Rackham's ruling as to the effect of that refusal; and the indifferent and irresponsible attitude of the Executive Committee at our last meeting when we were discussing what was to be the practical outcome of the Council's Decisions . . . make it clear that the Union is not going to put its heart and mind into this extension of suffrage work, as it has done into relief work.[42]

Marshall would resign as Parliamentary Secretary anyway, she wrote, but whether or not she would stay on any NUWSS committees such as the EFF would depend on whether members of the executive were free to express their personal opinions about the present war when speaking officially on behalf of the Union. She interpreted Mrs Fawcett's speech at Kingsway Hall to mean they could not.

We can only try to imagine the scene at the Union offices in Great Smith Street, Victoria, London, with the executive members, almost spanning three generations of suffragists, witnessing their political disintegration. This was no ordinary committee. These women had given their lives to the women's movement. They'd worked closely together for years, but now deeply held convictions were bitterly dividing them.

Being of a reserved nature and not given to passionate outbursts, Millicent Fawcett is unlikely to have betrayed much emotion over the news, although she was deeply hurt that Marshall had not told her beforehand and particularly shocked at the prospect of losing such a valuable Parliamentary Secretary. She wished to express the profound regret with which she heard of the intended resignations, she told the committee. She could not praise their work too highly and in her opinion the extraordinary value of the National Union as it existed today was very much of their creation. She was inclined not to fill up the posts, especially perhaps that of the Honorary Parliamentary Secretary, as this work was of a most difficult and delicate nature and Miss Marshall had conducted it with an extraordinary degree of success; she knew exactly how to approach the members of Parliament and there was no one who could really fill her place. Perhaps the societies could send in nominations for the office of Honorary Secretary only, she suggested.[43]

The next few weeks must have been trying for all concerned. Exhausted after five years' hard work on suffrage, with very few breaks for holidays, everyone was at a low ebb. Marshall was ill for most of March; Swanwick underwent an operation. The internationalists who had not handed in letters of resignation, stayed on in the belief that there was at least a mandate from the Council to implement peace education but Lady Balfour, Helena Auerbach, Millicent Fawcett and their supporters[44] would have none of it. They were on the alert now; they knew about the international congress and the 'peace propaganda' and wanted no part in it. The different shades of anti-war opinion on the committee and the ambiguity of the Council resolutions made it very difficult to vote the nationalists down; and Fawcett would insist on making further speeches on 'treason' and the war, which were automatically taken as the official views of the National Union. On March 22nd, Swanwick wrote to Marshall,

Mrs Fawcett wrote to offer to call on me here yesterday, so I invited her to tea and she came. I was absolutely blunt with her & told her that though we didn't retaliate, she couldn't expect us to sit under speeches like those she and Lady Frances had been lately dealing out to us – I tried to make her see that she couldn't decently call her colleagues traitors

& lunatics; but she just flushed & blinked & rambled away over all sorts of quite irrelevant things . . . just before she went I told her I intended to resign from the Executive & she implored me not to – 'There is so *much* to be done!'. . .

She is very miserable about it all but quite dreadfully embittered & unjust. Her mind is quite closed. I feel that so long as she dictates to the NU there is no place for me within it.

And in another letter on the following day:

As I see things now, there is no use whatsoever in making a prolonged misery of staying on the Executive . . . Mrs Fawcett *can* not see reason. Mrs Auerbach will be as difficult as stupid people always are & Mrs Rackham will exercise her power to suppress all objectors. Events (not only lately, dear Catherine, but for *months* past) have shown me that 'our lot' are not capable of making good *on that committee* & it seems . . . a dreadful waste of nervous energy. EFF is dead anyway & our Labour policy will *have* to be on different lines – Don't you see that? Can you see working a Labour policy with Mrs F???[45]

Feelings were very bitter all round with Marshall writing to Fawcett,

Thank you for taking the trouble to write and tell us what had happened about the Hon. Sec. of the NU – though I cannot help wondering that you should think it matter what is thought by people whom you consider capable of treacherous and dishonest action. . . .[46]

and then thinking better of the last comment and crossing it out. Kathleen Courtney felt bitter too: 'What I think so black about this affair,' she declared, 'is that she [Fawcett] is ardently ashamed of her speech but won't say so to those of us who were attacked.'[47]

Defeatism began to creep in, with the realisation that they were dealing with emotional prejudices which were unsusceptible to reason. Executive member Alice Clark thought that it was 'worth putting up a fight and giving the societies a chance to decide which way they shall go' but she doubted that the fight would be successful, as all the 'backward and ignorant societies will follow Mrs Fawcett. . . .'[48] Emily Leaf confided in Marshall,

> I don't know what is going to happen at the next
> Executive. . . . Personally I feel more and more . . . that the
> older section of the NU who want to do *nothing* (other) than
> ask for the vote – and feel that it is *undemocratic* to commit
> NU suffragists to the UDC or the International Congress
> must be left to go their own way . . . [they] will wish less and
> less to adapt themselves to the new ideas as time goes on – I
> don't consider that they are carrying out the resolutions of
> the Council by taking the line they do – but they either do
> consider it – or else they don't care. . . .
>
> [I] feel that our part of suffrage must show what it stands
> for and that will lead us to sympathy with the Radical
> Labour Party – and Socialist party on its International
> side.[49]

Nine more members of the twenty-four-member executive
resigned at an NU meeting on April 15th, together with Miss
Crookenden, the Secretary (a different job from that of
Honorary Secretary). Chrystal Macmillan was the only internationalist to stay on, presumably because she was in Holland
helping the Dutch suffragists organise the Hague Congress.
Since the executive split exactly in two, it is interesting to
speculate why the internationalists, rather than the nationalists,
resigned – especially since, as far as the officers were concerned,
if we include the editor of *Common Cause*, the ratio was four
to two in favour of international action. There seem to have
been three main reasons. Firstly, many executive members felt
that Millicent Fawcett had been President of the NU for so long
that societies would back her out of a sense of loyalty. As a
consequence they felt she was unlikely to resign and that as
long as she stayed they could not win their case. Secondly, the
internationalists did not want to be associated with the 'smash
the Germans view' some of their more vocal colleagues were
expounding. And thirdly, they believed the Union was becoming undemocratic.

It does not seem to have been the executive's decision
not to send official delegates to the Hague Congress, which
was the cause of this latter belief. Rather it was the decision
not to allow affiliated societies to send their own delegates
if they wished and the actions of certain NU executive
members between the executive meetings which both alarmed

and angered the internationalists.

An article by Oliver Strachey, who was married to Ray Strachey, a close friend of Millicent Fawcett, was condemned by Helena Swanwick in her resignation letter as apparently representing the Union's view 'on so narrow a basis [that] we should have never obtained the work, the talent, the sacrifices and the funds which have in the last few years . . . poured into the National Union'.[50]

Five of the other resigning members accused the executive of being undemocratic, while the others gave no reason for their resignations. The resigning Cary Schuster positively dipped her pen in vitriol:

> Not only has the majority of the Committee prevented what I believe to be the will of the Council from being executed but one of the means adopted by the Executive, for carrying into effect the resolution for the 'Promotion of Goodwill between Nations', has been thrust aside by the President, in the interval between the meetings of the Executive, and their decision has been thereby stultified; the position of the officer entrusted with the Press Department being also rendered untenable.
>
> Such an interference with the rights of self-government . . . is absolutely subversive of the democratic principle, and introduces into the Suffrage movement methods reminiscent of those by which the imperial Chancellor controls the Reichstag.[51]

Fawcett believed that, on the contrary, it was herself, and those who agreed with her, who were acting democratically and that members were resigning because, like Kathleen Courtney, most of them felt the views of the majority of the NUWSS society members were more in line with those of herself than their own. Many months afterwards she had not forgotten or forgiven Margaret Ashton, from the Manchester and District Federation, who, while she had apologised in writing for her personal insults to Fawcett, had never withdrawn her accusations that her late colleagues 'wilfully misrepresented the wishes of the 1915 Council'.[52]

Just how much support the internationalists had amongst the rank and file is hard to tell. Twenty-two societies sent resolutions protesting at their not being allowed to send delegates to the Hague Congress. There appears to have been something of a North/South divide with the Manchester and District Federation and the North-Eastern Federation sending particularly strongly worded protests, the former threatening to disaffiliate. Ten societies and twelve individuals declared a vote of confidence in Fawcett's leadership but only two letters came actually opposing the Hague Congress.[53] Out of 600 societies, this response does not show a very high interest in the subject, and there is some other evidence of apathy within the Union; only seventy societies bothered to vote for a new Honorary Secretary, for example.[54] Perhaps this is not surprising. War relief work could hardly hold such a large and diverse organisation together and there was a feeling amongst some members that the Union would have reached a turning point anyway, with a split between radicals and conservatives, largely caused by the generation gap. However, there was much debate over the Hague Congress in the letter columns of the *Common Cause*, with about equal views on each side.

The London Society for Women's Suffrage issued a questionnaire on the war, the results of which showed resistance to 'peace talk', but with some justification Marshall described the questions to be of the 'Have you left off beating your wife yet?' variety. Question 1 went: 'Do you consider that the NU should advocate anything, however good in itself, if by so doing it might impair its influence in Parliament and the nation and so endanger the cause of Women's Suffrage for which alone it was created?'[55]

Not for nothing had Marshall said in a speech to the North-Western Federation, 'Let us not succumb to temptation to do what wins us universal approval.'[56]

Although all the internationalists, except Macmillan, resigned from the executive, they did not completely give up on the NUWSS. They met, at Margaret Ashton's suggestion, for an informal meeting at the Sesame Club in London on May 9th to discuss possible tactics for re-electing a progressive majority on to a Special Council in June, held to fill the vacancies caused by the resignations, clarify what policies the societies wanted to follow and decide how free they were to pursue controversial policies. Five out of twelve of the internationalists were willing to stand again if the Council voted to take *action* on peace issues, and if it were decided to re-elect the whole executive so that there was a chance of a working majority. Four more were undecided. Marshall, who was one of those who thought the

Union would have split anyway, suggested putting an emergency resolution which proposed that the Union divide 'as a one-celled organisation divides into 2 cells when it has reached a certain stage of development'.[57] One section could do the controversial political work, the other devote itself to attracting as wide a cross-section of support as possible, she said, thus avoiding a damaging split. But only Emily Leaf supported Marshall on this and the idea was thrown out. Marshall was unsure whether to stand for re-election and such was her influence that Alice Clark thought the internationalists would 'hardly have much chance' if she did not.[58]

When the June Council was held, the internationalists seem to have had a following in some of the large towns but the majority of the smaller country societies were with Fawcett.[59] A strong argument held by many in personal sympathy with the peace propaganda advocates was that whatever might be the right course for individuals to pursue, the Union, as a corporate body, should steer clear of campaigning on divisive topics – and on ones for which it was not specifically formed. Neither Marshall, Courtney, Swanwick nor Maude Royden were at the Council. Courtney wrote to Macmillan, who was still abroad at the time, that they had 'planned to be in remote spots before the date was fixed' and that they were unable 'to alter things'. 'Besides I doubt whether it would not do more harm than good,' continued Courtney, revealing what was probably the real reason for their non-attendance, 'the reactionaries are having it all their own way in the NU & there is evidently only the tiniest minority for any forward policy. Well we must recognise facts. . . .'[60]

And yet there is further evidence that the rank and file delegates attending the Council were unclear about the issues put before them: 'The mass of people did not understand what the seceders really wanted . . . there was huge confusion of thought,'[61] wrote a suffragist from Cumbria, on behalf of her committee, and asking that Marshall, Courtney and Isabella Ford come and talk to them in a 'quiet, informal way'.

It would have taken a great deal of courage and deeply held principles to try and counter the anti-German hatred that brutalised British people in 1915. It would not have been easy to commit yourself to 'build up public opinion' for peace, even if in your heart you wanted to do so. Early in May, a British liner *Lusitania* had been torpedoed by the Germans off the Irish coast, with the loss of over a thousand lives, many of them women and children. A surge of hostility ran through Britain: German shops were attacked and looted in the East End and hundreds of top-hatted stockbrokers marched to the House of Commons to demand the internment of all Germans. Nineteen thousand 'enemy aliens' were already in prison but the Prime Minister, Asquith, was forced, by public demand, to announce that all such males of military age would be interned, and old men, women and children would be repatriated.

It is highly likely that if the National Union had made a wholesale effort at communication with 'enemy' women, or openly and persistently debated the foundations of a permanent peace amongst its members, female suffrage would not have come as soon as it did. Conscientious objectors were disenfranchised for five years after the war and women might have been kept voteless as a punishment, if pacifism amongst suffragists had been overt and widespread. It would have been a brave step indeed to risk half a century of women's struggle but given its former standing and established network, if it had wanted to, the Union could have played a major part in swaying public opinion away from hysterical jingoism and revenge. In turn, this might have put pressure on the government to seek a negotiated peace, and it is not impossible to imagine that if Lloyd George had not felt he had to 'play to the gallery', he might have tried harder to prevent the Treaty of Versailles from becoming the vindictive instrument it was, containing the seeds of future conflict.

In the short term, calling for peace could have lost the suffragists everything they were working for; but in the long term, when the full catastrophe of the war had been absorbed, the NU would surely have been respected for its political courage and foresight. However, it is not the job of history writers to contemplate what *might* have happened.

CHAPTER 5

Meeting across enemy lines

'Those of you who know what it means to organise, know that to get an international congress together from February to April, especially at a time when you cannot communicate, when you send out ten cables and do not know whether one of them reaches the person to whom it is addressed, at a time when you cannot write a letter in Europe without having it read by censors . . . you will realise [what it meant] for those splendid women in Holland [to get] together a meeting – an international meeting – with women from both belligerent and neutral countries, with fifty women from America and thousands of women from Holland within that short time. . . .

'People said, "All right we see they are coming but they will come and they will fight and not accomplish anything," but they did not fight. Then the people said that there would be just some talking and then the women would go home, and nothing will ever happen, and when you realise, as I shall tell you later, what did happen, you will realise that this congress was one of the greatest things that women ever achieved.' (Rosika Schwimmer in an impromptu speech, December 6th, 1915)

A hundred and eighty British women applied to be delegates to the Women's International Congress at The Hague, including some of the best known in British politics. Margaret Bondfield (formerly Secretary of the Shop Assistants Union and later the first women Cabinet minister in a Labour government – or any other government), Lilian Harris (from the Women's Co-operative Guild), Sophia Sanger (from the International Labour

Legislation), and Esther Roper (formerly from the Women's Textile Representation Committee and an active trade unionist in Manchester) were amongst the British Organising Committee members, as well as Pethick-Lawrence and Marshall, Macmillan and the other ex-NUWSS members. Mary Macarthur, founder of the National Federation of Women Workers and well respected in the labour movement, Sylvia Pankhurst, Charlotte Despard, Olive Schreiner, Emily Hobhouse, Lady Ottoline Morrell, Lady Courtney of Penwith, Katherine Glasier, Ethel Snowden and Eva Gore-Booth – Christabel Pankhurst's mentor – were also committee members. So, too, were Sarah Dickenson and Sarah Reddish, working-class trade unionists and suffragists from the Lancashire cotton district. Clearly, the Congress was not a minority interest amongst the thinking women of Britain.

Not that it did not have its opponents, of course. 'We suffragettes are no believers in that sham which is internationalism, which is really disloyalty and anti-nationalism'[1] went the lead article in the April 16th issue of *The Suffragette*, which, according to Sylvia Pankhurst, when writing of her sister and mother later, had suddenly 'burst into life' after eight months of silence. It was now 'a thousand times' more the duty of militant suffragettes to fight the Kaiser for the sake of liberty than it had been to fight anti-suffrage governments. In a speech given at Sun Hall, Liverpool, Emmeline Pankhurst condemned the Hague Congress and declared that France had to be defended 'to prevent her being crushed by the over-sexed, that is to say over-masculine ... Germany'. And with cruel irony she declared – to loud applause – that 'this terrible business, forced upon us, has to be properly finished to save us from the danger of another war perhaps in ten years' time'.[2]

Sylvia Pankhurst, who, together with other members of the East London Federation, enthusiastically supported the Congress, was severely reprimanded by the wealthy Lady Astor (later to become the first woman MP in 1919) who had just extended her valuable patronage to the Federation. She would not have done so, she said disapprovingly, if she had known Sylvia would attend such an international gathering. Other women also withdrew their support from the Federation and many returned to the WSPU, so endangering the Federation's work with poor East End unemployed women and their children, who were often threatened with eviction whilst their husbands were in the army. Sylvia Pankhurst wrote after the war,

> Many times before and since the choice came to me, whether for the sake of the work I was doing, to stay my hand and remain silent, or to speak and do what I believed to be right, knowing that through me, all else that I was prominently engaged in would suffer attack and perhaps extinction. I was guided by the opinion that freedom of thought and speech is more important than any good which can ever come of concealing one's views, and by the knowledge that in the hour of its greatest unpopularity the pioneering cause needs one most.[3]

In 1915, passports were a new invention. They were introduced for the first time at the outbreak of war so that passage abroad was impossible without permission from the authorities. Just a week before the 180 British women were due to travel in two contingents by boat to Holland, and when some of them had already been issued with passports, the British committee of the Congress received a bombshell of a letter from the Home Office. 'His Majesty's Government is of opinion that at the present moment there is much inconvenience in holding a large meeting of a political character so close to the seat of the war,' it said, and went on to add that the government was refusing permits to delegates, cancelling those which had already been issued.[4]

It was a bitter disappointment but, undeterred, Catherine Marshall decided to use what influence she had with Reginald McKenna, the Home Secretary. After much discussion, she managed to persuade him to issue twenty-four passports to women of his choice. However, there was no time to rejoice because the next blow was an announcement that an Admiralty Order had closed the North Sea to all shipping. The only consolation was that Chrystal Macmillan and Kathleen Courtney were already over at The Hague, having grabbed their passports earlier and gone over to help the Dutch with the organisation.

Meanwhile, the Congress was beginning to attract publicity. Several newspapers, *The Times* and the dry *Morning Post* included, published a strong rebuke from the 79-year-old French author Juliette Adam who had been invited to the Congress by a member of the British organising committee:

'They Burn, They Kill, They Violate: Are You Truly an Englishwoman?' went the front page headline in the *Daily Express*, which had already geared up its reporters for an orgy of ridicule by suggesting the previous day that the Congress should be held at St Helena in the middle of the South Atlantic. Under another heading 'Dismal Macawbers', the newspaper read as follows:

> When a Daily Express representative called at Queen Anne's Chambers yesterday for further information the secretary of the Cranquettes, a Mrs Hills, haughtily stayed in her room. She sent out a sorrowful spinster with the official notification that she had no news for the Daily Express.

Had they really expected otherwise? The report continued, in a series of nasty jibes,

> The disappointment of not seeing the bulbs in bloom, coupled with the dead seriousness with which the Cran-quettes take themselves as they work in their eyrie high above a cruel laughing world, make the offices of the British Women Peace Committee a sad place just now.
>
> Some day they may obtain a boat . . . perhaps the mothers of Scarborough and Hartlepool and the wives of the men of Mons and Neuve Chapelle and a few of the Belgians in this country who escaped from Liège and Malines with their lives and little else, will give them a parting ovation at the quay.[5]

At least Sylvia Pankhurst escaped the war of words with the *Daily Express*. Under no illusions that she would be one of the twenty-four chosen for a passport she had drafted a series of resolutions to send to the Congress. She wanted the abolition of secret foreign treaties, the creation of a permanent peace treaty uniting all nations, the abolition of national armies and navies and the democratisation of the international Court of Arbitration (founded by the First Hague Conference in 1899) with an extension of its powers.

When she showed the resolutions to Keir Hardie, broken as he was by depression over the war, he suddenly came alive and forcefully urged her to stress that the Congress take action to promote these ideas. The concept of international government – world government – seemed a good one but after leaving Hardie, and while waiting in Bishopsgate for the Old Ford bus, Sylvia Pankhurst had sudden doubts. People were only now gaining control of their national governments, she thought, when they got there would they find the power had gone to an international one? 'The belief flared up insistent that only from a society re-created from the root, replacing the universal conflict of to-day by universal co-operation, could permanent peace arise,'[6] she thought, heartily sick of the poverty and injustice around her.

A few thousand miles away in the middle of the Atlantic Ocean, the American delegates to the Congress were working on almost exactly the same proposals as those of Sylvia Pankhurst. Forty-seven delegates had sailed from New York on April 13th, at great danger to their lives, since the Germans were stepping up their submarine warfare in an effort to blockade British imports (in the same way Britain was very successfully blockading Germany) and were destroying many enemy vessels without warning.

Since the trip was not officially sanctioned, their ship, the *Noordam*, was unable to fly an American flag and so could easily have been mistaken for an 'enemy' ship and torpedoed. In any case, even vessels which were clearly flying a neutral flag weren't completely safe, since the Germans had found out that the British merchant navy was using neutral flags for disguise. Two ships had been sunk as the *Noordam* left New York. When the delegates left Jane Addams had told the press,

'We do not think we can settle the war. We do not think that by raising our hands we can make the armies cease slaughter. We do think it is valuable to state a new point of view. We do think it is fitting that women should meet and take counsel to see what may be done.'[7]

Of course, there was some strong opposition to the Congress in America too, even though Jane Addams's reputation lent the expedition an aura of respectability. Ex-President Theodore Roosevelt sent them on their way calling them 'both silly and base'. A Mrs Lowell Putnam, who happened to have a brother who was President of Harvard University, said that the Woman's Peace Party was

the most dangerous movement which has threatened our emotional people for some time. It was founded by an ex-militant [presumably she meant Emmeline Pethick-Lawrence], a woman who had been several times convicted of criminal acts which were far from peaceful.

This woman, to whom notoriety was the breath of her nostrils, got the ear of several emotional women whose hearts are so large that many people have mistaken them for heads.

They were told that, though they did not bear arms they bore armies, and similar catch-phrases. These good women, of whom the most prominent are childless and many of whom are spinsters against whom no breath of scandal has ever been raised, were lined up together and photographed as 'mothers of men' and no-one saw the absurdity of it all.[8]

Well, so much for sisterly solidarity. On the whole though the American press thought of the Congress as an impractical, if laudable, moral gesture, which didn't pose much of a threat to the American way of life.

It is worth tracing how Jane Addams came to be chosen as Chairwoman of the Congress. When the planning committee first met in Amsterdam, the Germans wanted Chrystal Macmillan to be Chairwoman, but the British women thought it better to have someone from a neutral country. So Frida Perlen wired to Schwimmer, 'Do everything, everything to persuade Mrs Catt and if you succeed send me a telegram.'[9]

Mrs Catt, however, had already decided she was having nothing to do with it. On the same day that Perlen wired Schwimmer, the Hungarian received a letter from the Alliance leader announcing that she had heard the first news of the Congress:

I have written to Aletta that I most assuredly will make no plans to cross the Ocean while the Germans are threatening neutral vessels and while neutral vessels are being struck in such a reckless fashion in all directions by floating mines which no-one seems to know anything about. I told her I was willing to die for peace, or for suffrage but that I wasn't willing to drown myself for nothing at all. Things may be better by April to be sure, but I have nothing yet which indicates that there is to be anything but a tempest in a teapot at the proposed conference.[10]

Having failed to make Catt change her mind, Schwimmer then turned to Jane Addams, who accepted. The quietly spoken social reformer could not have been a more brilliant choice.

The trip across the Atlantic went well, except for an incident with a gunboat drawing alongside, until the morning of April 23rd when the *Noordam* suddenly stopped in the English Channel, within sight of the cliffs of Dover. Passengers were informed that they could not land, or have anyone come on board. All traffic had been stopped and vessels waited on the horizon. No explanation was given.

The scene was strangely surrealist. The sea was calm and the sun shining as, out on deck, the delegates watched as groups of destroyers rushed past them; a mine exploded and they could hear the sound of a cannon booming in the distance. Tension grew when a series of irritating telegrams from the American Ambassador in London, Walter Hines Page, informed the women that there was nothing he could do since the matter was in the hands of the British Admiralty. This was a situation, they suspected, which would not greatly upset him, since they knew he referred to them as the 'Palace of Doves'.

British newspapers brought on board from neighbouring vessels revealed the contempt with which the American delegation and the whole Hague Congress were viewed: 'This shipload of hysterial women' (*Globe*); 'Folly in Petticoats' (*Sunday Pictorial*): 'This spring jaunt to anxious neutral Holland' (*Eastbourne Chronicle*); 'Pow-wow with the fraus' (*Daily Express*); and continuing in a similar vein, 'This amiable chatter of a bevy of well-meaning ladies' (*Northern Mail*).[11]

Little did the Americans know that the British contingent was feeling just as frustrated by a series of either intentional or inefficient – who knows? – bureaucratic bumblings which prevented them from travelling. Despite the Admiralty Order closing the North Sea, the British Organising Committee learnt that one last boat was crossing to Holland. On the strength of McKenna's promise of passports they decided to summon all the delegates by telegram. They laid on a special train from London to Tilbury. Everything seemed set until the Home Office declared that it could not, or would not, process their passports in time for them to catch the boat.

Returning to the Home Secretary the following day, (Wednesday, April 21st) they received an assurance that another boat would sail on Thursday (he had, he said, consulted the Prime Minister and the Lord of the Admiralty). But as if in some ghastly extension of the Cat and Mouse Act (see page 36), when they turned up the next day and McKenna handed over the passports – saying, for whatever reason, how delighted he was to be able to let them travel at last – he went on to add that unfortunately he had just been informed of another new Admiralty Order which was also closing all shipping across the North Sea for an indefinite period.

The women were furious. However, there was still a week to go until the Congress, and having made their way to Tilbury, they decided to wait for the first boat that sailed. Ten days later, when the Congress was over, they were still there. The *Daily Express* gleefully rubbed salt in the wound:

> All Tilbury is laughing at the Peacettes, the misguided Englishwomen who, baggage in hand, are waiting at Tilbury for a boat to take them to Holland, where they are anxious to talk peace with German fraus over the teapot.
> Longingly they gaze from the windows of their hotel at the Mecklenburg (a mail boat) at anchor in the river opposite . . . at present the only boat in Tilbury which would normally sail to Holland. . . .[12]

and so on in that mixture or ridicule and hostility, which newspaper journalists of a particular kind reserve for subjects to which their employers are politically opposed. 'Afraid of the Peacettes!'[13] the *Express* guffawed when Berlin radio announced that the North Sea had been closed to prevent British women from attending the Congress.

Questions were also asked about Marshall and her colleagues in the House of Commons. 'I selected women who represented organisations and well-known sections of thought,' replied Reginald McKenna in reply to a Parliamentary Question. The smiles changed to laughter when he added, 'As soon as the permits were given, communications between this country and Holland were suspended.'[14]

While the American contingent were stuck in the middle of the English Channel and the British delegates were sitting at Tilbury, Rosika Schwimmer had arrived at The Hague on Sunday, April 25th, three days before the Congress was due to begin. She had travelled with Lola Maverick Lloyd and her husband William and four children. Lloyd, who had met Schwimmer in Chicago in the autumn of 1914, was to become her life-long friend and co-supporter in peace campaigns.

This cartoon appeared in *The Daily Express* on April 28th, 1915. 'Even from the ranks of the super-cranks at the back of the Liberal benches,' the paper crowed, 'there rose no champion of the misguided women who have been trying to reach the Hague for an international chirrup.'

Together with some other Americans, the group had sailed ahead of the American delegation to Scandinavia, where Schwimmer made a whirlwind tour to mobilise delegations for the Hague Congress. A report in *Jus Suffragii* gives us some idea of the impression she gave onlookers at this time:

> Rosika Schwimmer addressed in Stockholm an audience which filled every seat in Grand Hotel's great state room, the same room in which four years ago the International Franchise Congress met. She reminded us how very full those bygone days were of happiness, enthusiasm, hope and confidence. . . .
>
> Rosika Schwimmer was greatly changed herself. She gave the impression of one who has suffered, who has lived in the very center of recent events, who has seen ideals topple . . . it was not merely her wonderful eloquence that held us all; it was the consciousness that her intense feeling of indignation . . . was . . . out of her innermost soul.[15]

Schwimmer and Lloyd had a tortuous journey from Malmö to The Hague, changing trains five times; being body searched at the German border and losing their luggage. When they met up with Chrystal Macmillan and Kathleen Courtney, Lloyd described them in her diary – perhaps because she was unused to British reserve – as 'tough nuts, cold as ice'.[16] No one wanted anything 'radical', Lloyd went on, and Schwimmer told her that all her old friends were against her. The two responses were connected because Schwimmer had already been thinking how the Congress could take *action*, instead of fading into glorious oblivion as a mere talking shop. She planned to add a controversial resolution to the agenda but didn't get much encouragement from her ex-colleagues.

Right from the very beginning, there were two schools of thought at the Congress: the out-and-out pacifists who wanted to stop the war immediately, and those who felt that the conference was definitely not a 'stop the war' congress but one to 'stop war happening again', and that a resolution demanding peace could not be passed without some statement as to terms, a task, they felt, that was beyond the power of the delegates.[17]

Many of the first group were Quakers, although Schwimmer was an obvious exception to this, and would not have supported the gathering if no attempt was to be made to stop the men killing each other. Frida Perlen and Theodora Wilson-

Wilson, two of this group, had drafted a controversial 'truce' resolution calling for an immediate ceasefire, which the others (Macmillan and Courtney, for example) were determined to rule 'out of order'. As it turned out, in the end everyone was satisfied.

The Congress opened on the evening of April 27th, with Aletta Jacobs, President of the Dutch suffrage society, making a stirring speech:

> 'We can no longer endure in this twentieth century
> civilization that governments should tolerate brute force as
> the only solution of international disputes.
>
> 'We women judge war differently from men. Men consider
> the first place the economic results, the cost in money, the
> loss or gain to national commerce and industries, the
> extension of power. . . . We women consider above all the
> damage to the race resulting from war, and the grief, the
> pain and misery it entails.'[18]

At 9 o'clock, the whole audience stood to applaud as Jane Addams walked into the hall and up on to the platform to take the Chair. The *Noordam* had been given permission to sail the previous afternoon and the ship had landed in Rotterdam, just half an hour before Aletta Jacobs began her speech!

As Rosika Schwimmer said afterwards, the most obvious historical significance of the Women's International Congress was that it happened at all. It took great courage and ability to organise such a gathering at a time when all other international movements were shattered by war-imposed animosity. That there would be a more peaceful world when women had political power was one of the main planks of women's suffrage propaganda, and when the most difficult test came, a significant proportion of the international women's movement proved they were true to their convictions.

 But the Congress was also the first international meeting to outline what the principles of any peace settlement should be. In January 1916, President Wilson told Jane Addams that they were the best plans put out by anybody and sure enough the famous 'Fourteen Points' which Wilson argued for at the end of the war (unsuccessfully) bear a striking resemblance to the suffragists' work. The Covenant of the League of Nations, which first met at Geneva in November 1920, is also remarkably similar to the resolutions passed at the Women's

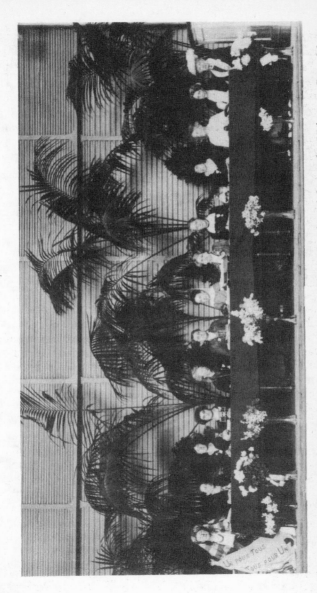

The platform at the International Women's Congress at The Hague: from left to right: Unknown, Rosa Manus (?), Lida Gustava Heymann (?), Rosika Schwimmer, Anita Augspurg, Jane Addams, Unknown, Aletta Jacobs, Chrystal Macmillan, Rosa Genoni (?), Mrs Kleman, Unknown, Unknown.

International Congress.

The main points of the twenty resolutions no doubt appear utopian to cynical generations battered by the seventy war-full years since the spring of 1915, but they are still valid as prescribing conditions for a war-free world, and only waiting for the human race to find the will to implement them. They were:

(1) No land should be transferred without the consent of the men and women in it, and the right of conquest should not be recognised.

(2) Autonomy and a democratic parliament should not be refused to any people and women should be granted equal political rights with men.

(3) Governments should refer future international disputes to arbitration or conciliation and bring social, moral and economic pressure to bear on any country which resorts to arms.

(4) Democratic control of foreign policy, with no secret treaties.

(5) Universal disarmament.

(6) Establishment of a permanent international conference (with women represented) with the authority to settle international differences arising from 'economic competition, expanding commerce, increasing population, and changes in social and political standards'.

(7) Representatives of ordinary men and women to take part in the final peace conference at the end of the 1914 war.

The delegates also put forward a practical solution for stopping the war which was raging around them: a *continuous conference of neutrals* as suggested by Rosika Schwimmer and another woman, a Canadian called Julia Grace Wales. Wales was a 33-year-old teacher at Wisconsin University and quite independently of Schwimmer had written an article about mediation in December 1914, which had been published anonymously by the Wisconsin Peace Society in February the following year. In April, it had been passed by the Wisconsin Legislature and sent to Congress. This proposal satsified both the apparently irreconcilable elements at the Congress, the 'peace at any price' versus the 'how to stop war in future' schools, and the contentious 'Truce' resolution was dropped.

'Only Madame Schwimmer could sweep the Congress off its

feet,' wrote an American delegate to a friend back home, 'and she did it several times.'[19] One of these occasions was before moving a major resolution entitled 'The Peace Settlement', when Schwimmer suggested a minute's silence for those fallen in battle. The delegates rose in unison; as always there was a strong undercurrent of emotion, checked by self-control. They had braved hostility and ridicule to meet together, while their fathers, brothers, husbands and sons were at war, not so many miles away across the Belgian border. Schwimmer described the women:

> we had one who learned that her son had been killed – and women who had learned two days earlier that their husbands had been killed, and women who had come from belligerent countries full of the unspeakable horror, of the physical horror of war, these women sat there with their anguish and sorrows, quiet, superb, poised, and with only one thought, 'What can we do to save the others from similar sorrow?'[20]

The soldiers in the First World War died not only from being mown down by machine gunfire as they went 'over the top', but from epidemics of typhus, cholera and dysentry which were soon to sweep through the filthy trenches. Under the constant strain of living under shellfire, with the din of explosions and guns, other men developed 'shell-shock'. Still others were tried by court marshalls and executed for leaving the trenches without permission, for supposed cowardice or for sleeping while on sentry duty. The only escape was if a man was badly wounded, and later in the war some soldiers deliberately shot themselves through the hand or foot. If it was discovered that their wounds were self-inflicted they were sentenced to death.

On the second day of the Congress, five Belgian delegates walked into the hall. Somehow they had managed to get travel permits from the German authorities occupying Belgium. Their difficult journey had involved driving by car to Esschen, where they were searched, and then walking for two hours to Rosendahl across the Dutch border, from where they got a train to The Hague. On hearing of their arrival, one of the German delegates on the platform, Anita Augspurg, leapt to her feet and invited them to join the other speakers. As they mounted the steps, the whole Congress stood and cheered.

Belgians Marguerite Sarten, Eugenie Hamer and the three

others from Antwerp had come especially to protest against the
'Truce' resolution which had been published in advance. No
peace settlement which allowed Belgium and France to remain
occupied would last for long, they argued; it would simply
postpone further military action. They were happy to learn the
resolution had been dropped.

Considering the short time in which the Congress was
organised, the response was indicative of the passion the
subject aroused. There were suffragists from Austria (6),
Belgium (5), Britain (3), Canada (2), Denmark (6), Germany
(28), Hungary (9), Italy (1), Netherlands (1,000), Norway (12),
Sweden (12) and the United States (47). French and Russian
women were not allowed to attend. Twelve out of the twenty-
six national suffrage societies affiliated to the IWSA had
representatives (albeit not always in an official capacity). But it
wasn't just suffrage groups. Invitations had been sent to both
women's and mixed organisations all over the world and 150
were represented. Just to give some examples, the Hungarians
sent a rep from the *Agricultural Women Labourers*; the Dutch
someone from the *League for the Protection of Children's
Interests*; the Americans, from the *Women Lawyers'
Association*.

A total of 1,136 voting members (plus visitors) packed the
largest hall which the organising committee could find in The
Hague, the Direntuin, a bizarre pseudo-Moorish building in the
Zoological Gardens. This location naturally led the *Daily
Express* (for which the Congress was 'more or less a practical
joke', while at the same time being 'remarkable for its extreme
dullness') to quip about 'Peacettes at the Dutch Zoo'.

The inside of the hall provided a suitably picturesque setting
for the historic debates. Balconies overlooked the main
auditorium and there were 'boxes' on each side of the stage, all
full to bursting and decorated with ornate ballistrades and
arches. On the platform, in front of a backdrop of enormous
potted palms, sat twelve members of the organising committee
behind a long trestle table. Emmeline Pethick-Lawrence made
the following observation:

A visitor who sat in the gallery was impressed by the
similarity in personality and dress of the delegates who
occupied the body of the hall. There was nothing in general
appearance to distinguish one nationality from another . . .

we realised that the fear and mistrust that had been fostered between the peoples of the nations was an illusion.[21]

The police presence, heavy at the start through anticipation of trouble, dwindled away when it was perceived to be unnecessary.

Procedure for the conference had been meticulously worked out. The criteria for voting was that delegates had to be female (men could attend as visitors) and in agreement with the resolutions sent out with the invitations, briefly, that international disputes be settled by peaceful means and that women have the vote. A Resolutions Committee (with two women from each country represented and Macmillan in the chair) hammered resolutions and amendments into a workable form and ironed out ambiguities in the different translations. The official languages of the Congress were French, German and English and everything said in one of these languages was translated into the other two. It was a magnificent piece of organisational work.

Discussions about which country had started the war and how it was being conducted were banned. This was a brilliant stroke of diplomacy which prevented arguments and encouraged positive thinking. However, as one American put it,

> Because there were no clashes along national lines, it must not be thought, however, that the Congress was stagnantly placid. People cared too much for the subject under debate for that to be possible. There were most vigorous differences of opinion over details, and some energetic misunderstandings, for which the necessity of translating each speech into two other languages supplied many openings. . . . One's every faculty was on the stretch hour after hour, and we wondered afterwards why we felt so exhausted.[22]

Besides the 300 messages of support which came from places as far away as India, Brazil, Spain, Serbia, Poland and South Africa, the Congress received thirty formal protests. The most controversial of these was from the National Council of French Women and the French Suffrage Union, deploring the holding of such a meeting while their country was under invasion: 'in order that future generations may reap the fruit of this magnificent display of self-sacrifice and death, French women will bear the conflict as long as necessary.'[23]

Congress members were accused of suppressing the protest because it was not read out at the Direntuin, but although the statement was published in Dutch newspapers a week before the Congress opened, it was not until the day after it closed that Jane Adams found a copy in her hotel room with the request that it should be read to the conference. In any case, none of the protests – and few of the greetings – were read out simply because there was not enough time.

However, the French response was not totally hostile. Not all the committee members of the National Council and Suffrage Union had signed the protest and the British delegation in London had received many letters of sympathy from French-women before the conference began. Sixteen of them (professionals, working-class women, students), including Gabrielle Dûchene, the President of the *Section du travail du Conseil National des Femmes Françaises*, signed a letter of support sent to The Hague:

> if other countries are now invaded, the women of those afflicted nations might quote our example, for refusing international co-operation, and the chain of mistrust and of hatred will bind for ever. . . .
>
> [women] are strong against war, because not making it they are not intoxicated by the joy of action. The so-called Gospel of Force which exalts brutal and material strength, is represented by some as the Virile Law, which despises pity and righteousness and the weakness of women.
>
> Women feminists who are so often accused of imitating men, oppose with all their strength this vile tradition. They wish to remain women, and they know that women's idea will triumph.[24]

As might be expected, the journalists attending the Congress were not much interested in the quiet drama of history: of women meeting across enemy lines in the greatest war the world had seen to 'consider in perfect harmony and straight-forwardness the most difficult propositions' and 'part better friends' than when they met. Schwimmer was constantly pestered by reporters at her hotel for 'behind-the-scenes' stories:

> It was said that the congress was so very, very disappointing because nothing sensational could be reported. One of our

correspondents, a very famous and great journalist of Europe, said 'I had a very hard time to get a commission to write up the congress, and when I did, the editor said: "All right, you may send one or two stories, except in the event they come to blows, then you can send cables or whatever you want!" '[25]

Evelyn Sharp, a British journalist, who had been one of those refused a passport, wrote a marvellous analysis[26] of the British press response to the Congress. *The Times, Manchester Guardian, Daily News, Daily Chronicle, Labour Leader, Christian Commonwealth* and *Herald* 'gave as good accounts of the proceedings as the meagre press telegrams enabled them to do,' she wrote.

> But I am dealing here with a mass of comments selected almost at random from numbers that appeared in the papers before the Congress took place; and their abusive impudence, their wilful inaccuracy, and the underlying note of fear that runs through them all, takes one back to the early days of the Woman's Movement.
>
> There seems to be a certain set of adjectives specially reserved in newspaper offices for women who set out to try and make the world better. 'Misguided' is fairly common, so is 'chattering'; 'hysterical', of course, has become a byword in the mouth of any one who wants to fling a sneer at a woman.

Sharp continued,

> 'Women peace fanatics,' says the *Evening Standard*, growing uneasy, 'are becoming a nuisance and a bore.' The *Glasgow Herald*, remarking airily – 'but perhaps we give them too much attention', proceeds to give them a good deal more, and adds – 'The irresponsible chattering is nevertheless offensive here at home, and those who are bearing the burden of the struggle [Query:- The staff of the *Glasgow Herald*?] have some right to be protected from annoyance.'
>
> The *Irish Times* opens a long leading article with the words – 'The Women's International Congress, which met at the Hague last week, was, of course, a fiasco.' Then why, one feels inclined to ask, devote a whole column or so to talking about it? *The Sunday Times* closes a longish paragraph on the proceedings at the Congress with the

invidious statement,

Doubtless amateurish peace projects need not be taken too seriously, but the impression on some of the observers of the proceedings was that the Governments of the world – both neutral and belligerent – would do well to put a quiet check on such schemes, lest they add to the embarrassments of the situation already difficult and delicate.

These gentlemen do protest too much to carry conviction with them that 'amateurish peace proposals' are not to be taken seriously.

All the newspapers declared that this was not the time to talk peace, reported Sharp. She went on,

Not now, says the *Daily Graphic*, 'while their husbands and sons and brothers are fighting and dying a hundred miles away!' Not now, echoes the *Sunday Pictorial*; and adds that 'The ladies who would sit with German women for the purposes of theoretical discussion show a strange want of imagination and of public decency, and a ridiculous sense of unreality.'

Not now! Then, in heaven's name, when? Only when the husbands and sons and brothers are all killed and life for those who are left has ceased to matter?

As in all progressive movements . . . it is fear that really runs through this outcry of the Press – fear lest the women might perhaps be right, might perhaps impress their belief on the women of other belligerent countries, might perhaps make this war really 'the last war', instead of merely talking about it as an unattainable ideal very useful as a recruiting cry.

Attendance at the Congress grew over its four days – sometimes there were over 2,000 in the hall. Public meetings held each evening were packed out. But the most exciting session came on the last day, with the passing of a resolution for direct action. Schwimmer and Lloyd had been planning it in their heads for weeks and they had persuaded Italian Rose Genoni to second it, and five other women (American and Scandinavian) to speak in support of it.

On Friday night (April 30th – the Congress had to be extended to a fourth day), Schwimmer and Lloyd 'whacked the resolution into shape'[27] in Lloyd's hotel room. The next morning Schwimmer dashed out at 8 a.m. without breakfast, in order to get the various translations of the resolution printed and prepare her speakers to be ready.

At the end of business, Schwimmer announced to the conference that she had brought in a new resolution, and in an impassioned speech from the rostrum, punctuated by cheering, she explained to the audience why she thought it was necessary that the Congress should elect some of its delegates as envoys to carry the Congress resolutions *in person* to the heads of belligerent and neutral governments and to the President of the United States. She did not wish, she argued emphatically, for the resolutions to be merely 'paper expressions of pious wishes' but to be a catalyst for international action. Neither was it enough to simply act as passive messengers; the envoys should report back to the Women's International Peace Party (or whatever it was going to be called) to decide on further action.

Each of the five supporting speakers pointed out additional arguments: three put their case in English, one in Italian, another in German. There was some debate on the platform, and much referring to minutes and rule books, as to whether Schwimmer's new resolution was legitimate. But, yes, it *was* put before the Resolutions Committee even though there had not been time to vote on it, so it was in order for it to go 'before the House'.

The resistance to this resolution was considerable. Having an international congress was one thing but acting as unofficial emissaries was another. Getting to the conference was bad enough but travelling around Europe would be impossible! The belligerent governments would greatly resent their citizens taking part. Delegates would be seen as usurping the role of those who governed, or perhaps they would be accused of spying, who knew the dangers? Chrystal Macmillan wasted no time in moving an amendment to take the stuffing out of the resolution. She proposed that Addams and Jacobs simply visit the appropriate ambassadors at The Hague. Jane Addams thought the Schwimmer resolution 'melodramatic and absurd', Kathleen Courtney too. She said,

'I strongly oppose this resolution. With the exception of Madame Schwimmer everybody who spoke in favour of it and appealed to our hearts came from neutral nations. I will speak in a calm manner and I don't appeal to your heart but to your head . . . it is not a really possible proposal . . . I don't want to take steps which look well on paper but which are not practicable.'[28]

Despite further appeals from the five supporting speakers, it did not look as if the resolution would be passed. But when Macmillan moved that the delegates vote on the issue, Schwimmer hurriedly asked to be allowed to speak for one more minute as a matter of personal privilege – it was conference policy for delegates to speak only once on a motion. 'I make a point of order and ask, whether Madame Schwimmer may speak,' Macmillan asked the Chair. A voice from the floor suggested a vote on it.

'A motion from the floor, that Madame Schwimmer shall speak, is moved, seconded and carried by the majority,' announced Jane Addams after the vote was carried.[29]

Schwimmer now knew that she had to use all her persuasive oratorical skills to try and convince the gathering of international women to have the courage to act on their words:

'Brains – they say – have ruled the world till to-day. If brains have brought us to what we are in now, I think it is time to allow also our hearts to speak. When our sons are killed by millions, let us, mothers, only try to do good by going to kings and emperors, without any other danger than a refusal!' (Hear, Hear, Hear!)[30]

'It was a close shave,' wrote Lloyd in her diary that night. 'Most exciting crisis of the whole Congress. . . . We trembled for its fate. The victory was all Rosika's but she wanted to go away and let them forget how she had forced things.'[31]

The vote had to be counted twice, but there were enough raised right hands to show that the motion was carried – to loud applause.

CHAPTER 6

To the rulers of Europe

Between May and August 1915, in the middle of the worst war which the world had seen up to that date, thirteen women delegates from the Hague Congress, split into two envoys, visited all the governments of Central Europe in an historic exercise in unofficial international diplomacy. It is hard to think of anything like it which has happened before or since. They visited top statesmen in fourteen capitals: Berlin, Berne, Budapest, Christiana (now Oslo), Copenhagen, The Hague, Le Havre (the seat of the deposed Belgian government), London, Paris, Petrograd (now Leningrad), Rome, Stockholm, Vienna and finally Washington in America.

As members of the female sex, barred from most of the world's parliaments, they were able to create a third force above the battle and therefore more open to confidences from politicians who would not have trusted their words to official diplomats. Shuttling back and forth between the chancelleries, in thirty-five separate visits, the Congress envoys gave the neutral governments information on what politicians were thinking in the warring countries.

By the summer of 1915, the fighting men of Europe, many of them now wounded and crippled, felt a growing gulf between themselves and civilians. They were disgusted by the bellicose hate campaigns and newspaper propaganda, which they witnessed when home on leave, and how those at the 'home front' were oblivious to the suffering of barbarous trench warfare. Meanwhile, the capital cities on the continent of Europe saw food rationing and appeals for War Funds and casualty lists plastered everywhere. Yet there was no sign of an end to the war.

Politicians seemed to be in a collective state of psychological paralysis. Officially all contact between the warring governments had been severed on the outbreak of war but there were secret meetings between emissaries from the two belligerent sides and a number of mediations from single neutral governments. But no one really trusted each other, and every diplomat suspected the other of seeking to make political capital out of the situation.

The belligerents said they wanted to cease hostilities but could not *ask* for mediation as this would infer that they were losing militarily. Several neutrals professed a desire to help but each was frightened of interfering lest it should be considered an 'unfriendly act' and damage their own national interests, and they seemed incapable of acting collectively. They might have done so if the American President had taken the lead but as if in some children's game, where each is waiting for the other to begin, the American President was waiting for the belligerents to ask *him*, something, of course, they would never do. 'We found on all sides the belligerents had said . . . "It is up to the neutrals to help us quit",' recalled Schwimmer afterwards.

Miss Addams said: 'But President Wilson has offered mediation.' They told her, 'Oh yes, President Wilson has offered, and the government of Spain has offered, and the government of Sweden has offered . . . and Switzerland . . . and Holland . . . but all have offered it in the wrong way. They have all said: Please let us know when you want our services.'[1]

Meanwhile, thousands of men went 'up the line to death', as if they had no individual lives of their own but were merely cogs in the war machine.

It is quite likely that the First World War would not have continued for over four years if the First Hague Conference of 1899 (called by Tsar Nicholas II), or the Second in 1907, had named *specific* countries whose role it was to mediate on the outbreak of war, in return for their neutrality. But in 1914, there was no international structure to deal with war on such an unprecedented scale. There was not even an organisation for the discussion of world affairs, as the League of Nations (later to become the United Nations) was a concept yet to be formed. The world was in chaos and Article 3 of the First Hague

Convention seemed like a utopian dream. It went:

> '. . . the signatory Powers recommend that one or more
> Powers, strangers to the dispute, should, on their own
> initiative, and as far as circumstances may allow, offer their
> good offices or mediation to the States at variance. . . .
>   The exercise of this right can never be regarded by one or
> the other of the parties in conflict as an unfriendly act.[2]

This was just what the women from the Women's International Congress wanted. They wanted the neutrals to set up a
mediating conference *on their own initiative*. They could see
there was a diplomatic stalemate before they began their visits
to the European chancelleries. What they set out to do was to
get the warring governments if not to agree to then at least not
to openly obstruct the setting up of a mediating conference, and
having reassured the neutrals that it was not 'an unfriendly act',
to goad them into action.

The organisation of such an expedition in wartime, when
there was strict censorship, no mail between warring countries
and restrictive border controls, must have been a nightmare.
Lists of suffrage contacts in the different countries were drawn
up and these contacts proved invaluable for providing accommodation for the envoys and helping to fix up interviews with
politicians and arrange public meetings. The Congress had
voted on the formation of two delegations, one to visit the
governments at war (which would have to be made up of
women from neutral countries) and the other to tour the
neutral countries. The former was led by American Jane
Addams and Dutch Aletta Jacobs; the latter – notice the
balance – led by Hungarian Rosika Schwimmer and British
Chrystal Macmillan.

Various other women went with them, some as personal
friends, such as Alice Hamilton, to help Jane Addams, and Lola
Maverick Lloyd, who wanted to travel with Schwimmer; and
some as official delegates like the Italian Rosa Genoni, who had
to drop out when Italy declared war on Austria-Hungary, and
American Emily Greene Balch. The latter was the unpretentious
Head of Economics and Sociology at Wellesley College for girls
near Boston, who taught pioneering courses in socialism. In her
late forties, she was tall and thin, reserved but not conservative,
someone who deliberately dressed plainly in order to be
classless and who had been known occasionally to wear her hat

back to front. Julia Grace Wales, as author of the pamphlet *International Plan for Continuous Mediation without Armistice*, travelled with the northern delegation in a private capacity until she became ill and returned to America. 'When you travel you . . . meet military authorities and they say "Please fall in line ladies, this side, gentlemen that side," ' Schwimmer told an American audience when later describing the crusade around Europe, in an impromptu speech.

> 'You have to go in and be searched. You have to undress. We women have to take down our hair and shake it out to show there is nothing in it . . . my shoes were put down and I was asked what are these numbers. . . . This powder paper here . . . in Europe one has to have paper to clean one's face, because one does not get towels or soap. This paper has passed the censor twice. It has been taken away from me because the maker's name is on it, and I had to leave it at the station.'[3]

It wasn't easy to pass from country to country, seeking and absorbing information and presenting the case of mediation to a war-mad continent, but having set off only with the attitude of 'leaving no stone unturned', the envoys met with success beyond their wildest dreams.

After an interview with the Dutch Prime Minister at The Hague, London and Berlin were the first stops for the Addams' delegation. In London, Catherine Marshall arranged interviews with the British Foreign Secretary and Prime Minister. The British Committee of the IWCPP had not yet been formed but, in a note which reveals the bitterness which still existed over the NUWSS split, Marshall asked Addams for a future declaration of her support:

> we shall have as handicap the openly expressed disapproval of Mrs Fawcett. Your approval and support would counterbalance this.
>
> Mrs Fawcett's name carries great weight with official people and with the Press. They do not know that the work of the NUWSS during the last few years . . . has not been done by her, but by a group of progressive and energetic people (Miss Ashton, Mrs Swanwick, Miss Royden, etc. and especially Miss Courtney). . . . The actions of the officers and Exec. Comm. will continue to carry the same weight as

before . . . therefore their attitude towards us is bound to do us harm. The irony of the situation is that it is *our* work and the effective machine which we have left in their hands, which enables them to do the harm![4]

Two days before the Addams delegation arrived in London the British liner *Lusitania* had been torpedoed, and in the circumstances it was surprising that the meetings which the British pacifist suffragists organised went off so well. 'A busy week with the meetings and parties in connection with the Hague Women's Congress,' wrote Kate Courtney in her diary. She was married to Leonard Courtney, a Liberal MP, and they both opposed the war. 'Besides Committee Meeting and party, we had a fine public meeting in Kingsway Hall. Every speech good, and no foolish, excitable word. I was surprised after the *Lusitania* at our success, numbers and quality.'[5]

'What are the neutrals waiting for?' Sir Edward Grey is reported to have asked Addams, Jacobs and Genoni when they saw him on May 12th. When the women told him that judging by the Dutch PM, the neutrals were waiting for the 'right moment', he was incredulous and asked them, 'When do they think the right moment is going to come?'[6]

The language of politicians does not alter very much from country to country, especially in wartime, and the women heard much the same words spoken in Downing Street as in Wilhelmstrasse, in Vienna as in Petrograd and in Budapest as in Le Havre. Not only were they all waiting for the neutrals to intervene but they were all, of course, fighting in self-defence and must 'push on to the end' for honour's sake.

In Berlin, the American Ambassador James Gerard (not on their side) met the envoy. He announced that he expected war to break out between America and Germany at any moment and was all packed ready to go. Privately, he thought them 'cranks', but succeeded in getting an interview for them with Foreign Secretary Herr von Jagow and Chancellor Theobald von Bethmann Hollweg, who, whether from guilt or contempt, apparently looked forward to meeting the women with 'unconcealed perturbation'.

Upon their entry into his office on May 21st, Jagow told his female visitors that it was 'the right of women to do this sort of thing', and he was surprised they had not done it sooner! Like the British Foreign Secretary, Jagow thought it was up to the neutrals to take any peace initiatives but was sceptical about America taking the lead because he doubted her neutrality. Anti-Americanism was rife in Germany. According to one German commentator the largest neutral country was like 'a great greedy vulture, feeding on the carrion of the battlefields of Europe, and growing ever grosser and more complacent as the masses of its gory food increased'.[7]

Jane Addams and Alice Hamilton became so weary of the attacks that they could hardly force themselves to answer, and they found the strength of feeling about it 'incredible'.

The Chancellor was less belligerent than his Foreign Minister; he had just lost a son at the front. He saw Addams alone. Kate Courtney wrote in her diary of their interview,

> No nation at war could begin [peace negotiations]. Neutrals were playing too feeble a part. Belligerents would not accept offer, but neutrals should begin and make propositions and go on making them.
>
> He struck Miss A. as a good man desiring some way out – representing civil opinion v. military, which perhaps was too strong for him.[8]

The German people, of course, saw the war in a completely different light from the British (and Americans, for that matter), and Alice Hamilton wrote to her family that 'no amount of mental gymnastics can put us where we can really see things as they do'.[9] To the great majority, England had planned the war from the start and was attempting to starve the German nation by blocking food imports. The fact that one small German submarine had sunk the *Lusitania* was boasted of as evidence of great military prowess and 'just deserts': the ship had been carrying ammunition and the passengers had been fully warned. Now with England's shipping lines under threat, victory was in sight! War maps were spread open eagerly and pored over in shops, offices and private homes.

The anti-English feeling (and it was England, not Britain) was whipped up into a state of frenzy: 'Gott strafe England' (God punish England) answered by 'Er strafe es' (May he punish it) was the standard greeting, both face to face and over the telephone. And postcards and newspaper cartoons featured Zeppelins destroying British cities.

Most of the Berlin women's organisations (not necessarily suffragist) appear to have been super-patriotic and when Lilly

108

Janasch, a prominent social worker, showed the Hague Congress delegation the German women's munition factories and workrooms, sometimes Addams was asked not to talk about the Congress as the German delegates to it had been denounced back home. Always anxious not to antagonise anyone – 'Your tongue cleaves to your mouth,'[10] she admitted when forced to talk peace and imply that people were dying for nothing – Addams complied with the request and concentrated on the social work techniques of Hull House. Aletta Jacobs, however, more uncompromising, slammed home the message of the Congress and the necessity for a peace conference.

But by no means all Germans supported the war. Bund Neues Vaterland (The New Fatherland) was a German equivalent of the British Union of Democratic Control, Helene Stöcker, who had been a delegate at the Hague Congress, was a member and the Addams delegation met up with them. 'The pacifists are now not the old set but a different type,' said Jane Addams when she returned home and talked of the British, German – and embryonic French – internationalist organisations. 'None of these are definite pacifists.'[11]

What Jane Addams meant about 'new' pacifists was that they did not simply oppose all war but wanted to construct international procedures to replace war. Bund, which mainly consisted of intellectuals and academics, bitterly fought a group of industrialists and land owners who publicly demanded the annexation of Belgium and parts of France for Germany, by putting out a manifesto of their own, demanding a just peace and a post-war league of nations.

While Bund tried to influence Establishment critics of German foreign policy, discontent over hardship caused by the war was already growing amongst working-class militants, with women in the forefront. By the end of 1915, food costs would have risen to one and a half times pre-war prices, and in March several hundred women gathered in front of the Reichstag and shouted for food and the return of their men from the trenches. In May, when Italy entered the war against Germany, there were over 1,000 demonstrators, with twenty-four arrests. The Social Democrat parliamentary group, which had so far supported the war, began to see angry debates within its ranks and disillusioned members resigned after twenty years in the party. By October, frustrated by its pathetic inaction, a group of enraged women felt compelled to storm an

SPD executive meeting and ask the men why they were not out there leading the discontented masses.

While the Addams delegation was visiting London and Berlin, Schwimmer and the others were planning to tour the three Scandinavian capitals to test whether the neutrals (Denmark, Norway, Sweden, Holland, Switzerland) would act in concert and initiate a mediating conference, if they knew that America would agree to attend. Lola Maverick Lloyd had travelled with the Addams delegation to Berlin so that she could report back to Schwimmer the results of the German interviews (Addams had communicated the British response on her way through Holland) but for some reason, perhaps not realising its significance, Addams seems to have been reluctant to pass on the information to her and all Lloyd could report back by telephone was that Addams was 'satisfied'.

Of all the interviews that the Schwimmer delegation had in Scandinavia, their most promising response came in Sweden. Knut Wallenberg, the Foreign Minister, was the sole politician to see them but he was worth all the rest. 'We always went three or four persons . . . at all times,' recalled Schwimmer, when describing how the northern delegation had organised their round of interviews.

'When we came home, each of us told how she heard of the things, what she remembered, and each of us wrote it down. Then we compared our notes. We found there were differences. We understood different things, and so we got the thing quite clear, then we repeated it to each other verbally so often that we were like parrots, and could not make a mistake.'

Not wanting to risk reports being scrutinised by the censors, Schwimmer said, 'We had to do that, because we had no other means of keeping records of the things.'[12]

They had rehearsals for the interviews, with Julia Grace Wales acting the part of the male politician. Taking it in turns to speak, each woman would practise making a particular point, and when one of the delegates dried up, another would chip in with a further argument. In this way they could keep the interview going for as long as possible, in order to drive their arguments home. However, with the King of Norway, their plans went rather awry. They bought white gloves for the occasion and tortuously rehearsed court etiquette but to their surprise they found the man

> so fine and simple, we did not get a chance to use any of the
> words we had practiced. Finally towards the close of our
> conversation . . . an American member [this must have been
> Emily Balch] . . . said 'Yes, Your Majesty', and we nearly
> laughed. Afterwards she said: 'I felt it was too bad we had
> all that work for nothing. I wanted to see how it sounded!'[13]

Knut Wallenberg, the Foreign Minister of Sweden, was an
elderly dynamic man with a pointed beard who came from a
great Swedish banking family. His country had already taken
two peace initiatives since the war began: in December 1914,
the Swedish King Gustav V had arranged a meeting with
the Norwegian and Danish kings, at which it was resolved that
the three countries should stay out of the war. And in May
1915, the Swedish Prime Minister had gone to Berlin to sound
out possible Swedish mediation, but was given a cool reception
by the German Chancellor who appears to have abruptly ended
their talk after only half an hour.

In their interview with Wallenberg on June 2nd, Schwimmer,
Macmillan, Balch and Ramondt-Hirschmann played on the
man's national ego. It was evident that he was eager for any
conference that was set up to be held in Sweden. His statements
became increasingly bold, and he eventually declared that the
Swedish government would be willing to take the initiative if he
had 'sufficient evidence' that it would not be 'unacceptable' to
the governments of the countries at war. When asked what
would be 'sufficient evidence', he said it would be enough if one
of the women brought a note from 'the two chief representatives of both sides'.

The women couldn't believe their luck. During the war it was
almost impossible to get diplomats to say anything so definite
and, encouraged by this breakthrough, the Schwimmer delegation began to plan a journey to Russia. The usual route by sea
from Stockholm to Abö in Finland was closed and it was
necessary to make a three-day train journey around the Gulf of
Bothnia over the northernmost Swedish territory.

However, the delegation had to split. Lola Maverick Lloyd
was booked to sail for America on June 4th and Julia Grace
Wales, who had been ill with a fever in Copenhagen, was
persuaded to go with her. Schwimmer, being a Hungarian, was
unable to enter Russia as it was enemy territory, and she left to

The northern envoy from the Hague Congress after their audience with the King of Norway on May 31st, 1915: left to right: Emily Greene Balch, Cor Ramondt-Hirschmann, Rosika Schwimmer, Chrystal Macmillan. The taxi driver who took them to the interview kept driving around the palace because he would not believe that they had an appointment to see the King.

travel to Budapest via Copenhagen and Berlin for a ten-day
visit to her family. She was very close to them and had not seen
them since the war began. The plan was that she would meet
up with the others, and with the Addams delegation in
Amsterdam where they would compare notes and discuss
what further action to take. 'Baroness Ellen Palmstierna
[Swedish] who you perhaps remember from the Congress . . . is
our 4th member for Russia,' wrote Emily Balch to Jane
Addams on the train to Petrograd.

> [She] is proving a charming addition to our already most
> enjoyable party. I can't tell you the pleasure it has been to be
> so closely associated with these fine and so agreeable
> women. Travelling is supposed to show up people's
> weaknesses – well, they have been trumpy at every point.
>   Madame Schwimmer is as considerate of their welfare in
> the smallest details as if she had nothing bigger on her mind.
> I have grown to both admire and love her.[14]

On arriving at Petrograd, they were met by the President of
the Russian League for Equal Rights for Women, who put them
up at her home. A ban on public meetings meant that it was
impossible to make many sympathetic contacts, but after a
week, the women managed to secure an interview with the
Russian Foreign Minister, Sergei Sazonov, on June 16th. After
being ushered into his office, they were asked to sit opposite his
desk in classic interrogation style, with lights behind the
minister shining into their faces. Not surprisingly, their
carefully planned dialogue fell into disarray. This was the first
government this envoy had contacted whose country was at
war and they were nervous.

However, after the interview in Sweden, it was important to
collect as much written evidence as possible and having gained
his permission, Macmillan wrote out a statement from
Sazonov. Russia would not regard a mediating conference of
neutrals as an 'unfriendly act', he said, but he did not think it
would have any 'practical results'. Macmillan put down her
fountain pen and handed him the sheet of paper, whereupon
Sazonov, having been initially startled by the request to record
his views, recovered his composure and ended the interview by
reading and approving his statement.

The greatest success the Addams delegation had was in
Vienna. The Austrians had been hit particularly badly by the

war; people were already starving; the bread ration was a two-inch-square chunk three times a day. After repeating the Congress resolutions to the Prime Minister, Baron Karl von Sturgkh, Jane Addams felt rather intimidated by the silence of the big, grim-faced, ponderous man and blurted out,

'It perhaps seems to you very foolish that women should go about in this way; but after all, the world itself is so strange in this war situation that our mission may be no more strange nor foolish than the rest.'

'Foolish?' roared Sturgkh in reply, banging the table with his fist. 'These are the first sensible words that have been uttered in this room for ten months!'[15]

When she returned to the United States, Jane Addams told various newspapers that the envoys from the Hague Conference had been received seriously and solemnly by all the European politicians; they were not considered a joke as they had been in America, she emphasised. Nor were they seen as interfering. 'We were not official, but we were felt,'[16] she said.

She reported that in each country a division existed between the military establishment and the civilian government, with the former being much more resistant to the idea of a negotiated peace. Civilians were alarmed at the removal of one safeguard after another against permanent militarism and worried about whether democracy would be restored.

From Vienna, the Addams delegation went on to Budapest, Berne, Rome, Paris and Le Havre. On June 4th, Italy had entered the war, and when the women met the Foreign Minister, he struck them as being like a young boy with a new toy. Convinced that Italy's manpower would stop the war, Rome was bubbling with excitement, full of soldiers in fresh uniforms. The Pope gave his support to Addams in a private interview.

In Paris, the delegation met an American nurse who showed them her ghoulish collection of German military ephemera presented to her by French soldiers returning from the front. They also talked to an American writer, who told them while sprawling on a sofa in their hotel lounge that he would 'sacrifice the last Frenchman in the trenches'. Resident Americans all over Europe, wrote Alice Hamilton, were always more bellicose than the locals.

They were followed everywhere by police in France. The

nightmare of being invaded made almost everyone they met intensely anti-German. Madame Schlumberger, who had written to Schwimmer at the beginning of the war asking Carrie Chapman Catt to take action, now had a son at the front and was against any talk of internationalism. The French Prime Minister and Foreign Minister were bellicose, although after some persuasion the former, René Viviani, grudgingly agreed that he would not resent the creation of a continuous mediating conference. Their final interview on the continent was at Le Havre, the temporary seat of the Belgium government, and the sad-faced Belgian Foreign Minister told them he would far rather the German troops in his country retreated as a result of negotiations than the country be fought over all over again.

As has been said, the original plan of the delegations was to meet up in Amsterdam after the visits. Both Emily Balch and Chrystal Macmillan wrote to Jane Addams on June 8th to confirm this. 'Of course it must be most inconvenient for you and your own people must want you back badly for many things,' went their letter, written on the train between Stockholm and Petrograd. 'This, however, is more important because it concerns the whole world.'[17]

But for some reason Jane Addams did not wait to rendezvous with the others in Holland but sailed for America with Alice Hamilton on June 18th. Schwimmer never forgave her for deserting the cause at the crucial moment. Perhaps Addams believed that only President Wilson could make any effective peace initiatives and that she would be more use in America than Europe, but it seems that she was also tired and eager to get home to rest and relax. A welcome meeting was being arranged for her in New York and she had told her Hull House colleagues, some time back, that she would return around the 15th to 20th June. She had her doubts about the wisdom of returning home but she had never been as enthusiastic about the mission as Schwimmer and some of the others were.

After nearly two months of making endless travel arrangements, suffering delays at borders and incessant questioning, body searches, bouts of flu and alarms about spies (one man followed them on the train in Scandinavia, and a German woman tried to pump one of the unofficial Congress delegates for information), the northern envoy were dismayed when they returned to Holland and discovered that Addams and

Hamilton were half-way across the Atlantic. 'Jane Addams left on St Louis without meeting Scandinavian party. Ignorant of our important achievements,' cabled Schwimmer to Lloyd of July 2nd. Her draft continued angrily, 'leaving us ignorant. Why rushed home though needed her presence. Lola shall find out more and cable information' – but for some reason this was later crossed out and the final version merely went on to say, 'Headquarters needs ten thousand dollars at once. Important steps depend on funds which cannot raise quickly enough in Europe. Could Chicago not contribute it quickly. Lola's money not received. Urgent need.'[18]

Lloyd had promised Schwimmer $1,000 for peace activity. It took a long time to arrive but on the strength of the promise Schwimmer was able to borrow money from Hungary. All the women's efforts at unofficial peace diplomacy had to be self-financed; the people involved were mainly from comfortable middle-class backgrounds but that didn't mean they had limitless money of their own. Madame Wilhelmina van Wulfften Palthe, a friend of Aletta Jacobs, was the only one in this group who was wealthy. The Palthes had sugar plantations in Java. Funds for international travel were not easy to come by as there were currency controls in some countries and it was always a case of balancing the budget and borrowing from each other.

Schwimmer, Macmillan, Balch and Hirschmann did at least meet up with Aletta Jacobs at The Hague, and it was decided that if the Dutch government, which seemed to be warming to the idea of initiating a mediating conference, did not announce this intention in a few days, then they would return to both Berlin and London – in the hope of bringing 'a note' from both sides to Wallenberg as proof that these belligerents did not consider an initiative by the neutrals as 'an unfriendly act'. They planned to present this written evidence to the Swedish Foreign Minister hoping it would finally push him into action.

On their way back from Russia, the northern delegation had again visited all the Scandinavian capitals. In Sweden there was a wonderful reception waiting for them with a series of peace rallies, one with 3,000 people. Wallenberg, to whom they showed the Russian Sazonov's statement, seemed keener than ever. Schwimmer believed that the neutrals had finally realised that a mediation attempt might be a guarantee of their own defence ensuring that they weren't dragged into the war, which was always a possibility.

A few days later, with no sign of action from the Dutch politicians, the women went to get the German and British 'notes'. 'Herr von Jagow says that Germany would find nothing unfriendly in the calling of a conference of neutrals but asks whether it would have practical consequences,' Schwimmer and Hirschmann recorded in Berlin on July 15th. The German Foreign Minister said he agreed with them that now might be a good time to initiate peace proposals from the neutrals because the military situation was about equal. Neither side would appear to dictate terms or would risk humiliation.[19]

It was 'heart-rending' to see the thousands of soldiers with 'empty resigned faces go towards an unwanted death',[20] wrote Schwimmer to Lloyd, as they travelled near the Western front. The two were held at the German border and their papers confiscated. This may have been because before leaving Berlin, they had contacted Bund Neues Vaterland and offered to distribute leaflets outside the country. In any case, it was only after Schwimmer cabled to Jagow that they were released.

Back in Stockholm, Schwimmer presented Wallenberg with all the information she had (he had replied almost immediately to her request to see him). The Dutch government was split, she reported. One section favoured the Hague Congress plan, the other wanted peace terms decided first, before any negotiating conference was established. She presented the note from Herr von Jagow. She told Wallenberg about the activities of Bund Neues Vaterland, the UDC and Anti-Orloog Raad, a similar Dutch peace group.

Knut Wallenberg kept covering his face with his hands. It was obvious to Schwimmer that he was worried about saying too much. The elderly Swedish man was sitting opposite a dynamic woman whose forceful eloquence he must have found hard to resist. Wallenberg would not have found it difficult to start proceedings for a conference of neutrals, if he so decided, his only obstacle would be to persuade the Swedish Prime Minister. 'A new era will begin in mankind's history, the day invitations are sent out,' Schwimmer told him.

'It is not Sweden's ambition,' insisted Wallenberg, 'it is not competing. Its only wish is to be of useful service . . . if it is better that Holland . . . let it be there. Swedish and Dutch governments ought to meet to discuss this. Anyway, it would have to be done through diplomatic channels. Not one but a whole group ought to act together.'[21]

On the day that Schwimmer and Hirschmann had talked to Herr von Jagow, Chrystal Macmillan and Emily Balch had met Lord Crewe at the British Foreign Office in London. He was acting as Foreign Secretary in Sir Edward Grey's absence. Afterwards, Balch remained in London, waiting for a boat to America, but before they parted she gave Macmillan a sum of money to spend on further peace envoys. Meanwhile, Schwimmer waited in Stockholm, anxiously wondering what written evidence the British Foreign Office had given her colleagues. It was so difficult to get anyone, anywhere, in power to say anything definite in this war. Arriving at Stockholm's railway station to meet Macmillan's train, she bought a rose for her hat and waited expectantly. She was soon to find out that the taciturn Scot had managed to secure a statement from the British Foreign office which Schwimmer felt like 'shouting abroad to the world!'[22] It went, 'You . . . asked whether it might be said that the Government accepted the idea of the immediate cooperation of the neutral countries in instituting a Committee to examine the subject' (i.e. peace), wrote Eric Drummond on Lord Crewe's behalf to Macmillan, in a report of her London interview

> Lord Crewe answered that he did not like the word 'accept' to which a meaning would probably be attached going beyond anything to which his Colleagues and he could agree, but you could say that the Government would not place any obstacles in the way of the formation of such a body or make any protest against its existence if it should come into being.[23]

With this evidence Knut Wallenberg finally promised Macmillan and Schwimmer that the Swedish Cabinet would discuss the possibility of initiating a mediating conference. They had given him their collected information about all the interviews (except those which Jane Addams had conducted alone) in a written report which concluded,

> considering the impossibility for any belligerent government *to invite* the formation of a neutral conference, it is obvious that no stronger evidence on this point can be given than these statements taken together.[24]

Aletta Jacobs had never been enthusiastic about the second

trips to Berlin and London. She preferred, perhaps out of national pride, to concentrate on the Dutch government, who seemed to be on the brink of making a decision. While the others were away, she made further attempts to see the Dutch Prime Minister, Cort van der Linden, which resulted in his sending her to Washington to enquire of President Wilson whether America would participate in mediation. When Macmillan and Schwimmer returned to the Hague, they found yet again that 'their bird had flown'. Schwimmer was all for following the Dutch woman immediately, but at a meeting of the International Committee of Women for Permanent Peace she met opposition. Madame Hubrecht and Rosa Manus voiced doubts about whether this was a good idea since Aletta Jacobs had already left Holland and was on an official mission. But they were swayed, and on 28th August the Scot and Hungarian embarked for the United States, wiring to Jacobs asking her to wait for them. If there had been time to organise it, they would have preferred to have taken both a French and a German woman with them as well, but it was important for continuity that they saw the American President with Jacobs, as she had been one of the European envoys, and they did not want to miss her in mid-ocean.

During the past few weeks, it had sometimes seemed to Schwimmer that a conference of neutrals would be 'called the next day', but before sailing for America, she wrote an unusually pessimistic letter to her Hungarian friend Vilma Glücklich. Asking Vilma to burn her papers if the ship be torpedoed, she continued,

> National ambitions and selfishness hold back those people whom we have seen during these past weeks. . . . Each one wants something. . . . Today I loathe the neutrals more than the others. There is no doubt any longer that of the belligerents *not one would oppose* a neutral conference. But on the part of the neutrals there are conflicting interests which still stand in the way of the first step. We hope with this American trip to bring about a decision. . . . In the meantime, the world perishes.[25]

Tragically, American politicians proved to be just as unimaginative and concerned with their own national image as the politicians of the European neutrals. All through the summer and autumn of 1915, President Wilson listened and debated, in often hour-long interviews, with people who argued for a conference of neutral government representatives. Jane Addams and Lillian Wald saw him first, then Emily Greene Balch, then Aletta Jacobs, then Rosika Schwimmer. It was not just the women from the Hague Congress who failed to persuade him. In November, the President also had further long discussions with David Starr Jordan, the chancellor of Stanford University; Louis Lochner, Secretary of the Chicago Peace Society, and Henry Ford, the automobile millionaire, as well as on other occasions with socialist delegations. It was not that he was totally unsympathetic; all his life he had dreamt of international law superseding warfare, but nothing could make the man take action, and we will find out the reason why later.

It was July 5th when the American liner *St Louis*, carrying Jane Addams and Alice Hamilton, drew alongside the dock in New York harbour. A heavy downpour drenched the women as they descended the gangway, to be greeted by the fifty or so peace activists, wearing white ribbons inscribed 'Welcome Jane Addams', and a strong wind lashed the rain across the quay. Fanny Garrison Villard, Crystal Eastman and Florence Kelley were amongst those waiting and seventeen peace societies were represented in the gathering. While the ship had still been down the bay, Addams had received an encouraging telegram from President Wilson, saying that he was sorry he could not be in New York to welcome her but would be delighted to receive her in Washington, when she could come.[26]

Reaction in the press to Jane Addams's European visit had been mixed but on the whole her popular reputation had survived. However, this was not to last long, as she was soon to inadvertently challenge one of the most potent myths of American masculinity, by an almost throwaway remark at a large public meeting held in her honour at Carnegie Hall on July 9th. At the end of a quiet speech, in which she said it was an old man's war in Europe in which the young were dying, and told how one soldier confessed to her that he never shot to kill and of five others who committed suicide rather than return to the front, she added,

'We heard in all countries similar statements in regard to the necessity for the use of stimulant before men would engage in bayonet charges – that they have a regular formula in Germany, that they give them rum in England and absinthe in France . . . that they have to give them "dope" before the bayonet charge is possible.'[27]

Now in America – if not the rest of the world – soldiers were always courageous and strong, glorious and glamorous. To be a soldier was to be a 'real man'. You fought for the protection of others – especially women and children – not because you were *drunk*!

Of course, Jane Addams wasn't challenging the men's bravery, she was merely telling the truth; it wasn't surprising that soldiers needed alcohol to dull the horror of trench life. But that was not how the reporters saw it. 'Troops drink-crazed, says Miss Addams,' went the headlines the next day and a flood of hostile criticism was unleashed upon her for the next two months. 'Jane Addams is a silly, vain, impertinent old maid,' said the *New York Topics* in a fit of apoplexy, 'who may have done good charity work at Hull House, Chicago, but is now meddling with matters far beyond her capacity.'[28]

The occasion provided a wonderful opportunity for opponents of female suffrage:

> statements like this are characteristic of the suffragists. I have been debating with them for two years, and have met and heard their principal orators. They mean well, perhaps, but are always making positive statements which show ignorance of the fundamental facts of human nature. No fable is too gross for them to swallow if it reflects on the tyrant man.

And another, in fury:

> Miss Addams evinces an utter and amazing ignorance of the elements of human nature . . . if the woman conceded by her sisters to be the ablest of her sex, is so readily duped, so little informed, men wonder what degree of intelligence is to be secured by adding the female vote to the electorate.[29]

'Human nature', of course, proved that men were not only far superior to women but, by golly, had no qualms about killing in cold blood! If women could give life, then men could take it away.

Addams was bewildered by these irrational attacks on her. She was someone who believed that ultimately people responded to informed, rational argument and she was oblivious to the emotion invested in the American superman myth. She had also, of course, completely ruined any propaganda she might have made for an American lead in setting up a peace conference, because all public attention was transfixed by the repercussions of men needing alcohol to see them through bayonet charges.

Her interview with Wilson was postponed and she and her colleagues began to worry that it might be because of the Carnegie Hall furor. When it did eventually come, after she had been kept waiting much longer than at any European capital, the President was friendly but non-committal. She also saw Colonel House, Wilson's personal adviser, who later wrote to the President, 'Jane Addams came on Monday. She saw Von Jagow, Grey and many others and for one reason or another they were not quite candid with her, so she has a totally wrong impression.'[30]

Ironically, whether or not the European politicians were totally candid with Addams, they certainly weren't with Colonel House in the two visits *he* made to them during the war.

Schwimmer and Macmillan arrived in America at the beginning of September and tracked down Addams to her summer house at Bar Harbor on the East coast. They were shocked to find that she was already involved in another peace scheme, this time to set up an unofficial mediating conference, with three 'internationally minded' women and men from each neutral country. They managed to persuade her that she couldn't just drop the Congress plan at her whim and, with some concrete details of the interviews which she had had with the politicians at war, Schwimmer, Macmillan and Jacobs, who they had also met up with by this time, drafted a manifesto to 'the Governments of Europe, and the President of the United States', which both Addams and Balch signed. Published on October 15th, 1915, an unpretentious and moving document, it concluded,

> The excruciating burden of responsibility for the hopeless continuance of this war no longer rests on the will of the belligerent nations alone. It rests also on the will of those neutral governments and people who have been spared its shock but cannot, if they would, absolve themselves from their full share of responsibility for the continuance of war.[31]

However, by late 1915 the whole atmosphere had changed in America. People were finding it hard to remain neutral and dispassionate. The *Lusitania* disaster, which had killed a hundred Americans, had hardened attitudes towards the Germans. Schwimmer and Macmillan did some lecturing but they found, for example, that the New York suffragists treated them coolly, fearful that any peace activism, which was now considered controversial, would harm the New York State suffrage campaign.

Addams, Balch and Jacobs persistently assured the other two that President Wilson would not give any interviews to women or men from belligerent countries. So it was not until November, when a Detroit reporter asked the White House why Wilson had not received Schwimmer and Macmillan and was told that no such request had been made, that such an interview was quickly set up.

By this time, Chrystal Macmillan had gone to Canada to set up a women's peace group there but Ethel Snowden, an active British socialist and NUWSS suffragist, was in America on a lecture tour. She was married to the MP Philip Snowden and was well known in the British Labour Party. Schwimmer had spoken on suffrage platforms with her in Europe before the war. They were a favourite pair with organisers of feminist conferences, as their styles of rhetoric were as different as their appearances. The Hungarian, as dark as the Englishwoman was fair, was as satirical and humorous as the latter was serious and thought-provoking. Ethel Snowden recalled that in 1911, for example, 'the grave and the gay of the women's question was divided between the black and the blonde' at the Opera House in Stockholm.

Schwimmer had more or less given up on Wilson taking action by this time but as a final effort she orchestrated a campaign through the Woman's Peace Party. For three days, 12,000 telegrams from party members (paid for by Clara Ford, who was married to Henry Ford the car millionaire – but more of this later) poured into the White House demanding that the President start a conference of neutrals, and on November 26th, while the cables were still streaming in, Schwimmer and Snowden had an interview with Wilson. An enthusiastic crowd escorted the two women to the presidential building from a preliminary public meeting and stood outside while the meeting took place. But yet again, Wilson could not be persuaded.

As has been said, it was not that the President wasn't searching his soul for a way to stop the war;[32] he had humanitarian instincts but he dreaded even more making the wrong move at the wrong time to the detriment of both himself and America. Until June 1915, he had had William Jennings Bryan as his Secretary of State. Bryan was a passionate pacifist and had begged Wilson to call a neutral conference, saying that this was America's responsibility.

But the President's other close confidant, Colonel House, his political advisor, was never really neutral. He waxed and waned from either thinking that war with Germany was inevitable, to actively wanting to provoke it. He thought that if Germany won, then America would 'be next' and not only were Americans unprepared, went his fantasy, but with the Allies crushed, there would be no one to help them stand up to the first shock. He told Wilson that a peace move would be unwelcome, futile and offensive to the politicians in the belligerent governments and would probably damage any future influence America might have. When Bryan resigned, Robert Lansing took over as Secretary of State, and so, he being of like mind with House, the men through whom the President received much of his information were both against intervention.

The official reasons for not calling a conference were that the United States could not ignore the South American countries and to include them would make the gathering too large and unwieldy – and that the Central Powers had at that time a military advantage. The real reason was that, unknown to the pacifists, Colonel House had worked out a plan of mediation of his own, in which America would hold all the trump cards.

In no way did he intend involving the other neutrals in a serious arbitration attempt but planned instead for the President to demand an end to the war with the prior secret agreement of the Allies. That way, if the Central Powers agreed, America would get all the kudos for saving the world; and if they refused, then America would have an excuse to enter the war against them, before German troops tramped through Europe and crossed the Atlantic.

In September 1915, when the pacifists were having their string of interviews with the American President, Sir Edward Grey, the British Foreign Secretary, inadvertently gave House the impression that the British government wanted Wilson to act. Having excited House, Grey did not dare to offend the President and in the next few months (House left for Europe under the President's authority on December 28th, 1915) there began a string of diplomatic interviews in which the American emissary was flattered and misled by politicians in London, Berlin and Paris.

While House was under the illusion that the American government was about to play a masterstroke of diplomacy by which it could not lose, the European politicians put his visit down to the fact that it was US Election Year. In any case, the Europeans doubted whether they could trust the American President to give them the terms they wanted in any peace conference, and the French especially did not want to lay France's future at the feet of a foreign head of state. Surely they would get a better deal if they won an out-and-out military victory, they reasoned.

These attitudes to House showed the impossibility of trying to get the belligerents to *ask* for peace; they were bound to be suspicious of a single arbitrator. Even the Allies did not trust the American President and he was supposedly saying he might join them in the fight. It was also impossible for all the Allies (and the Central Powers too) to agree amongst themselves to what peace terms they wanted, and as the war went on, views became more entrenched and embittered. Only a truly neutral, strong, collective force could have possibly brought about agreement – and that would have been difficult enough. The continuous, mediating conference of neutrals, which the Women's International Congress demanded and lobbied for, would have been the only solution. But the leaders of the neutral countries were too frightened, or unimaginative, or selfish, to act collectively. The idea of acting for humanitarian purposes and not for state power was beyond the mentality of national politicians.

CHAPTER 7

Most dangerous pacifists

AFTER the Women's International Congress at The Hague in April 1915, while the multinational envoys were scurrying from European capital to capital in search of rational politicians, other delegates made their way home intent on doing what they could to stop the war in their own countries. By November 1915, there were twelve national sections of the International Committee of Women for Permanent Peace (the rather cumbersome title of the organisation which came out of the Hague Congress) in Austria, Belgium, Britain, Germany, Denmark, Italy, Norway, Sweden, France, Hungary, the Netherlands and the USA. In Australia, the Sisterhood of International Peace had affiliated.

As with most voluntary international networks, the reality of 'headquarters' was a skeleton staff of three or four, working out of a small office with very little money. Their base was in Amsterdam, and most of the women were Dutch, although Chrystal Macmillan worked there as Secretary and Emily Hobhouse, of Boer War fame, stood in for the three months while Macmillan was in America and Canada. Besides a 323-page report of the Hague Congress published in book form in both German and English (the US Public Affairs Information Service called it 'one of the most significant volumes which the Great War has brought forth'!), Central Office also wrote and distributed a newsletter entitled *International*, of which fourteen issues were distributed; but it was always uncertain whether it would get through to its intended readers. Suzanne Dûchene, one of the rebel French-women who had sent greetings to the Hague Congress, wrote to Amsterdam from Switzerland, begging to be put in touch with likeminded women in other countries. Information sent to her from 'headquarters' had obviously never arrived.

In the August newsletter came a request for five women from each national section to become members of the International Committee. 'These women should *not* act as representatives of any society to which they may belong,' the letter stated. 'But as *individuals* representing their country and if possible its various sections and classes.'[1]

There were two main objectives of the ICWPP, which were stated in print at the top of its headed notepaper. The first was to publicise what was said, and decided, at the Hague Congress. The second was to hold another Women's Congress, to coincide with the official political one which they knew would have to be held at the end of the war. They knew that whoever 'won', the European statesmen would have to meet to decide peace terms and their idea was to try and influence those terms by lobbying and propaganda.

The five women chosen from each national section were asked to spearhead the work for both objectives in whatever way was suitable in their own countries. Money would certainly have to be raised to finance the next Congress. It was hoped that at least twenty women from each country would attend, but in any case the five on the Committee should 'hold themselves ready' to travel abroad, once the end of war was declared.

Seventy years later, it is moving to try and imagine these small pockets of female anti-war resistance, operating under great difficulty all over Europe. British Dorothy Buxton helped set up the tiny Ligue International des Femmes Pour La Paix Durable in Paris, along with the Paris correspondent of the *New Statesman*. It was led by Gabrielle Dûchene, the wealthy feminist and socialist President of the Section du travail du Conseil National, who, the reader will remember, wrote to the Hague Congress to protest at the 'Virile Law' which despised women.

Nationalist sentiment probably ran highest in France but nevertheless the group bravely decided to state its position publicly. In a pamphlet entitled *An Urgent Duty for Every Woman* it declared, 'Peace will not come by itself. One must not wait for it as for a miracle; one must prepare for it as a task which will be what the efforts of all will make it.'

But even this seemingly moderate statement was fiercely

attacked in French newspapers and provoked a police raid on Dûchene's flat and denunciations from other women's organisations. It was not until the summer of 1917 that anti-war discontent appeared to surface on any scale in France. Women teachers, working through their union, played a prominent part. A number were arrested and sent before court marshalls. Hélène Brion, for example, a prominent trade unionist, was charged with displaying posters in the Parisian workers quarters exhorting every woman to protest with the words, 'Women Want Peace!' and 'Enough Men Killed! Peace!'[2]

Munich, the home of the 2,000 strong radical Women's Suffrage League, led by Anita Augspurg and Lida Gustava Heymann, was the centre of the German women's war resistance. During the first nine months, the war had gone virtually unopposed in Germany – except for the small socialist caucus led by Rosa Luxemburg, Karl Liebknecht and Clara Zetkin – so that when Augspurg and Heymann returned from The Hague, invigorated by the international spirit, they were easily picked out by the authorities.

The German section of the ICWPP presented a copy of the resolutions from the Women's International Congress at the Hague to every member of the Reichstag, the German parliament. It sent a petition against any future annexation of Belgium to Chancellor Theobald von Bethman Hollweg, and later in the war protested against deportations of Belgian workers, the Brest-Litovsk Treaty which took land from the Russians and the German offensive in 1918. The Bavarian War Ministry devoted a third of its secret report on the peace movement, compiled at the end of 1915, to the role of women and international feminism. Heymann was banned from public speaking as early as November 1915 (later she was forced to leave Bavaria and forbidden to return for two years). By March the following year, the entire Munich branch of the Suffrage League was prohibited from holding private or public meetings and the League's journal *Zeitschrift für Frauenstimmrecht* was heavily cut and censored.[3] But despite all the harassment, German women set up peace groups in forty different cities.

In Hungary, anti-war propaganda was equally suppressed. There was simply no way the word 'peace' could be said or written publicly, even though the hardship caused by the war had generated a great deal of sympathy for a negotiated end to the fighting. In Budapest, the money in the ICWPP group's bank account was confiscated, the women involved were taken before police courts, all their meetings were banned, foreign mail was stopped and their journals censored. But Hungarian architecture came to the rescue.

A certain sort of apartment block which housed forty to fifty families was common in Budapest. It contained a common passage on each floor and if the caretaker wanted to relay a message he would summon the tenants with a bell to assemble there. Of course this method was ideal for anti-war propaganda, and one women's peace group soon adopted it. Members would stand on a crate in the hallway, telling the female tenants of the senseless massacre of their men. Sometimes the police were informed but other women soon took the place of those arrested. In the provinces, house-to-house canvassing was done wherever possible.

Rome and Milan were the centres for the two peace groups in Italy. Rosa Genoni circulated a petition asking for peace by arbitration, which resulted in the Milan group being investigated by the police, but they managed to continue to meet once a week. In the neutral countries, campaigning was easier, of course. In Norway and Denmark, the National Council of Women supported the aims of the ICWPP as did other well established suffrage groups. In Norway it was not considered necessary to form a separate organisation and in Denmark the membership of the ICWPP section rose to 15,000. On June 27th, 1915, there were 343 meetings all over Sweden, calling on the government to take action; nearly a million signatures were collected supporting the Women's International Congress resolutions.[4]

What wonderful moral support the knowledge of these events would have been to women all over Europe who despaired at ever seeing an end to the war; who spent agonising hours trying to imagine what life was like for their loved ones in the trenches; who searched in vain for food while they watched their children starve; who were imaginative enough to see that how the war ended would settle the fate of Europe for many years to come. But even the ICWPP women in neutral Switzerland knew little of what their sisters were doing in the warring countries. Such scant news came through.

In Britain, peace agitation appears to have begun slowly during 1916 but increased during the last two years of the war. Throughout the period it was always greater the further away from London one travelled. Scotland (especially 'Red' Clyde-side), Wales (especially Cardiff) and Lancashire (especially Manchester) pulled the largest anti-war audiences. For example, Captain Townroe from the West Lancashire Association Territorial Force wrote to Lord Kitchener as early as July 9th, 1915, saying that 'over a hundred organisations in West Lancashire had distributed "Stop the War" literature in the last six weeks'. In the autumn of 1916, Helena Swanwick was addressing crowds of up to 2,000 in Cardiff, although very often these meetings were broken up by groups of 'patriots'.

Ethel Snowden and her husband did a tour of Wales in June 1916 and found a sympathetic response. After the war, Ethel Snowden wrote,

> a deep and widespread desire for some attempt at an honourable peace by understanding had existed in Great Britain for nearly two years before the end of the war came. A working woman's organisation, the Woman's Peace Crusade, collected in a few weeks nearly 60,000 signatures to a petition for negotiated peace; and at 133 public meetings addressed in less than a year by myself, with an average attendance of 1,000 persons, was carried a resolution on similar lines, with fewer than 30 dissentients in all. These were small things in themselves, but symptomatic.

Sylvia Pankhurst remembered this:

> Anti-war feeling was by no means confined to sophisticated intellectuals. One found it perhaps most firmly rooted amongst the simple, unlettered people of rural areas. In the tiny, small-paned windows of country cottages cards with red crosses indicated that a member of the household was fighting at the Front. On the parlour walls, among the flower-illuminated cards bearing scriptural texts, and the faded pictures of parents and grandparents, were photographs of soldier sons and husbands and cheap magazine colour-prints of khaki heroes. Yet the talk in the cottages was not of Victory, but grief and bereavement, scarcity and high prices. . . . Those who had relatives in the Channel seaports told heart-rending tales of the grievous return of vast numbers of wounded.[5]

In a file marked 'Anti-recruiting and peace propaganda' kept by the Home Office during the war, out of 115 peace groups listed throughout the UK, the British ICWPP section, known as WIL (Women's International League), is marked as one of the most prolific at distributing literature. By the end of the war WIL's official membership was 3,687 but it must have had many more sympathisers. It had fifty branches and worked closely with the Union of Democratic Control and the Independent Labour Party. By 1918, the UDC, to which all peace groups were affiliated, claimed to have an affiliated membership of over half a million (650,000).[6]

The majority of women involved with WIL came from the stock of ex-NUWSS executive members and others who had wanted to go to the Hague Congress.[7] There had been an unofficial committee for some time but in September 1915 Helena Swanwick was elected to the Chair, with Margaret Ashton, Maude Royden and Kathleen Courtney as Vice-Chairs. Emmeline Pethick-Lawrence was Treasurer and Catherine Marshall Honorary Secretary.

However, poor Catherine Marshall, who had already been ill due to nervous exhaustion in the summer of 1915, was soon obliged to make another agonising choice about where she should put her energies. The trouble was that valuable political experience like hers was hard to find, and there were too many progressive causes begging for it. After a year, she was absorbed into the No Conscription Fellowship, which was set up to help conscientious objectors on the introduction of conscription in 1916. Marshall thought this an effective form of war resistance, which she hoped would be the catalyst for a wider peace movement. But more of this later.

Her replacement, Irene Cooper-Willis seems to have been more than up to the job, with Swanwick remembering her as 'absolutely reliable', accurate, a witty and original speaker, unegotistical and reserved. Willis wrote *England's Holy War* between 1919 and 1921; this was a study of the contortions of the Liberal press during the war. It is not known whether or not she was paid by WIL but previously she had scraped together a living by doing research and secretarial work for Vernon Lee, the writer (real name Violet Paget), with whom she had a long and stormy relationship, and for Bertrand Russell. During the war she also worked for the No Conscription Fellowship and was a member of the UDC, the Women's Labour League and the ILP. She, too, had been another one to live at 1 Barton Street, as a tenant of Mary

Helena Swanwick, a 'very consistent and intrepid feminist', intolerant of fools and with an extraordinary intellectual power.
(Photographer: Lizzie Coswell Smith, London. Date unknown.)

Sheepshanks.[8] At the end of 1917, someone with a different sort of suffrage background, Margaret Haley, an ex-WSPU group organiser in Birmingham, became Honorary Secretary. But unfortunately we know little about her (as yet anyway).

Charlotte Despard was one of the ordinary committee members (there was a twenty-four-strong executive, with six officers) and became increasingly active. Sylvia Pankhurst was a committee member too, in the early days, but she never really fitted in and soon left. She felt the group was too tame, dominated by 'seceders from Mrs Fawcett's National Union' who assumed a 'cautious and moderate tone', she thought, and who 'felt the fierce opposition to our Peace efforts more sharply than Suffragettes and Socialists, who had already borne the brunt of championing unpopular causes.' She didn't like the exclusion of foreign women from membership nor the refusal to put 'Peace' in the League's name (as in Women's International Peace League).[9]

There is some other evidence of WIL's style being perceived as over-cautious. Helen Crawfurd, Secretary of the Glasgow branch and an ex-WSPU member, felt she couldn't conform with WIL's policy of always submitting literature to the censor before publication. She resigned from being Secretary but stayed on as an ordinary member. 'The Executive accepted my resignation rather hurriedly, afterwards telling me that they did not want to be held responsible for what I might do,' she remembered later.[10]

The WIL executive seem to have been wary of being associated with more overt radicals. They were very much against Emily Hobhouse being appointed temporary Secretary in Amsterdam, while Chrystal Macmillan was away in America. As in the Boer War, Hobhouse was again being publicly denounced in the British press as a traitor. This time, it was because she had gained permission from the German Chancellor to visit Belgium and was allowed access to prison camps. She reported back to London that reports of damage to the invaded country by the Germans were much exaggerated. On her return to Britain she was strip-searched and Edward Grey, the Foreign Secretary, refused to grant her an interview. When her reception by the WIL executive committee was also somewhat frosty, she resigned her membership. This was another occasion when Sylvia Pankhurst violently disagreed with WIL, and she later recalled sending Hobhouse a note begging to see her, to express her sympathy and support.

According to Chrystal Macmillan, some of the WIL executive members also disapproved of Macmillan and Schwimmer going to America because they 'distrusted' the Hungarian. Nevertheless, they were not quite such a frightened lot as Sylvia Pankhurst made them out to be. Even the intrepid Pankhurst had to admit that 'all Peace work laboured under the weight of harsh adversity' and she herself, torn between alleviating misery in a practical way where she could and speaking out publicly against the war, chose the former most of the time. Her long-term goal was to fight the poverty she saw in the East End of London. Even if war ended tomorrow, she argued, the wretched families she worked with there would be no better off. Much of her energy was absorbed in the running of subsidised canteens, a children's nursery and a toy factory.

WIL had an enormous task. To promote the concept of internationalism and urge women war workers and soldiers to stop feeding the war machine, when the nation had had its instinct for self-protection so inflamed, was a daunting prospect. WIL had to be 'for peace' without mentioning the word. The Liverpool and Birkenhead Women's Peace and Arbitration Society actually invited Catherine Marshall to speak at their meeting but requested that the word 'Peace' not be in the title of her talk! And London, home of the executive committee (the exact address of the WIL office was 12 Little College Street, Westminster) was probably the most jingoistic part of the country. Take the experiences of Florence Lockwood, whose husband was a woollen manufacturer in the Colne Valley, Yorkshire, when she came on a visit to the capital:

> One only had to move about and stay in hotels and hydros among the rich and realise what an 'eccentric' my tendencies had made me. When I talked to people, their primitive views and arguments, if they had any, astonished me. . . . They said: 'It is so good for the ignorant and uncivilised to be under British rule; we have built up our Empire by our armies'; 'We *must* have wars, it says so in the Bible. It is God's will'; 'Discipline is so good for our young men.'[11]

American Jane Addams was particularly aware of the loneliness of a pacifist in wartime and the British WIL women must have felt this just as keenly. She analysed the human instinct to agree and co-operate with others:

> There is a distinct physical as well as moral strain when the instinct is steadily suppressed or at least ignored. . . . The large number of deaths amongst the older pacifists in all the warring nations can probably be traced in some measure to the peculiar strain which such maladjustment implies. More than the normal amount of nervous energy must be consumed in holding one's own in a hostile world.[12]

In 1915, at least, WIL was an isolated minority trying to change the hearts and minds of a majority. It is in this context that it must be judged. It is perhaps understandable that it did not want to 'ask for trouble'; it is also true that most of the leading women involved were not overt rebels like Sylvia Pankhurst, Rosika Schwimmer and Emily Hobhouse who thrived on, or at least were hardened to, controversy. Also two of the main London protagonists dropped out. Courtney went off to Corsica and Marshall went to work for conscientious objectors. The state of mental seige the women were under exacerbated any personality clashes and as the interminable 'war to end wars' dragged on, tempers, as Helena Swanwick, who was holding much of the responsibility, recalled, 'grew as thin as muslin.'

The work must have felt just about as effective as throwing peas at an elephant as they sat down to discuss, for example, the impact of a fact-sheet on *The Problems of Organising*, with such thorny perennials as 'How to start a branch' and 'How to interest the industrial and professional worker' or 'The woman at home'. WIL responded to British events like conscription or the exploitation of women workers by lobbying, publishing pamphlets and writing letters to the press. They did the same with international events when they could find out what was going on. Above all, they tried to educate *themselves* about international affairs in small, private groups. WIL also held a great number (Swanwick says 'thousands') of both indoor and outdoor public meetings between 1915 and 1918. However, no one would have known this from reading the newspapers. These events were either boycotted by the press or only reported when unsuccessful. Newspaper editors 'pursued the same tactics as they had during the suffrage movement,' remembered Swanwick.

For example, a blaze of publicity followed a meeting by Ethel

Snowden in Consett, County Durham, which was broken up by violence, whilst her hundreds of well-received talks in Bradford, Leeds, Bristol and Glasgow went uncovered. Swanwick wrote,

> In the North of England, in Scotland and in Wales, I addressed meetings on Peace by Negotiation which were attended by enthusiastic crowds but I learnt that, though our papers were never weary of repeating that I was a Hun, in the pay of the Huns, they never had space to print what I actually said.[13]

In London, and occasionally in the provinces, organised gangs of louts, and even children, would disrupt any peace meeting which was advertised more than a few days in advance. Certain newspapers would encourage this. For example, over five days in November 1915, the *Daily Express* foretold the UDC's 'Peace Crank Congress'. The copy ran,

> Make a Note of the Date . . . those who protest against it are as surely fighting for their country as if they were standing in the trenches . . . it can only be hoped that a number of them [tickets] are already in the hands of loyal people. . . . Opportunity will be afforded tomorrow to heckle. . . .

To which the UDC replied with an underlying tone of desperation,

> Our aim is merely to see whether, when the time comes to draw up terms of settlement, such a settlement cannot be arrived at as will give some prospect of a permanent peace in Europe, instead of merely sowing the seeds of future wars.[14]

On the day, the meeting was broken up by Australian and Canadian soldiers, who got in with forged tickets, stormed the platform, roughed up the audience, let off stink bombs and displayed posters provided for them by the *Daily Sketch*. Swanwick remembered that they

> pulled one lad backwards over the top of a bench. Being afraid they would break his spine I laid my hand on the arm of one of the soldiers. He turned on me a face convulsed with fury and, with tears running down his cheeks, fairly sobbed out, 'If that – woman – in a – green hat – doesn't let – me – go – there'll be murder done!' One gathered that they had been so filled up with lies that they really believed

the German Emperor had 'ordered' this meeting to be held.

The *Financial News*, quoted by the *Daily Express*, reported that the Kaiser was furious at the failure of the meeting and ordered the immediate organisation of many others![15]

At a meeting in South Wales on December 3rd, 1916, Ethel Snowden gave examples of how fake photographs were being used in the press: 'the photograph of the corpses of men, women and children destroyed in the Russian pogrom of 1905 was printed in the Allied Press as an illustration in 1915 of the German atrocities committed in Poland. The photographs were identical in every respect.'[16]

At another meeting in Southgate Church in North-East London, Helena Swanwick, Irene Cooper-Willis and another WIL member, Eva Macnaghten, were attacked when a drunken mob broke in through the church windows and smashed up some furniture to use against the audience. The man who appeared to be the ringleader kept shouting, 'Let the women deal with the women!' But when he goaded one woman into raising a stick of wood above the heads of the WIL women, they just gazed at her placidly until she walked away muttering. 'I have a picture in my mind of Miss Cooper-Willis, with one arm over a girl-rioter's shoulder, talking earnestly with her, while another girl accompanying us called to a band of approaching rioters, "They're *not* Germans! *Strite*, they're not!" ' wrote Swanwick later, adding, 'It was funny, but it was pathetic too.'[17]

WIL members had their telephones tapped and overseas mail very often never arrived, so that contact with international pacifists was almost impossible. Helena Swanwick, in particular, was pilloried in *John Bull* by the immensely popular jingoist Horatio Bottomley, and there were several attempts to discredit her as a 'German woman' in the House of Commons. Violence and abuse at meetings which questioned the war was so prevalent that Philip Snowden MP asked a question in Parliament demanding protection for speakers. He also wanted action on the incitement to violence from newspapers.

The British Home Office was constantly considering whether anti-war speeches were illegal under DORA, the newly introduced Defence of the Realm Act. But most of the time they decided, like the German authorities, that it was expedient not to make martyrs. Margaret Ashton, Maude Royden, Helen

Crawfurd, Sylvia Pankhurst, Margaret Haley and others are all to be found in Home Office records of the period; the Snowdens had a file all of their own. Chief Constables all over the country were scribbling verbatim reports at public meetings and sending them to the Home Secretary for advice on whether to take action.

Very often it was other civilians who did the 'spying':

> I write these few lines to warn you of a woman called Mrs Crawford . . . this woman is causing a Terrible discontentment among the munition workers and I am just suspicious of her Being a British subject. Shall I keep in touch with this Woman for the sake of our empire. Write and let me know what to do in this case.

So wrote one William Kelly, whilst a Mrs Lawrenson brought her 11-year-old daughter Doris into Holyhead police station to complain about a Father O'Brien at the convent, who had said that England 'shouldn't have interfered'.[18]

London authorities soon began to prevent WIL from holding public meetings in London by 'warning' the managers of halls that there might be disturbances on such occasions, and that the police would not be prepared to intervene. However, WIL continued to operate under false names. A great deal of trouble seems to have been taken behind the scenes not to be overtly repressive and yet – illogically – the law was sometimes used against peace activists for the most minor activities. For example, two members of the East London Federation were arrested whilst canvassing for the *Peace Memorial* in Leytonstone. This was a petition asking for a negotiated peace which was started in the spring of 1916 by the Peace Negotiations Committee, an alliance of feminist, labour, religious and pacifist organisations chaired by Helena Swanwick. By August 1917, it had collected 221,000 signatures.[19] The two women, Ethel Tollemache and Mrs Brimley, both ex-WSPU members who had joined the ELF because of their opposition to the war, were held for six hours' questioning and warned that they would be arrested for contravening DORA if they continued.

Clara Cole, an ex-postal worker, was sent to prison for five months with her friend Rosa Hobhouse. Cole had started a group called the League Against War and Conscription (which appears in the Home Office files) because she could not bear to nurse injured men in a war hospital, only to see them at risk of being torn apart again in the trenches. In the summer of 1916 she set out on the road with Hobhouse, talking to people they met about the brutality at the front and asking if it was necessary. But after only five days, they were arrested at Kettering in Northamptonshire. A note which was found in Cole's pocket with the impassioned plea, 'Is there no strength in your cold madhouse to cry halt, cowards, cowards, and again grey-bearded cowards!' apparently sent the judge into a blind fury.[20]

Alice Wheeldon, a second-hand clothes dealer from Derby, who was an ex-WSPU member and a radical socialist, was sentenced to ten years in prison at the Old Bailey in London in March 1917. In an extraordinary case, in which Emmeline Pankhurst gave evidence, she was charged with planning to assassinate Lloyd George with poisoned darts (supposedly a WSPU tactic planned but never used). Wheeldon regularly sheltered conscientious objectors and claimed that she had been framed by two *agents provocateurs*, who had posed as army deserters and asked her to procure poison to get rid of guard dogs working at an internment camp. She was eventually released from prison after going on hunger strike.[21]

At the end of 1915, after seventeen months of fighting, it seems that the British anti-war resistance was anxiously waiting for a leader to emerge or an event to happen which would act as a catalyst and goad the British people into angry rebellion. The various groups were as follows: WIL was essentially a small educational group, with the impossible task of trying to debate rationally with a frightened populace the possibilities of a federated world. The UDC was of a similar complexion – save that its members were mostly male, with well-known MPs in its ranks. The ILP, although officially opposed to the war, decided not to launch a national peace campaign. And the East London Federation of Suffragettes continued to fight the exploitation of women, but in the early days of the war it did not make many public demands for peace. It was only after September 1915, when Sylvia Pankhurst's beloved Keir Hardie died of pneumonia at the age of 59, that she doubted the wisdom of her previous judgment: 'I wished with an intensity which seemed to burn up all other feeling,' she wrote later, 'that while there was yet time, I had gone with him as a missioner through the country denouncing the War.'[22] Keir Hardie had been devastated by the events of August 1914, since he had believed that the growth of socialism was such that working men would refuse to fight. He saw all his hopes for the future shattered.

At the beginning of the war, Sylvia Pankhurst had been approached by Lucy Thoumaian, a Swiss woman, who wanted to organise a thousand women to make their way to the front and 'fling themselves between the contending armies'. The war was 'man-made – it must be woman-undone!' she told Sylvia. Not usually one to turn down a challenge, Sylvia was inspired but felt that she could not leave the work she was doing in the East End of London, and Thoumaian was unable to get other support. Dorothea Hollins wrote to several newspapers, signing herself 'X', with the same idea. She was a wealthy woman who lived in Chelsea. A number of private meetings were held at her house but nothing materialised.

The two leading working-class women's organisations, the Women's Labour League and the Women's Co-operative Guild, gave their thoughts to the question of how war could be prevented in future and generally adopted an anti-militaristic tone but do not seem to have directly organised any peace propaganda. In January 1915 *The Labour Woman* printed a letter from Clara Zetkin, the International Secretary of Socialist Women, and announced that although the Annual Conference had been postponed for that year, every district should hold a local conference to discuss 'the terms upon which a lasting World Peace should be built up'. In April (just before the Women's International Congress at The Hague) Margaret Bondfield, Mary Longman, Marion Phillips and Ada Salter went to the International Socialist Women's Conference in Switzerland. And when the first WLL conference of the war was finally held at Bristol on January 24th, 1916, Katherine Glasier (a leading activist in the ILP) reported in *Labour Leader*, 'never have I heard fiercer anti-militarist speeches or more complete acceptance of them by any previous audiences.'

The Women's Co-operative Guild raised a special fund to send four members to the Women's International Congress at The Hague and letters were sent to Co-operative women in other countries, urging them to attend. In the spring of 1915, local Guild conferences (there was no national conference that year) passed almost unanimously a resolution urging the formation of a League of Nations. In June 1916, the first national Guild conference of the war, with 800 delegates, voted against conscription and for a negotiated peace. The *Labour Leader* report went as follows:

> The vast hall, which the largest Labour Conference last year only half filled, was very nearly completely filled for two whole days by working women. But I saw none of our Labour leaders among the audience and hardly a representative of Labour organisations. The loss was theirs, to put it plainly, for if they had been present they would have had an object lesson in efficient organisation, combined with a natural genius for politics. . . .
>
> One must remember that the Guild is in no sense a selected body, either of militarists or pacifists. It is a body of some 30,000 women scattered over the face of England. . . . One can imagine the sort of scenes which would take place today at a Congress . . . in which Arthur Henderson and Thorne . . . sat cheek by jowl with Snowden, Jowett. . . . Now among the women there were those who disagreed quite as fundamentally about the war. But on both sides the spirit, the tone, and the temper were equally admirable. Speakers and audience seemed to realise that on political questions no-one has a monopoly of truth and honesty.

That fundamental disagreement was not illustrated until summer 1918, which appears to have been the date of the next Congress, when a radical resolution for a 'People's Peace by Negotiation' was defeated by 399 votes to 336, with 80 abstentions. However, June 1918 was one of the tensest months of the war in Britain, with the German army only forty miles outside Paris.[23]

But let us return to the end of 1915, to our list of peace groups and their apparent powerlessness. At the end of that year, the introduction of conscription was being threatened by the government. Pacifists everywhere saw it as the spread of militarism to British shores, the defeat of everything for which Britain was supposedly fighting. They would resist it, they decided, and in doing so, galvanise the dormant anti-war feeling they believed existed in the British people.

Catherine Marshall was one of those swept up in the anti-conscription movement. At last, she thought, here was a positive way to oppose the killing. In November 1915, the No Conscription Fellowship was formed and the principle of conscientious objection, to refuse to kill and be killed for the state, was established. No other country in the war, except America, formed such an organisation because conscription in the rest of Europe was accepted as the norm; even Karl Liebknecht, the hero of all German pacifists, became a soldier.

The President of the NCF was Clifford Allen, a charismatic young man who had studied history at Cambridge and been converted to socialism. He had worked for the first British Labour daily paper *The Daily Citizen* but left in 1914 because of its stance on the war. Fenner Brockway, the young editor of *Labour Leader*, was another leading light in the NCF. Most of its members – it had 12,000[24] at its peak, about half of whom were serving prison sentences – were ILP men of military age who were religious pacifists, particularly Quakers. The original idea came from Lilla Brockway, who was married to Fenner.

Industrial action was threatened. The South Wales miners voted by a large majority to strike if conscription was brought in. On the Clyde, thousands walked out as a sign of protest. ILP branches enthusiastically organised demonstrations. But when the first Military Service Act was passed in January 1916, conscripting all single men between the ages of 18 and 41, opposition seemed to melt away. Only thirty-six MPs voted against it and all remained peaceful on the industrial front. Arthur Henderson and two other Labour ministers threatened to resign but were pacified when Asquith promised that the legislation would not be extended to married men. This promise only lasted until May 2nd, by which time the three Labour politicians appeared to have forgotten their indignation.

'When conscription came,' wrote Sylvia Pankhurst after the war, 'Clara Cole stood in Trafalgar Square with a badge "Stop the War"' and a banner against Conscription. She was arrested and brought into Court; but the charge was dropped, though she many times repeated the demonstration.'[25]

On April 8th that year, Sylvia Pankhurst was herself involved in a protest demonstration in Trafalgar Square. The ELF slogans were: 'Complete democratic control of national and international affairs!' and 'Human suffrage and no infringement of popular liberties'. The *Daily Express* and *Globe*, amongst others, denounced the coming meeting as 'open sedition'. Sylvia Pankhurst later described it thus: 'As usual, friends saluted us on our march through the East End, crowds gathered to speed us; they had struggled with us for a decade; they supported us still, though our standard seemed now more Utopian, more elusively remote.'

At Charing Cross, the group met a crowd of people cheering and clapping (*The Times* estimated the numbers as 20,000):

> In their jolly kindness some shouted: 'Good old Sylvia!' I gave my hands to many a rough grip. They pressed round me, ardent and gay, sorrowful, hopeful, earnest. Many a woman's eyes brimmed with tears as she met mine; I knew, by a sure instinct, that she had come across London, overweighted with grief, to ease her burden by some words with me.

But again colonial soldiers had been organised to disrupt the meeting and as there were so few police in the crowd (which Sylvia Pankhurst thought was a deliberate policy), the demonstration was fated from the start.

> As we entered the Square a rush of friends, with a roar of cheers and a swiftness which forestalled any hostile approach, bore us forward, and hoisted a group of us on to the east plinth, facing the Strand, whilst the banner-bearers marched on . . . but the north side was packed with soldiers who fell upon the approaching banners and tore them to shreds.

Norah Smyth, Charlotte Drake, her small daughter Ruby, Sylvia Pankhurst and two other women faced the crowd alone. Male supporters who wanted to mount the plinth and join them were prevented from doing so by the police. Red and yellow ochre was hurled, splattering the women and nearby reporters.

> The soldiers from the north were now forcing their way towards us, resisted by the crowd on the east. After a brief tussle the soldiers prevailed, and came surging forward to storm the plinth. As the head of one of them topped it, Norah Smyth lunged at him vigorously and thrust him down. The other women sprang to help her; but two of them were dragged to the ground, and dozens of soldiers swarmed up. . . . 'They say you are paid by the Germans!' one of them blurted, shamefaced.[26]

Needless to say, Sylvia Pankhurst explained she was not,

before being marched off by 'two burly police inspectors'. As always after such demonstrations, the mother and child clinics (which a thousand mothers attended in 1915), day nursery, canteen and factory which ELF ran, suffered the immediate loss of donations. Emmeline Pankhurst, who was on a tour of America to promote the Allies' case, read a press account of the demonstration there, and sent a cable to Britain repudiating her daughter. This was broadcast over the radio and helped to alienate even more of the old WSPU members who still supported the ELF. Sylvia must have been dismayed.

By April 1916, Catherine Marshall was thoroughly involved with helping conscientious objectors. She had gone as a WIL delegate to the inaugural conference of the NCF and been inspired by Clifford Allen's dynamism: 'We have got to make the task of building a new social order so enthralling that the glamour of war will cease to attract,' he said in the summer of 1916.[27]

Marshall organised a deputation to Parliament, which consisted of prominent people who were anxious to press for improved methods of dealing with conscientious objectors, now suffering torture and humiliation in military prisons. The 1916 Military Service Act set up tribunals to determine what should happen to individual conscientious objectors. Some men resisted any sort of war work and were immediately jailed ('absolutists'), while others were prepared to do non-combatant service. The main role of the NCF was to monitor cases coming before the tribunals and give support, advising the men how to present their cases and keeping track of those who were arrested. If necessary, help was given to dependants. Railway stations also had to be watched to see that no objectors were secretly shipped abroad.

Within six months most of the men were in prison and Marshall had taken over the running of the organisation. She set up a Political Committee which drew on the support of MPs who opposed conscription. Philip Snowden, for instance, was particularly useful; Ramsay MacDonald was more cautious because the conscientious objectors were breaking the law. Marshall would table questions for Snowden and others to ask about conscientious objectors in the House of Commons, and sometimes the Ministry of Defence had to ring her up to get the answers! It was largely because of the influence of this political section that the NCF was able to save thirty-four conscientious objectors who had been shipped to France in the summer of 1916. They had still persisted in refusing to do military service and were sentenced to death but Asquith intervened at the last moment. 'I think,' Marshall wrote to Helena Swanwick about the NCF, 'that I have been able to help them in some degree to develop and make good the positive and constructive ideals involved in their attitude about war.'[28]

She worked closely with Bertrand Russell, who was already famous as a mathematician and philosopher and had been thrown out of his fellowship at Trinity College because of his stance against the war. Marshall wrote to him daily during March 1916, beseeching his help. The philosopher thought many pacifists were an 'awful crew' and hated their cold-hearted theorising but he was attracted to the humanitarian stance of WIL and the immediacy of NCF[29] action. For the next year and a half Marshall and Russell worked together – but it was a complicated relationship. She was, according to the *Labour Leader*, the 'ablest woman organiser in the land' whilst Russell hated detailed administration. She gave him daily lists marked 'BR to do' and kept an assiduous check on whether or not he kept up to date. He loathed the desk job which he had taken on at the NFC, so in the circumstances it is not surprising that he resented Marshall's scolding and thought her auto-cratic. Both of them found criticism hard to bear and were overwhelmed by feelings of impotence against the war. She respected him but was determined not to be overwhelmed by his reputation or powers of persuasion, and yet her upbringing as a woman inhibited her from playing the necessary leadership role with him. At the same time, Russell's hatred of his own hopeless organising skills made him particularly sensitive to a woman boss.[30]

There were a number of other militant and non-militant suffragists who worked for the NCF. Violet Tillard, who came from an army family, ran the Maintenance Organisation for the relatives of conscientious objectors and in 1917, she became the NCF General Secretary. Lydia Smith, a teacher from Brighton, and Joan Beauchamp, a farmer's daughter from Somerset, who had worked with Sylvia Pankhurst, ran the press and publications office and Smith edited the NCF journal *The Tribunal*, which had to go underground. They travelled around the country, recording and then publicising the case histories of conscientious objectors who had experienced ill-treatment in army prisons. Many conscientious objectors were forced to live in filthy, dark and cramped conditions with inadequate food; they were beaten up, and mentally and physically tortured. Many had their health permanently ruined and some committed suicide.

There were several police raids on the NCF offices, which were under constant watch from Scotland Yard detectives stationed in the house opposite. All three women were eventually prosecuted under DORA but Smith was released because she looked so young, and, in any case, the police were convinced that the editor of *The Tribunal* was a man.[31]

Catherine Marshall calculated that the number of times she had broken the law in aid of conscientious objectors meant she was liable to a total of 2,000 years' imprisonment. She was under great strain during 1916 and 1917. She had to cope with Russell's inefficiency, with overwork, with harassment both official (Scotland Yard) and unofficial ('Mr Glover of the Anti-German Union ... and his hooligan New Zealanders') and with criticism over her political work (the Quakers thought objectors ought to take the brutal treatment meted out to them without comment). She was also taxed by worries about Clifford Allen, with whom she had fallen in love. He was court-marshalled three times and was eventually taken to hospital with tuberculosis.

Added to this, her old friends at WIL were unhappy about Marshall's allegiance to the NCF. In the begining Marshall worked for both organisations but by August 1916, Helena Swanwick was writing to her,

> I want also to tell you that I feel and I believe most of our colleagues do too, that unless you can come back to us in the autumn we must try and find another Hon. Sec. This 'hope deferred' about you has made my heart very sick – we go on and on and your return is always tomorrow, not today – I can't feel that what you are doing now is wide enough. But if you do, it's right you should do it. Meanwhile the work of the WIL simply doesn't get done. . . . I do as much of the Hon. Sec.'s work as I possibly can but it is absurd that I should be expected to be Chairman and Hon. Sec. rolled into one and with all my other work [Swanwick was involved with the UDC and ILP as well] I can't do it properly. . . . We must be preparing for the Congress. We ought to be

planning our delegates – this is untouched and is urgent.[32]

Margaret Hills and Maude Royden are also on record as feeling ambivalent about conscientious objectors (or at least their tactics) but were concerned not to hurt Marshall's feelings. Margaret Hills, who had worked closely with Catherine in the NUWSS Election Fighting Fund, wrote,

> I don't think we'd really quarrel about CO's I'm not quite as bad as I made out – I think it is just the sense that one's own man's conscience keeps him in hourly peril, agonisingly against the grain, that makes it impossible to feel tender to the man whose conscience keeps his body safe even in HM prisons. But I know that is merely sentiment – anyway, we won't squabble! . . . My man has just been home on his first leave and I still live in the after-glow.[33]

When Marshall finally resigned from the Honorary Secretaryship of WIL in September 1916, dictating her letter in great haste because she had been cabled to go and see men released from jail in Suffolk, she said that she had never in her life been 'so torn in two' between work that she loved and considered of the most vital importance 'on either hand'. But she did assure WIL that the conscientious objectors were all becoming 'ardent Women's Suffragists'. 'Your letter of resignation was read to the Committee amidst loud outcries and wails,' wrote Swanwick as part of an informal note attached to a formal reply. 'Be sure of this, Catherine dear,' she added, 'we shall all never cease wanting you back.'[34]

> Are the Socialist women of Britain less mindful of their men than the women of Germany? It is now twenty-two months since war started, and as far as my knowledge goes there has not been one public demonstration against this wholesale slaughter of our menfolk.
> This has not been the case with the German women. They have had several. . . . Surely we women must make a strong effort to stay this terrible slaughter that grows in numbers every day.

And so it was that this letter, which appeared in the *Labour Leader* on May 18th, 1916 from S. Cahill of Lewisham,

147

inspired an exciting new development against the war in Britain. Within three weeks, Helen Crawfurd from the Glasgow branch of WIL was writing to the same letter columns saying that since Cahill's plea, she had been approached by several women to see if they could get up a demonstration in Glasgow: 'We in Glasgow have not had the terrible persecution which Pacifists in the South have had, and we are realising every day that there is a common desire for Peace among the common people.' There would be, she said, a meeting at the Central Halls in Glasgow on June 10th, to which all women's societies were invited, to discuss the feasibility of starting a Women's Peace Crusade.[35]

Helen Crawfurd was the working-class daughter of a baker. The fourth child in a family of seven, she had been born in the Gorbals, a Jewish working-class district of Glasgow. Political discussion was a prominent part of her upbringing. Although a strong trade unionist, her father was a staunch Conservative and her mother, as well as being devoutly religious, was a member of the Primrose League (the Conservative Women's Club). Most of Crawfurd's childhood was spent down south in Ipswich, but it was her return to Glasgow which started her asking questions about how society was run. She was 17 and shocked at the poverty, dirt and deprivation which she saw:

> These despised rivetters, boiler-makers, moulders, returning from their work, had been building ships that sailed the seas with strength, dignity and grace. Yet these skilled creators of the city's wealth were living in squalor, in hovels unfit for human beings. I began to think there must be something wrong with a system that could allow this.[36]

When she was 21, Crawfurd married a clergyman (it seems she was not very keen on him but didn't like to keep refusing in case it was 'God's mission') and gradually, during her twenties, became both a feminist and a socialist.

> I had always resented any suggestion of the inferiority of women. I can remember once as a girl I was given a sixpence while my brothers got a shilling to spend at a fair in Ipswich. I somewhat shocked my parents by throwing it down and saying, 'Damn!'[37]

She was particularly active in the WSPU. She had great

admiration for Emmeline and Christabel Pankhurst; Charlotte Despard and Clara Zetkin were other well-known feminists who were acquaintances. She soon became famous in her area: 'I always took the lead in things. I didn't mean to put myself in the forefront, but when I believed a thing was right, I wanted to bring other people to see it my way.'[38]

Her own particular brand of rhetoric was punctuated with quotations from the Bible and illustrations of the wrongs meted out to the poor. The women of Scotland, she felt, were still bound 'hand and foot' to the Church but because she had been 'extremely religious' herself she was able to understand and communicate with them. When making the decision whether or not to go on the 1912 WSPU raid, breaking windows down in Whitehall with seven other Scottish suffragettes, she prayed for a message from her husband's sermon. It turned out to be about Christ making a whip of cords and chasing the money changers out of the temple, and she thought, 'If Christ can be Militant so can I!'

Smashing the windows of the Ministry of Education (she went there in a taxi, armed with the two stones with messages attached to them given her by the WSPU organisers), and pouring corrosive materials into letter-boxes, ended with a month's prison sentence. Years later she gleefully remembered that when the judge passed sentence, a row of middle-aged women sitting in the front row of the court opened up their handbags and took out crab apples to throw at him! However, prison did not deter her from future suffrage activity and in March 1914 she was one of Mrs Pankhurst's bodyguard, protecting the by now notorious suffrage agitator from arrest, at St Andrew's Hall, Glasgow. Mrs Pankhurst had been released from a three-month sentence after suffering exhaustion from hunger striking but had then absconded to Canada for three months, and on her return in December 1913 was under threat of re-arrest. Helen Crawfurd was one of those who wrestled with police as they stormed the stage at St Andrew's Hall the following March. The men lashed out with batons as a 4,000-strong audience looked on in a pitch of intense excitement: 'I found myself in the Kent Road in the hands of two policemen, minus my hat, my hair streaming down my back, and every button off my costume jacket. I was small fry and they let my go.'[39]

Crawfurd was disappointed in Emmeline and Christabel

Pankhurst's militaristic response to the war. Ironically, at one public meeting (date unknown) in the very same St Andrew's Hall, she confronted Christabel Pankhurst, who had come to urge Scottish women to enter munitions work. Members of the audience began singing revolutionary songs and the Lord Provost of Glasgow, who was chairing the meeting, sent white-overalled women munition workers, who had been sitting on the platform, down into the audience. They began hitting the singers with their hands and with sticks. Crawfurd was disgusted by this and marched down the central aisle, mounted the Reporters' Table and shouted, 'Shame on you, Christabel Pankhurst, to get these women to do your dirty work. It is an insult to womanhood!'

From the very beginning Crawfurd spoke out against the war, travelling around the country. Soon she was part of the 1915 Rent Strike which was to make the Clyde internationally famous. It ended in the government creating the Rent Restriction Act that year, in order to protect people from unscrupulous landlords, who wanted to make quick profits from the influx of workers into industrial centres for munitions work. Glasgow had been one such centre but when the landlords put the rent up, the tenants refused to pay any at all.

Great masses of women came together for the Rent Strike. They organised themselves so that one woman would sit on guard in the hallway of each tenement block, and when the bailiff appeared to evict non-rent payers, she would ring a bell as a signal for the others to come and pelt him with flour and wet cloths. This went on for several months until every hall in the working-class districts of Glasgow was packed out with public meetings. When nine strikers were taken to court, thousands of men from the Clyde shipyards and engineering workers came out in support and the judge postponed the cases until after consultation with the government. It was then that protective legislation was introduced.

During the Rent Strike Helen Crawfurd met Agnes Dollan. She was to play a leading role in the Scottish Women's Peace Crusade. Ten years younger than Crawfurd, who by this time was 37 and a widow, she had a 'fine speaking voice', with a love of literature and political philosophy. In later years, she was to go on to be a member of Glasgow Council and to sit on the National Executive of the Labour Party. By 1914, she had been married for two years to Patrick Dollan. An ILP city councillor, tall and curly-haired, he was a journalist who contributed to the ELP's *Women's Dreadnought*, amongst other newspapers, and was eventually to become Lord Provost of Glasgow from 1938 to 1941. A supporter of the WSPU, Dollan had her first row with her husband when the suffragettes blew up all the telegraph and telephone wires between Glasgow and London, and Patrick couldn't phone through his copy to waiting news editors!

Helen Crawfurd and Agnes Dollan worked together in the Glasgow WIL branch until the meeting on June 10th, 1916 which launched the Women's Peace Crusade. Two hundred delegates representing sixteen women's organisations attended. There does not appear to have been any break in relations with WIL, since Helena Swanwick was one of the main speakers. Just six weeks later, on July 23rd – a Sunday – the WPC held a 5,000-strong demonstration on Glasgow Green. Despite an attempt at organised disruption, Patrick Dollan reported in the *Women's Dreadnought* that

> Not one woman was subjected to interruption. At several points the audience cheered most heartily, and in many other ways indicated their approval of a settlement of the war by negotiation. . . .
>
> The demonstration was arranged entirely by women, and carried through by women, who have been well led by the able and enthusiastic Mrs Helen Crawfurd, who has no leisure hours that are not devoted to furthering the cause of Peace.[40]

Besides Crawfurd and Dollan, there were six other speakers on two platforms around which the crowd gathered. They included Margaret Ashton, from Manchester, and Muriel Matters, the famous suffragette who had chained herself to the grid of the Ladies' Gallery in the House of Commons before the war. A resolution urging the government to seek a negotiated peace at the earliest possible opportunity was enthusiastically passed. 'At the opposition "meeting" (about 200 people) a resolution urging the vigorous persecution of the war to a finish was not submitted to the vote, yet was declared, and reported in the Press to have been carried.'[41]

It is interesting to look at not only *what* these women did for peace (and there was another WPC demo in Edinburgh not long after, which met with a 'most encouraging response') but *why* they did it – and why they organised *as women*. They do not seem to have written much about their philosophy themselves but no doubt Patrick Dollan gave a reasonably accurate account of their thinking when he wrote in a front-page article in the *Dreadnought*:

War is the enthronement of force and the dethronement of reason, and the history of women's progress makes it plain that women have everything to gain by the dominance of reason, just as they have everything to lose by the domination of force . . . it has only been where militarism has been brought under control that women have made headway in any progressive direction.

Militarism means the subjection of women, imposing, as it does, the right of the State to take from woman the men whom she has brought into the world to be comrades and friends of her sex.

Dollan noted with some bitterness that women were being exploited in the war. Three hundred men had been dismissed from the Glaswegian Civil Service to be replaced by women at lower wages:

Women have only been allowed into industry in great numbers because their labour is necessary to militarism, and not because of any desire on the part of the State, built up by force, to recognise the right of women to earn their own maintenance . . . it should now be apparent to most observers that women are being used in industry to make the prosecution of the war in all countries more easy. After the war the labour of women will be used to cheapen men's wages in the interests of capitalism.[42]

1916 saw the start of the really horrifying battles of the First World War. During the first half of the year, the French lost 350,000 men in defending Verdun, a city which was held in special affection and which became a symbol of defiance against the Germans. Trenches collapsed; many men were buried alive and the troops had to live and fight with corpses all around them. The German death toll was 300,000. July 1st, the first day of the Battle of the Somme, saw the worst slaughter ever suffered by a British army in a single day: 19,000 were killed, with 57,000 casualties. The attack was meant to be secret but the Germans knew all about it. 'Waves' of 1,000 men formed a human battering ram but died struggling through reinforced barbed wire, while the Germans knocked them over in rows from deep bunkers. By November a total of 1,223,907 French, German and British men had died, with over a million more injured.[43]

Any men who had come out to the front full of idealism and the glory of war lost their innocence from that time on. As news of the casualties trickled back, through letters from friends, nurses and army chaplains – long before the official army telegrams – British civilians no longer bothered to offer each other condolences, as so many were now in mourning. Despite the press censorship, the British home front was beginning to understand what life in the trenches was all about.

CHAPTER 8

Keep America out!

IN THE MIDDLE of November 1916, Woodrow Wilson was re-elected President of the United States of America. The election campaign divided suffragists and it was a tense time; women, it seemed, could not be allowed peace *and* political freedom. Wilson opposed federal action for female suffrage but he seemed to promise continuing neutrality with his slogan 'HE KEPT US OUT OF THE WAR', usually printed under pictures of happy family scenes. The Republican candidate, Justice Charles Evans Hughes, on the other hand, was quite happy to give women the vote but advocated gearing up the American military to prepare for war 'just in case'.

The choice of whom to support presented feminists who opposed the war with a cruel dilemma. In the end, all the leading women in the peace movement, Jane Addams, Emily Greene Balch, Lillian Wald, Fanny Garrison Villard and Crystal Eastman, campaigned for Wilson but Alice Paul's Congressional Union (renamed the National Woman's Party in 1916) organised for Hughes. Crystal Eastman had been one of the original executive members of the Union since its beginning and was in the unenviable position of endorsing the candidate whom some of her closest friends were heckling. One colleague, Inez Milholland, seemed to single her out for attack:

> Do not let anyone convince you that there is any more important issue in the country today than votes for women. . . . There are people who honestly believe – HONESTLY BELIEVE! . . that there are more important issues . . . it makes me mad. . . . We must say, 'Women First.'[1]

However, once the election was over the hostilities between suffragists were soon forgotten. The political philosophies of the two groups had never been that different anyway, it was just a case of conflicting priorities. Eastman couldn't be accused of renouncing her feminism because to her the vote was only a small part of it. Her vision was a total one of women freed from physical and mental servitude. Her demands ranged from short hair and comfortable clothes, birth control, shared housework, equal pay and access to jobs, to giving women a chance to compete at sport and what we would call today 'non-sexist' education. She believed passionately that the international women's peace movement was 'unique and priceless' and she urged women to 'stand by it and strengthen it no matter what other peace organisations we may identify ourselves with'.[2] Her support for Wilson could not be portrayed as a betrayal. Nor could Alice Paul and her colleagues be classed as warmongers because by the beginning of 1917, when it was becoming obvious that Wilson's slogan 'HE KEPT US OUT' was strictly in the past tense, they were vigorously opposing any suggestion that America enter the war.

However, we must backtrack a year and find out what happened to the envoys from the Women's International Congress, after their series of frustrating interviews with President Wilson in his first term of office. By the end of 1915, the women had all gone their separate ways. Chrystal Macmillan went to Canada to set up a national women's peace organisation there, returning afterwards to work with Aletta Jacobs (first Vice-Chairman) and Rosa Manus (Assistant Secretary) at ICWPP headquarters in Amsterdam (Macmillan was Secretary). (Upon her return, Jacobs soon came under pressure because a new Constitution Bill was proposed for Holland and she had to organise suffrage lobbying. The ICWPP Treasurer Madame Hubrecht also fell seriously ill, and there was still much work to be done with Belgian refugees. In December, the Dutch parliament debated the idea of a neutral mediating conference, but the discussion came to nought.) Writing to Jane Addams in January 1916, Macmillan paints a sorry picture of how Jacobs seemed to have lost all her courage on her return to Europe and would not even agree to send the Manifesto, written and signed by the envoys in America, to the European press.[3]

In 1915, Jane Addams was the most respected woman in America. Loved by many, she literally made others more peaceful in her presence. However, Carrie Chapman Catt called her 'slippery Jane' and Rosika Schwimmer said Hull House reminded her of her convent school.

Jane Addams's time, meanwhile, was to a large extent spent resuming the day-to-day responsibilities of running Hull House. Her settlement colleagues Marie Smith and Louise Bowen had never been very enthusiastic about her peace campaigning and were anxious to solve some of the problems which had piled up while she had been away. However, there were also other demands on her. The 'drunken bayonet charge' story led to a demand for more interviews and lectures and she was still President of the Woman's Peace Party and on the executive of the American Union Against Militarism. This was an organisation which had been set up at the beginning of the war with the aim of analysing the economic and social effects of militarism, as well as to lobby Washington. The members of these groups looked to her for leadership but she hoped that now the President himself would take the initiative in any peace moves.

Rosika Schwimmer had no such delusions. By December 4th, 1915 she was aboard Henry Ford's Peace Ship, sailing for Scandinavia to set up a people's mediating conference. If politicians couldn't be persuaded to face up to their responsibilities, then ordinary citizens would have to do it instead. The story of how Henry Ford, the millionaire inventor of the 'universal car', came to sponsor such a grand unofficial peacemaking exercise is little told in the history annuals of the First World War. Throughout the summer of 1915, the man had been letting his opposition to warfare be known and by September he had pledged ten million dollars to fund an effective scheme which would take *action* to stop the insane bloodshed in Europe. The only trouble was that he was guarded around the clock and it was almost impossible for pacifists to talk to him. He received 600 letters a day propounding every kind of scheme, and Jane Addams was one of the many who tried and failed to get an interview with him. Meanwhile, much to the frustration of the penniless peace movement, those valuable dollars lay idle.

Rebecca Shelley, a teacher from the Mid-West, and Angela Morgan, a poet, two young women who had both gone to the Women's International Congress, were convinced that if they could get a meeting between Schwimmer and Ford then exciting things would happen. The Hungarian feminist had become their mentor ever since her evangelical speech in the closing minutes of the Women's International Congress. Throughout the autumn, the two of them organised street

157

demonstrations and huge mass meetings in Detroit, home of the car manufacturer, with the hope of getting his attention. Publicity was surprisingly good and by November local editors were competing over which newspaper was going to orchestrate the meeting between Schwimmer and Ford.

Shelley must have felt desperate when she went to see the editor of the Detroit *Journal* on the day of Schwimmer's final visit to the city. Schwimmer had decided to leave America on November 27th and try and persuade the Scandinavian, Dutch, Swiss and Spanish governments to set up a conference themselves. It seemed that the Hungarian would never meet Ford, but by a stroke of luck a cub reporter named Ralph Yonker overheard the conversation between Shelley and his boss. He was one of Ford's favourite young reporters and within minutes he had made a short telephone call and fixed up an interview between Schwimmer and the car manufacturer.

Just two and a half weeks after Schwimmer met Ford, the expedition set sail. The idea for a Peace Ship came from the 1914 Christmas Ship, which had been chartered by President Wilson to deliver seven million gifts to war orphans in Europe. A thousand American newspapers had encouraged school children to send in their pennies for presents and the liner had been well received at all the German, French and British ports at which it docked. Henry Ford, who had a great sense for publicity, adored the suggestion and couldn't wait to get started. Unfortunately, he was always more interested in the Peace Ship than the unofficial mediating conference planned for its Stockholm destination. Despite his sincere hatred of warfare, it was difficult for journalists to take Ford seriously.

Within eighteen days, Ford, Schwimmer and Louis Lochner (the 28-year-old secretary of the Chicago Peace Society, who had attended the Hague Congress as a guest) arranged accommodation on the Scandinavian-American liner *Oscar II*. They sent out invitations to hundreds of suitably internationally minded Americans and wired to Scandinavia peace contacts to organise festive reception meetings in Norway, Sweden and Denmark. Beseiged with reporters, pacifists and publicity seekers, the New York Hotel Biltmore, where the expedition had its headquarters, buzzed with excitement and the days were frantic.

To her disappointment, many of the feminist pacifists whom Schwimmer had hoped would come declined their invitations.

Lillian Wald, Fanny Garrison Villard and Anna Howard Shaw refused. So did Crystal Eastman, because she believed her fight was at home. Emily Greene Balch declined because she felt duty-bound to resume her work at Wellesley College after such a long absence visiting European politicians (although later she spent several months working at the unofficial conference in Stockholm). Jane Addams planned to come but was worried about the sensational publicity the Peace Ship was receiving and begged Lochner, with whom she had worked closely, to keep to the subject of the conference, but

> the people in New York in charge of the enterprise believed that the anti-war movement throughout its history had been too quietistic and much too grey and negative; that the heroic aspect of life had been too completely handed over to war, leaving pacifists under the suspicion that they cared for safety first and cherished survival above all else.[4]

Despite her reservations, and her remonstrating friends, who urged her not to become associated with anything so open to ridicule, she still felt committed:

> [I] believed that at the worst it would be a protest from the rank and file of America, young and old, learned and simple, against the continuation of the war which in Europe was more and more being then regarded as inevitable.[5]

She reassured herself by reflecting that Henry Ford probably understood the mentality of the 'ordinary working man' better than she. However, a few days before the ship was due to sail, she collapsed with kidney trouble and had to be taken to hospital. She promised to make her own way to the conference once she had recovered – but she never did.[6]

None the less, despite these disappointments, there were prominent women from the American suffrage movement on board. Inez Milholland (who was later to chastise Crystal Eastman for thinking there was anything more important than votes for women) was one whom the rest of the party looked forward to meeting. She had gained a certain notoriety for leading a suffrage parade down Fifth Avenue, in New York, wearing a Grecian gown and riding a white horse. More importantly, she was a tireless campaigner for a range of progressive causes, and during 1915 had spent six months in Italy as a war correspondent before being deported for her

159

pacifist articles. Sadly, she was to die suddenly from pernicious
anaemia late in 1916.

Seventy-year-old May Wright Sewall, co-founder of the
National and International Councils of Women and Chairwoman of the Woman's Peace Party's Northern California
Branch, was also there. She was a friend of Schwimmer, who
had met the ship when the Hungarian first arrived in America
in August 1914. Helen Ring Robinson from Colorado, the first
woman ever to be elected to a state senate, came along. She had
shared suffrage platforms with Carrie Chapman Catt and Jane
Addams many a time. And Alice Park, who wore badges all
over her chest and had travelled from Europe to Hawaii for
suffrage and social justice, was glad to answer the following
telegram of invitation, which was sent out to everyone:

> With 20,000 men killed every twenty-four hours, tens of
> thousands maimed, homes ruined, another winter begun, the
> time has come for a few men and women with courage and
> energy, irrespective of the cost in personal inconvenience,
> money, sacrifice and criticism, to free the goodwill of Europe
> that it may assert itself for peace and justice, with the strong
> probability that international disarmament can be accom-
> plished.[7]

Katherine Leckie, a well-known newspaper woman, who had
been Schwimmer's speaking agent in 1914, was employed to
try and keep the press corps happy (all forty-four of them), and
Rebecca Shelley was responsible for the welfare of the twenty-
five-strong student contingent. Henry Ford paid $900 to
compensate the University of Wisconsin for the absence of Julia
Grace Wales (the author of *International Plan for Continuous
Mediation without Armistice*). He paid, too, for Lola Maverick
Lloyd's three children to sail with her as she was in the middle
of a marital breakdown and divorce was pending. There were
not many nationally known figures amongst the party; the cruel
invective and relentless ridicule of the American press deterred
anyone with a reputation to protect.

At the time, Schwimmer's persuasion of a millionaire to
sponsor an unofficial mediating conference seemed like a
miracle in the absence of any governmental action. But the
expedition was a mixed blessing, and after the war Schwimmer
reflected that it might have been better if she had returned to
Europe as planned on 27th November. She resigned as Ford's

organiser in March 1916 and collapsed with heart trouble, unable to work for three months. She had been working almost non-stop since August 1914, and for long hours ever since she was 18. Bedevilled by illness in childhood, it was not surprising that the strain of public activity and the hostility shown her on the Ford Peace Ship and at the subsequent conference finally caught up with her.[8]

On a personal level, the expedition seems to have been racked with dissent from the beginning. Power struggles and intrigues are not unfamiliar scenarios in politics of any complexion but perhaps being incarcerated in an ocean-going steel box, three or four to a cabin, in the middle of a stormy mid-winter sea, with the threat of being torpedoed at any time, made friction between the party members particularly bad. Neither did taking along almost as many journalists as delegates make for harmony: complex discussions on inter-national affairs make bad copy, and personality clashes are much better.

Schwimmer was resented by many for having been given control by Ford (no doubt there was some sexism here) and for not revealing her 'secret documents' which she carried every-where with her in a large black leather bag. These were the notes from the German, Russian and British politicians implying acceptance of the setting up of a mediating confer-ence. The constant complaint from some sections of the party was that she was secretive, autocratic and extravagant. For her part, Schwimmer felt on no account could she break the confidence with which the European politicians had entrusted her. As the sea voyage continued, she became increasingly anxious that the expedition would be sabotaged, either by the journalists or by some of the delegates whose judgment she did not trust. Ford himself had already made the blunder of saying at his first press conference in New York that he wanted to 'get the boys out of the trenches by Christmas', an intention which, considering the *Oscar II* was due to sail on December 4th, was predictably hailed as ridiculous. Thus began a series of critical front-page reports in an American press which was already increasingly pro-Ally and out of sympathy with pacifists.

On a more public level, the importance of the Ford Peace Expedition in the context of the war was that it broke through the war-censorship of an embattled Europe. Although it was despised and ridiculed, peacemaking was at last headline news for several months: 'It is probably difficult for you in America to realise how little or how absolutely nothing with any meaning in it, was put in the European Press before the arrival of the Oscar II,' Chrystal Macmillan wrote to Jane Addams on January 14th, 1916.[9]

Unfortunately, the dramatic spectacle of a Peace Ship – always meant to be of secondary importance – completely overshadowed the purpose of the voyage, which was to set up a standing conference in Stockholm, with delegates from not only America but also Sweden, Norway, Denmark, Holland and Spain, which would go on proposing peace terms between the two belligerent sides no matter how many times they were rebuffed. It was hoped that this would at least create a more suitable climate for peacemaking. In the event, the conference (the first meeting of which was on February 8th, 1916) became a focus for European peace groups, not only inspiring greater confidence but also acting as a clearing house for ideas and information. Most importantly, perhaps, it helped keep the small neutral countries out of the war, when there was great pressure on them to join.

What a surprise it must have been for British WIL members to read that Schwimmer had joined forces with Henry Ford, the car millionaire. And what must Mrs Fawcett have thought! In December, Catherine Marshall received a letter from someone called M.E. Hirst, who said she was sending out copies of *Towards Permanent Peace*, the Hague Congress report, as Christmas cards:

> Gertrude (an American friend) went to see the Ford ship sail and said the crowd was very large and sympathetic. But what a fool his secretary must be not to see that they took honest reporters with them. And I think Frau Schwimmer would have been well advised, as a belligerent, to travel on another boat! However, I was delighted to see that they had a good meeting of students in Christiana.[10]

And Madame Löfgren, a Swedish sympathiser, visited the WIL offices in London with the news that 'Rosika Schwimmer's meetings' had been a success in Sweden. True to plan, the Ford Expedition made its round of public rallies in Scandinavia. They were joined by distinguished Swedish, Norwegian and Danish peace advocates and travelled by sealed train through Germany to Holland, having first been ordered to spend an afternoon soaking and scraping labels off bottles and jars to clear any suspicion that they were carrying messages to war-ridden Germany.

The International Committee of Women for Permanent Peace decided not to back the Ford Expedition. This was surprising, since Ford had pledged $200,000 to the ICWPP headquarters. And it was ironic, too, since the idea for a continuous mediating conference, albeit an official one, had been exactly what the Hague envoys had been promoting on their crusade around Europe the previous summer. Nevertheless, when Aletta Jacobs wired Jane Addams to ask her what the relationship between the Ford Expedition and the ICWPP should be, Addams replied that it would be best for the ICWPP not to affiliate to the Expedition but for members to co-operate as individuals, if they wished. She added that this was what she was doing. After receiving this advice, the ICWPP Amsterdam office sent brusque telegrams to Schwimmer, refusing to have anything to do with Ford.

Badly shaken, hurt, and ignorant of Addams's 'advice', Schwimmer, who by this time was totally immersed in the daily frenetic activity at the Hotel Biltmore, felt she had no option but to resign as Second Vice-Chair of the ICWPP. She only eventually learnt of Addams's telegram to Jacobs when the *Oscar II* landed in Norway. She couldn't believe that Addams would send such a telegram, but the President of the ICWPP wrote that she had done so.

When the Ford Expedition meetings were a success in Holland and not silenced by the Dutch government as Jacobs had imagined they would be, she and Rosa Manus became more interested. However, by this time, Schwimmer was too resentful to come and talk things over. Chrystal Macmillan, who saw Schwimmer as a friend several times in Holland, stood by and watched all this, knowing that relations between Schimmer and Jacobs had been bad since the latter left independently for the US the previous August. Macmillan had tried to defend Schwimmer's integrity to Jacobs, and soften the words in the telegrams sent to the Hotel Biltmore, and she wrote to Addams to explain why Schwimmer was so hurt, and why she had resigned.[11]

In April 1916, a month after Schwimmer had left the Ford Conference, and three months since it had started, American political pundits were astounded when Henry Ford won the

Republican Presidential primaries in Michigan and Nebraska despite all the withering ridicule which had been heaped on him. Peacemaking was not such a political poison after all. And the Peace Expedition had become part of American folklore. Even Tin Pan Alley sang out in ragtime:

> And they'll all cheer for the
>   nation
> That had taught them arbi-
>   tration
> Mister Ford you've got the
>   right idea![12]

Only when America broke diplomatic relations with Germany in February 1917, prior to entering the war on the Allied side, did Henry Ford withdraw his financial support for the unofficial mediating conference in Stockholm.

However, before America broke diplomatic relations with Germany there was an almighty fight by American pacifists to keep their country out of the war. In early 1916, when most of the Americans on the Ford Peace Ship returned home from Holland, they still believed that their country could remain neutral. And no sooner was she on US soil, than Rebecca Shelley began organising another campaign.

This time she teamed up with another close friend, Lella Secor, from Battle Creek, Michigan. One of seven children, Secor had had an eventful childhood, having been brought up by her mother after her carpenter father abandoned the family. As a young girl aged 11, she was made responsible for the sales promotion of the family boarding house! Now 28, she worked as a journalist for various newspapers and, never one to miss a chance, she had borrowed $76 and travelled for 5 days from the West Coast when Shelley got her a reporting job aboard the Peace Ship. She even climbed aboard with a fake passport because there wasn't time to get a real one.

Secor was appalled by the behaviour of the press corps on board ship:

> The avidity with which these members of my profession
> seized upon the smallest incident which could be woven into
> a lurid story, or invented incidents if need be, shocked and
> amazed me.[13]

And she was impressed by the idea of a continuous mediating

conference. Never having given either peace or internationalism a single thought before, she became convinced of the logic behind the expedition. So much so that on one occasion, at a stormy meeting held in the ship's dining-room, she rose to defend Schwimmer.

Twenty years later, she still vividly remembered the cramped journey through Germany by sealed train:

> The blinds were drawn, but peeping beneath them we could see Germany – so black, so still – only here and there a light shining dimly in a window. Once we stopped on a siding to let a train pass – carrying men mutilated in battle. It seemed almost as though the hand of death hung over Germany – all life subdued, waiting, bending to the threat.[14]

At 4 in the morning, they got off at Bremen, stiff and tired, and were shepherded into a dimly lit waiting-room where they waited, expecting their luggage to be opened and themselves to be strip-searched. To their amazement it was announced that they could pass through Germany without being examined:

> I have never experienced a moment of such dramatic intensity. A completely soundless second while the announcement registered. Then the most stupendous cheer – all the pent up emotions . . . there were calls for the German officer – he was lifted bodily on to the table – a shy, embarrassed, gentle youth of a man. He spoke softly, haltingly. We were welcome to such hospitality as Germany could offer – he prayed God that we might bring speedy peace to Europe.[15]

When Secor returned to America, she decided to stay in New York and help Rebecca Shelley with a new campaign called the American Neutral Conference Committee. She got a job on a magazine called *Every Week* but spent all her spare time 'debating Rebecca's schemes, helping her with letters, typing out appeals, and such like'. They believed that it still wasn't too late to get President Wilson to act and that if only enough public pressure could be put on him, he would do so.

The ANCC had a list of wealthy sponsors a hundred strong: 'We early learned the technique of interesting one or two prominent people, then using their names as bait for the others,' wrote Secor later.[16]

Jane Addams was one of their supporters, as was the author

Charlotte Perkins Gilman and 70-year-old Fanny Garrison Villard, who had organised and led the Peace Parade down Fifth Avenue on August 29th, 1914. The latter was the daughter of the famous abolitionist William Lloyd Garrison. She was Chairwoman of the New York state branch of the Woman's Peace Party. One of her sons, Oswald Garrison, inherited his father's position as owner/editor of both the New York *Evening Post* and *The Nation*, two leading liberal newspapers.

It was Oswald Garrison who contacted Emily Greene Balch, one of the Hague Congress envoys, when she returned from Ford's unofficial Stockholm conference in July 1916. He wanted her to work with Shelley and Secor because she was older, more experienced, and could be a 'steadying partner'. They were, he said, both brilliant and original, but he felt he could not risk his financial support unless Balch joined them. Having come back to find a strong fight against increased military spending in full swing, Balch had already lent her active support to Lillian Wald's American Union Against Militarism and Crystal Eastman's Woman's Peace Party of New York. Now she was to get further involved in what was commonly known as the 'anti-preparedness movement'.

To give her unqualified support was a brave thing to do, because she must have known the risk to her university career. Working out of attic offices and mixing with the politically radical and sexually liberated Greenwich Village set would not endear her to the upper echelons of university hierarchy. Being chosen as a 'steadying partner' makes her seem conservative, but in the inevitable controversies about tactics between pacifists, she tended to back radicals like Crystal Eastman and Rosika Schwimmer, and she was prepared to put her livelihood on the line for what she believed to be right. Many years later, she talked about her experiences in the war:

> 'Working for such organisations meant headlong collision with prevailing public opinion in favor of formally joining the hard pressed Allies, with the press in particular, and above all with governmental policy. . . .
> 'This still seems to me to have been right. That war seemed to me to have been essentially a struggle for power between the empires of Britain and Germany. . . . I thought with abhorrence and dread of a Europe dominated by

Prussian ideas . . . trained by drill sergeants. . . . Nevertheless it seemed to me that war was not the remedy. Of course no man can say what would have been the course of history had the United States stayed out nor what sort of world would have resulted had Germany won a substantial victory.'[17]

At one of its lavish dinners at the Waldorf Astoria, paid for by 'our charming millionaires', the ANCC publicised an 'Open Letter to the President' from Bertrand Russell, who by that time was working with Catherine Marshall on behalf of the British conscientious objectors. Lella Secor remembered the letter as

> a magnificently clear and lucid plea to America to play the roll of arbitrator rather than to throw her military forces into the grim business of war. Mr Russell wrote it out in his minute script on thin sheets of paper which were concealed by a young lady who travelled to America. . . . She brought the letter to our office that morning. . . . We begged her not to show it to anyone. At a carefully arranged moment, she was to make her dramatic entrance into the dining-room and the letter was to be read.[18]

At the same time as Shelley and Secor's ANCC was gathering support throughout the country, Crystal Eastman had launched the Truth About Preparedness Campaign in November 1915, from her position as executive director of the AUAM. She wanted to expose the profit motive behind certain industrialists' clamours for increased armaments to 'clear the air of suspicion'; she also wanted the nationalisation of all the defence industries. AUAM members lobbied vigorously against a step-up in military spending. Jane Addams, testifying before the Military Affairs Committee of the House of Representatives in January 1916, said the desire to prepare for a hypothetical enemy was part of war hysteria, which came primarily from men who were more emotional than women. To which the leader writer of the *Ogden Examiner*, a newspaper in Utah, could think of no better riposte than the time-honoured platitude that Miss Addams needed 'a strong, forceful husband' – presumably to physically keep her in her place![19]

But when Wilson ignored appeals and ordered the training of 400,000 civilian soldiers, the Truth About Preparedness Campaign stepped up its activities. A fifteen-member executive grew to an organisation of 6,000 members with local branches in twenty-two cities and a press office which served over 1,500 newspapers and magazines.[20] The Woman's Peace Party of New York began to organise public debates with businessmen connected with the Navy League and other military organisations, who stood to gain financially from the war. The radical feminists didn't give a hoot about Establishment sacred cows and vigorously booed and hissed the profiteers. They also organised a hard-hitting exhibition called War Against War which drew crowds of 5,000 to 10,000 New Yorkers a day for several months. The centre piece was an enormous metal dragon representing the war machine of Wall Street. And in January 1917, the Party launched a new publication called *Four Lights*, modelled on *The Masses* (co-edited by Crystal and Max Eastman) and subtitled *An Adventure in Internationalism*. A four-pager, in its first editorial it proclaimed itself to be 'the voice of the young, uncompromising peace movement in America, whose aims are daring and immediate'.[21] Its editors, responsible for its irreverent, impulsive and witty style, were Frances Witherspoon, from the conservative Deep South, Jessie Wallace Hughan, a plain-speaking Scot, and another woman, Tracy Mygatt, about whom we know little.

That Christmas, both the German government and the American President had made announcements which gave hope to pacifists everywhere. With an eye on their internal, as well as their external, enemies, the German Chancellor, Theobald von Bethman Hollweg, and President Woodrow Wilson issued separate peace appeals, after a series of behind-the-scenes manoeuvres.

By the end of 1916, Bethmann knew that the German people, now starving as a result of the food blockade imposed by the Allies, were near to being beaten. He knew too, that the German military were itching to begin all-out submarine warfare to impose a similar blockade on France and Britain. Bethmann was frightened that if they did this, not only America but Holland and Denmark too would be provoked into the war on the Allied side. Through cautious communications between the German and American Ambassadors, the Chancellor tried to encourage Wilson to make a peace call soon, warning him that all-out submarine warfare was imminent and that he would not be able to act once his ships started going down.

Wilson, meanwhile, did not want to act – and did not act – before the American election. Once he was re-elected he drafted an Appeal For Peace, but waited so long to actually send it that Bethmann, realising that he could not hold back the German military for much longer, decided he had to issue his own Peace Note. The German Chancellor reasoned that if all out sub-warfare was declared, the US would come into the war and the German people would not have the heart to go on, unless they knew that their government had made some attempt towards peace. He also hoped that America might remain neutral, despite submarine attacks, if Germany made a peace move first and the Allies rejected it.

The German note was sent out on December 6th, the American one, finally, on December 18th. The German note was rebuffed by the Allies almost immediately because it demanded too much of the territory which Germany had taken by force. And the American note succeeded in annoying both the Allies and the Central Powers, not because Wilson suggested a peace conference with himself included, which both belligerent sides feared, but because he made great play of asking, 'What was the war about?' He was, he said, struck by the familiarity of each side's war aims. Everyone in the world was suffering, yet the concrete objects for which the war was being fought had never been definitely stated!

Even Bethmann was upset by this because Wilson asked the governments to *publish* their war aims and he had only preserved internal unity by appearing to be all things to all people on this subject. And the Allies were outraged that Wilson could not see that they were fighting to Save the World for Democracy! However, American Secretary of State, Robert Lansing, who was eager for the US to enter the war and wanted to sabotage the peace plan, soon reassured the British and French Ambassadors that the President hadn't really meant what he'd said in the note, he was just preparing the American people for war.

Despite the rebuffs, Wilson did not give up but kept open communication channels with the Central Powers and the Allies. He had a message from the American Ambassador to Austria-Hungary saying that the people there were starving and longing for peace. Wilson wired this information to Britain hoping that Lloyd George would make a separate peace with Austria-Hungary but the British Prime Minister replied that he wanted to keep Austria-Hungary in the war because it would be a drain on Germany. And when, he asked the American

President, was America going to come into the war to help make peace at the end?

On January 15th, Wilson made his famous 'Peace Without Victory' address to the Senate, which he especially wanted to communicate to the peoples – not the governments – of Europe:

> Victory would mean peace forced upon the loser, a victor's terms imposed upon the vanquished. It would be accepted in humiliation, under duress, at an intolerable sacrifice, and would leave a stirring, a resentment, a bitter memory upon which terms of peace would rest, not permanently, but only as upon quicksand. Only a peace between equals can last.[22]

But it was too late for America to mediate. Submarines had already left the German ports and were off the west coast of Ireland. On January 31st, the German government wired to Wilson that all ships would be destroyed without warning around Great Britain, France and Italy from February 1st, after a period of grace for neutral ships to get out of the war zones. The American Union Against Militarism immediately telegraphed Wilson that the United States should 'refuse to allow itself to be dragooned into war at the very end by acts of desperation committed by any of the belligerents'[23] and printed the wording in an advertisement in the *New York Times* with the signatures of Lillian Wald, Emily Greene Balch, Crystal Eastman, Oswald Villard and several others. But on February 3rd, America broke off diplomatic relations with Germany and the German Ambassador was sent home.

This was not war yet but it looked perilously close. Rebecca Shelley, Lella Secor and Emily Greene Balch hastily called their American Neutral Conference Committee executive committee together. Most of the members promptly resigned. 'We were now without funds or financial backing and I had given up my job with *Every Week* to devote my full time to the anti-war movement. Courage was about the only thing we had left, and so with that we bought a page in the *New York Times*,' remembered Secor.[24]

Out of their tiny office on the ninth floor of a building in Fifth Avenue, they wrote an advertisement for the newspaper. 'WIVES, MOTHERS, SWEETHEARTS' it began, in enormous type across the top of the page, and went on to appeal for money and help. The next day, postmen arrived with sackfuls of letters and hundreds of people, who had come to give money in person, blocked the corridors and lifts. 'The people were largely poor women from the East side who knew what war meant,' recalled Balch later.

> They all came with dollar bills in their hands. There were so many and we were so crowded . . . that the dollar bills were temporarily held in waste-baskets. . . . In an unlucky moment, one was carried into the hall. . . . It was quickly salvaged but it made a good story at our expense.[25]

At dawn, the three women finished counting the $35,000 they had collected and the Emergency Peace Federation 'to defend American ideals of liberty and democracy in wartime and to work for an enduring peace' was born. Together with the Woman's Peace Party, the Socialist Party, the Socialist Labour Party and the Church Peace Union, the EPF held a mass rally on February 5th. William Jennings Bryan, formerly Secretary of State, made an emotional appeal for a referendum, as the American people were not willing 'to send American soldiers . . . to die on European soil in settlement of European quarrels. . . .'[26] Other speakers called for a general strike and Lillian Wald sent a report to Wilson – supported by some liberal newspapers – recommending the formation of an armed league of neutral nations to protect all legitimate neutral commerce.

During February and March 1917, the women pacifists worked around the clock to keep America neutral. There was a real fight to keep the United States out of the war. Historians differ as to the state of mind of the American people at that time, as the women pacifists appear to have done. Lella Secor recalled that the EPF grew to amazing proportions within a few days of the German Ambassador being sent home:

> We extended our work right across the continent. Thousands of individuals joined, and hundreds of organisations with large memberships affiliated. Branches sprang up all over the country. There can be no doubt that at that time the American people were opposed to war.[27]

But Jane Addams, who helped form the Emergency Peace Federation, watched as people changed:

> The long established peace societies . . . quickly fell into line

expounding the doctrine that the world's greatest war was to make an end to all wars. It was hard . . . to understand upon what experiences this pathetic belief in the regenerative results of war could be founded. But the world had become filled with fine phrases, and this one, which afforded comfort to many a young soldier, was taken up and endlessly repeated with an entire absence of the critical spirit.[28]

Wilson was probably not surprised when his political opponent, ex-President Theodore Roosevelt, raged on about his 'lack of manhood', but he thought American clergymen were going crazy when they began to preach war sermons from their pulpits. Soon businessmen (including Henry Ford) began to offer the President not only money but their factories for prospective munition making and university academics seemed to embrace the prospect of war unanimously. On February 23rd, Carrie Chapman Catt, President of the National American Women's Suffrage Association, called an executive meeting to decide the organisation's policy, should war come. It was a long and difficult meeting but the final outcome was that suffragists should offer their services to the government, although their first objective would be to continue to fight for female suffrage. The decision was hailed in newspapers across the country and as a result the Woman's Peace Party of New York dropped Catt's membership in disgust.[29]

Crystal Eastman, meanwhile, had been working sixteen to twenty hours a day to try and stem the rising military tide, despite the fact that she had just had her first baby. Her special concern was that the demand for conscription and compulsory military training be dropped: 'We must make this great democracy know . . . that military training is bad for the bodies and minds and souls of boys,' she argued, '. . . that free minds and souls undrilled to obedience are vital to the life of democracy.'[30]

She wrote that the radical peace movement had three aims: to stop the war in Europe, to organise the world for peace at the end of the war, and to defend American democracy against the subtle but pernicious dangers of militarism.

Two events seem to have tipped Wilson into war. Firstly, by March 3rd, German subs had torpedoed three American ships. But perhaps more important was the Zimmerman telegram. This was a telegram intercepted by British intelligence, proposing a Mexican-German alliance. Whilst the American leadership had been negotiating with German rulers for peace and reconstruction, so Wilson thought, those same rulers had been conniving to entice bankrupt and war-ravaged Mexico into attacking the United States. If they could do that, they would stop at nothing. He was shocked and angry.

By March 20th, the entire American Cabinet was for declaring war on Germany, and Wilson, persuaded at last, called Congress to special session on April 2nd. The peace movement rallied one last final effort and most of the burden seems to have fallen on the Emergency Peace Federation organisers. Having already arranged a delegation to Wilson in February with Addams, Balch and two socialist men, they now deluged the President with letters, petitions, proposals and requests for interviews. They drew up a new peace plan with several alternatives to going to war – they suggested submission of German-American disputes to a joint high commission or a conference of neutrals – and publicised it in other full-page ads in the *New York Times* and other newspapers, this time declaring 'WAR IS NOT NECESSARY'.

As a climax to a round of public meetings hurriedly organised in many different cities (the ECF sent 'Twelve Apostles of Peace' out of New York to do this), over 1,000 EPF demonstrators descended on Capitol Hill to gather in the stone corridors of the Senate and House office buildings, pleading with senators and congressmen when they arrived on April 2nd. At 8.30 p.m., Wilson arrived to deliver his speech – to ask Congress for a declaration of war. America could not be humiliated by submitting to defenceless attack, he said, and merchantmen could not adequately defend themselves without declaring war.

On April 4th, after much debate, the vote in the Senate on the war resolution went 82 to 6. The final step was the vote in the House of Representatives. Ironically for the women pacifists, Jeanette Rankin from Montana, the first woman to be elected to the House, took her seat for the first time on the night Wilson advocated war. Carrie Chapman Catt had given her breakfast at Washington's Suffrage House and rode with her at the head of a trail of decorated cars to Capitol Hill. Not only that, but the women's suffrage amendment was to have been the first item of business until the war speech took precedence. When Rankin introduced it later, she was loudly applauded by her new colleague.

When the vote on war was finally announced at 3 o'clock in the morning of April 6th, Frances Witherspoon, with Emily Greene Balch and about twenty other pacifists, pressed against the wall in the gallery so they would not be seen, heard Rankin say, 'I love my country but I cannot vote for war.' She was one of the fifty opposers, against 373.[31]

> 'Once lead this people into war and they'll forget there ever was such a thing as tolerance. To fight you must be brutal and ruthless, and the spirit of ruthless brutality will enter into the very fibre of our national life, infecting Congress, the courts, the policeman on the beat, the man in the street.'[32]

So said President Wilson to a newspaper editor in the early hours after he had made his speech. He seemed to know that now there would be no lasting 'Peace Without Victory', either within or without the American federated state.

During the war, Jane Addams, who was by this time vilified by the press as a symbol of everything un-American – even the National Federation of Settlements opposed her – redeemed herself somewhat by working for Herbert Hoover's Food Administration. She toured the country appealing to women to conserve and grow more food. Lillian Wald chaired the Council of National Defence's Committee on Public Health and Child Welfare and both of them offered their settlement buildings for the registration of men for the army. After the war Addams wrote,

> In they came somewhat heavily, one man after another, most of them South Italians. I knew many of them had come to this country seeking freedom from military service quite as much as they sought freedom of other sorts . . . the traditional belief in America as a refuge had come to an end and there was no spot on the surface of the earth to which they might flee for security.[33]

When she goes on to describe how one man told her it would be her fault if he died in the trenches because she had got his name on the official records by encouraging him to come and learn English, it is hard to understand how she could have done it. *Four Lights* devoted a whole issue to women like Jane Addams and Lillian Wald who they thought had compromised their principles. In *The Sister Susie Number*, Witherspoon and the others criticised 'Hoover Helpers' for accepting their position 'beside the garbage cans as they have always accepted what God and man has put upon them to endure'.[34] Some branches of the National Woman's Peace Party, declared the magazine, spent the entire war feebly knitting socks!

In fact, the WPP opposed the Espionage Bill, the Conscription Bill and the military training of schoolchildren in 1917, and Jane Addams was under surveillance by the Department of Justice but this paled beside *Four Lights*'s open welcome of both the first and the second Russian Revolutions, which it heralded with 'MAD, GLAD JOY!'[35] Mygatt, Hughan and Eastman did the socially unacceptable job of helping conscientious objectors. And Shelley, Secor and Balch formed The People's Council of America, inspired by the revolutionary events the other side of the world, and were threatened with lynching in Minneapolis and by the troops in Chicago. The American people forgot 'there was such a thing as tolerance' pretty quickly – and it was not only pacifists who were persecuted; in East St Louis, dozens of black people were sadistically mutilated and murdered soon after the declaration of war against Germany.

CHAPTER 9

Hail the Revolution

Our mother is perishing. Our mother is Russia. I want to help save her. I want women whose hearts are loyal, whose souls are pure, whose aims are high. With such women setting an example of self-sacrifice, you men will realise your duty in this grave hour![1]

So rang out the voice of Maria Botchkareva to a vast audience at the Mariynksi Theatre in Petrograd (now Leningrad) in the summer of 1917. Wild cheering and thunderous applause broke out. Botchkareva was a fierce patriot, an agricultural worker from Irkutsk, way over in the east of Russia. Alarmed by the defections of Russian soldiers from the eastern front, she had decided to form a Russian women's fighting unit, under the title of the 'Battalion of Death'. Her idea was to get at least 300 women to the front where they would fearlessly lead a division 'over the top'. This, she thought, would serve as an example to the entire army and shame them into fighting. The Mariynksi Theatre speech launched her recruiting drive and 2,000 women volunteered as a result.

Six months earlier, the winter of 1916-17 had been a particularly cold and harsh one for the Russians. Ever since the war began, Russia's huge army had been incompetently led and poorly equipped. The seemingly inexhaustible supply of fighting stock drawn from its 165 million population did not compensate for the lack of artillery, shells, bullets and rifles, for the slow replacement of supplies held up on ancient railways and rough and often impassable roads, or for the painfully primitive medical treatment. By March 1917, with starvation in the cities and the continuing heavy death toll (over two million men), riots and strikes broke out in Petrograd. Tsar Nicholas abdicated and a new democratic Provisional Government was formed under Aleksandr Kerenski, with a commitment to immediate amnesty for all political prisoners, the freedom to form trade unions, the establishment of a free press and the introduction of universal male suffrage.

Dr Schishkin-Javein, President of the All-Russian League of Women's Enfranchisement, wrote to Mary Sheepshanks with details of how Russian women had successfully won inclusion in the new franchise.[2] In a demonstration outside the Winter Palace on 19th March, 40,000 women declared that they would stand there in the cold and wet until their demands were met: 'Women also have filled the prisons, and boldly marched to the gallows. . . . We have come to tell you that the Russian woman demands for herself the human rights to which she is entitled as a human being,' went their statement.

All parties in the new government, except the Bolsheviks, thought Russia should stay in the war but wanted a negotiated peace 'with no annexations or indemnities'. However, by the summer of 1917, it was clear from the increasing desertions at the eastern front that the will of the Russian people to stay in the war on *any* basis was fading fast. It was in this context that Botchkareva had persuaded Kerenski to let her form a women's battalion.

Russian soldiers were not the only ones who were throwing away their guns. In 1917, French troops on the western front mutinied for about six weeks from the end of March to June. They were tired of being slaughtered in thousands for the gain of only a few yards. If the Battles of Verdun and the Somme had not been enough, the onslaught on the valley of the River Aisne, led by their new commander-in-chief General Nivelle, who claimed 'to have the formula!', was a disaster. Two hundred thousand men were killed as they clambered uphill, through uncut barbed wire. Soldiers on leave began to riot at railway stations and refuse to return to the trenches. Inspired by the Russians, some threatened to march on Paris and overturn the government. If the Germans had known about this they could have marched on Paris themselves and won the war.

With the western front weakened, it was important for the Allies that Russia should stay in the war. Lloyd George and Emmeline Pankhurst, who was by now his confidante, decided that she should visit Russia to rouse the people. On its June cover, the WSPU magazine *Britannia* featured the sober-faced Pankhurst and Jessie Kenney[3] ready to embark on their three-month journey. They were to sail from Aberdeen to Norway whence they would travel by train to Petrograd. To her delight, Pankhurst saw Labour's Ramsay MacDonald turned off the boat by the Seamen's Union. He had wanted to travel to Stockholm for an International Socialist Conference inspired by the Russian Revolution but the Union thought this unpatriotic. Pankhurst had always disliked MacDonald for his stand against women's suffrage. Now she detested him because he had resigned from the government in protest over the war.

But her own mission was eventually thwarted too. Although people in Petrograd knew all about the suffragette campaign (she discovered that her autobiography was being studied at a girls' high school) and journalists flocked to see her, she was forbidden to hold public meetings because this might cause trouble. And when she and Kenney had an interview with Kerenski, he seemed to resent their presence.

Meeting Maria Botchkareva raised her spirits. She was most impressed and publicly called her the greatest woman of the century, comparing her to her own idol, Joan of Arc. In St Isaac's Square, Pankhurst and Botchkareva watched the 'Battalion of Death' at drill and saluted the women soldiers as they marched past with their rifles on their shoulders. It made a strange scene: Mrs Emmeline Pankhurst, now 58, the internationally known celebrity of women's suffrage, sent by the British Prime Minister, elegantly dressed as usual in hat and long-skirted costume, next to Commander Maria Botchkareva, an agricultural worker from the Russian interior, in heavy boots and soldier's uniform.

Despite their national and class differences, Pankhurst and Botchkareva held many attitudes in common. Both were intensely patriotic; they wanted their respective countries to 'win' no matter what the cost. They both thought that committees or any sort of consultative system of organising was both time-wasting and inefficient. Some British suffragists repudiated what they saw as the Pankhursts' autocracy, but it is true that the Pankhursts never set out to create a mass organisation but more to inspire a mass movement. And they wanted, above all, to get results: 'Deeds Not Words' was their motto. For her part, Botchkareva wanted her Russian female fighting unit to be a tightly knit, moral trouble-shooting force amongst the male army ranks and was extremely frustrated when the women wanted to elect a committee to decide policy (a popular idea put into their heads by a Bolshevik agitator): 'Suppose we had a committee and the moment for the offensive arrived. Then the committee suddenly decides not to advance and our whole scheme is brought to nothing,' she argued.[4]

Emmeline Pankhurst had used almost exactly the same scenario – only in her case, of course, it was allegorical – to justify the way she and Christabel ran the WSPU. But this time, with real lives at stake, back came the rebellious answer: 'Certainly. . . . We should want to decide for ourselves whether to attack or not!'[5]

By the summer of 1917, there was an increasing number of street fights between supporters of Kerenski and the Bolsheviks. Watching the women's battalion depart from the railway station, Jessie Kenney was badly hurt in one such skirmish. Nikolai Lenin, Leon Trotsky and other Bolshevik leaders were now free men and Kerenski's days were numbered. Lenin had returned from exile in Switzerland. He had been helped by the Germans, who transported him through the country in a secret 'sealed' train, because they knew his party wanted to take the Russian people out of the war. Trotsky and others had been released from prison, under orders from Kerenski himself. They began encouraging industrial workers to strike, peasants to overthrow their landlords and seize land for themselves and the Russian troops to leave the hideous trenches and come home. Starving and tired of the killing, the Russian women and men needed little persuasion.

By the time Pankhurst and Kenney left Russia in September, they could foresee the October Revolution. Together with Grace Roe, Flora Drummond and Christabel Pankhurst, who had returned from Paris, they spent the last year of the war touring the industrial centres of Britain denouncing 'Strikers, COs, pacifists and Bolsheviks', often amidst the clatter of plates in factory canteens. They demanded the internment of all enemy aliens, military conscription for all men and industrial conscription for all women. A 'knock-out blow' was needed, they said, to obtain victory – and peace. In June 1918, Emmeline Pankhurst went to America with Maria Botchkareva, to urge that the Allies send Japan to militarily intervene in Bolshevist Russia.

All through the war, the stance of Emmeline and Christabel

Pankhurst and what was left of the WSPU members had been at one with the most extreme of jingoist sentiments. Between them they had, by the summer of 1917, made three visits to America and Canada to whip up pro-Allied sentiments. While Christabel Pankhurst was in Paris, writing critical editorials for *Britannia*, on the ineffectiveness of Asquith and Grey as war administrators, her mother was holding regular 'patriotic' meetings in Hyde Park, Trafalgar Square and the Albert Hall.

In the summer of 1915, the WSPU organised a huge women's demonstration at the request of Lloyd George, then Minister of Munitions. He wanted to overcome the munitions shortage by recruiting more women into shell production, but he faced opposition from the male-dominated trade unions, and even from his colleagues in the Cabinet. The procession, which was an elaborate two-mile-long affair marching on a circular route through central London, was for the benefit of these men. The occasion received a blaze of publicity. Ninety bands played the 'Marseillaise'. There were contingents of nurses and other war workers; 400 women in white dresses carried crooks with red roses, and a 'Pageant of the Allies' was led by a woman in a long dress carrying a tattered flag, who represented Belgium. Seven hundred banner bearers carried messages including 'SHELLS MADE BY A WIFE MAY SAVE A HUSBAND'S LIFE'; 'FOR MEN MUST FIGHT AND WOMEN MUST WORK' and 'DOWN WITH SEX PREJUDICE'.[6]

A similar demonstration in 1916 demanded 'HUGHES ON THE WAR COUNCIL'. Billy Hughes was the Labour Prime Minister of Australia and the hero of all bellicose nationalists. By this time, the WSPU had begun a £10,000 Victory Fund to campaign against a 'compromise peace'. In September, Annie Kenney visited Melbourne in Australia, bearing a memorial from 'the women of England', which pleaded for the return of Mr Hughes. 'Do you realise that the women of Great Britain will be the laughing stock of Australia?' wrote one Margaret Lane from Brisbane to the *Labour Leader*. 'All the funny cuts are at work already. Even Hughes cronies have to laugh albeit a trifle ruefully at what is felt to be an exhibition of national insanity.' And the Australian *Worker* reported that mass meetings of women and men had unanimously passed resolutions bidding Kenney 'good riddance'.[7]

Both the WSPU marches ended with speeches by Lloyd George to the assembled masses. In 1915, there was a crowd of

60,000 on the Victoria Embankment, despite wind and pouring rain. The following year, Sylvia Pankhurst remembered with irony that at the end of the march, the 'mutinettes', as they were called, saluted the politician with 'livid yellow hands'. Handling high explosive powder turned the skin a deep yellow.

Lloyd George got his female munition workers. His tactics had been astute. For weeks, the WSPU 'HQ' in Kingsway was deluged with mail from women wanting to do war work. By the end of the war, 900,000 women had been involved in the production of shells, guns and aircraft for the British fighting forces. Munitions absorbed the biggest proportion of women war workers. Another 792,000 went into industry, taking on heavy and dangerous work. Only stevedoring, underground mining and iron and steel smelting remained all-male bastions. Twenty-three thousand voluntary nurses (VADs) and 15,000 orderlies were recruited and smaller numbers went into police work, or to work on the railways and buses. Further thousands took over clerical jobs. By 1919, 230,000 had gone into the Land Army. The Women's Army Auxiliary Corps was formed in 1917 and employed 60,000, 10,000 of whom went to France. The WRNS and WRAF came a few months later. Five hundred WRAF women went to Germany in 1919 as part of the occupying forces. Altogether, at the end of the war, there was a British civilian war work labour force of about three million to demobilize, compared with five million soldiers.[8]

Much has been made of the emancipating effect this war work had on women, not only in Britain but all over Europe. But in Britain at least, even before the war, there was an ever-increasing number of clerical jobs open to the middle classes and working-class women had always done monotonous, tiring, and sometimes dangerous and heavy work. Sorting refuse was considered a good job for a working-class woman before the war; being outdoors was better for your health and it paid a reliable wage. However, the war was certainly the first time that many upper- and middle-class women had had an income of their own; out of a total female population of fifteen million before the war, only about four million did paid work.[9] And for poor women, the pay was better in munitions than it had been in domestic service or the sweated female trades, in which they had previously been employed.

That is not to say that conditions in war work were not harsh. In munitions, the working day was split into two twelve-hour shifts (ignoring the pre-war Factory Acts, which limited hours to ten and a half per day) in order to facilitate round-the-clock production. There was often an hour or more's walk to the factory. Accommodation was inadequate because of the sudden relocation of workers. In some boarding-houses, beds were never aired, as they were used alternately by different shift workers.

All protective legislation was ignored, and by 1918, 300 munitions women had been killed, either as a result of explosions or from TNT poisoning. The latter was absorbed through the skin and could render a woman sterile. Protective gloves and respirators were provided in high-risk jobs, but the first inhibited the necessary dexterity, and the second rubbed the mouth raw. They were little worn.

There was a constant fight by women socialists like Sylvia Pankhurst, Mary MacArthur and Margaret Bondfield to get equal pay for women in the jobs which they had taken over from men (known as 'dilution'). But by 1918, the flat rate for female workers in the National Shell Factories was half the male rate. Re-organisation of industry, with many jobs being sub-divided or new ones being created, meant it was difficult to make equal pay claims. Margaret Bondfield led a recruitment drive to get women into unions and numbers increased to nearly two million from 360,000[10] – but male trade unionists still jealously guarded their employment empires and often actively obstructed the recruitment of women, regarding them with amused contempt when they were taken on.

Male agricultural workers were a good example of this, when the 'breeched, booted and cropped land-girl' shocked socially fossilised, rural Britain: 'Many of us were Cockneys who didn't know wheat from barley – and we were all sorts – housemaids, schoolmistresses, singers, painters, writers, women of leisure, factory packers, sick-nurses and shop assistants,' wrote a member of the Women's Defence Relief Corps in *The Lady* in March 1916.[11] In what seemed like perpetual rain they mastered the back-breaking tasks of flax pulling, hoeing and, worst of all, the smelly job of bean gleaning: 'nothing, nothing in this world could be more monotonous than hoeing; but then I knew nothing of bean-gleaning' (gleaning is going up and down the lines picking up loose beans and breaking off any that the binder had not cut).[12]

Land-girls were given a month's free training, travel expenses and working clothes. They slept on the floor of a spare barn; or in the farmhouse attic. In the evening, these places would be full of women talking, writing, smoking, and singing the latest musical-comedy hits. Of all the war work women did, perhaps this was the most pleasant. It was certainly better than the life of the VADs in field hospitals, who saw at first hand the awful, brutal reality of the war: young men with mask-like faces blinded and burnt by gas attacks; pus and blood and stinking bandages; amputated limbs stuck in buckets.

Life could never be the same for women after such experiences. Old traditions were questioned: there was a looser sexual morality and a breaking down of class barriers. Many of the genteel niceties which bound women seemed irrelevant; women bought themselves pretty clothes which they could often afford only for the first time; they rolled their own cigarettes and went to see Charlie Chaplin at the 'picture palace'. Hand in hand with this liberation-at-a-price came criticism. Fur coats became known as 'munitions overalls'; there were accusations of promiscuity and drunkeness; illegitimacy was said to have increased enormously. There was surveillance of soldiers' wives who had separation allowances, to make sure they were behaving themselves, and laws which allowed police to arrest and intimately examine any woman suspected of being a prostitute were re-introduced. All this contrasted with the tone of astonishment, often mixed with sickly sentimentality, used by Fleet Street at the beginning of the war when describing women war workers: 'Isn't she wonderful? Didn't know she had it in her!' the hacks had gushed.

What the war did was to make female abilities public. For the first time it entered the national consciousness that women were perfectly capable workers. They were *seen to be* doing skilled and/or heavy work, and it was this which changed their own self-image and the attitude of men towards them. However, the acquisition of this liberating self-confidence did not mean that the world run by men would change to accommodate them after the war. The *Daily Graphic* was soon to write,

The idea that because the State called for women to help the nation, the State must continue to employ them is too absurd for serious women to entertain. As a matter of grace, notice

183

should be at least a fortnight and if possible a month. As for young women formerly in domestic service, they at least should have no difficulty in finding vacancies.[13]

But back to 1917 and the events in Russia, which brought hope to the women and men all over the world who wanted to see peace and freedom and justice. 'Wasn't yesterday wonderful?' Catherine Marshall wrote to Bertrand Russell in March, upon hearing of the abdication of the Russian Tsar.

I felt simply intoxicated with a sense of freedom and joy and *frustration* – the frustration of the heroism and sacrifice and suffering that has been preparing for this miracle in Russia – the joy it was to tell the prisoners about it. The warden let me talk without interruption and I told them . . . *everything* and saw them go back to their cells radiant and with renewed *vitality*.[14]

All the leading lights in WIL and the Women's Peace Crusade greeted the March revolution with joy. It was the 'first real gleam of hope that we received' remembered Helen Crawfurd. The cold harsh winter had affected much of Europe, as well as Russia, and Britain had not escaped. Hardship was not as bad as that in Russia, Germany and Austria-Hungary, but food and fuel were growing scarcer. The rich had special deliveries (soon butcher boys were held up and looted) while poor women stood in queues, shifting their double burdens of babies and baskets, for a little meat, margarine or coal, which was collected in prams.[15] Hopes of a negotiated peace raised by the German and American Notes of December 1916 had been dashed. But here at last was proof that the world could be changed, if people would only revolt! 'It is hardly necessary to dilate upon the League's joy at the news of the Russian Revolution. . . ,' began the section entitled 'Russia' in the 1916-17 WIL Report. 'Women suffragists all over the world will welcome the liberation of the hundreds of millions of inhabitants of that vast empire. . . ,' Mary Sheepshanks wrote in *Jus* on 1st April, 1917.[16]

In the same month, nurses and wounded soldiers outside Poplar Hospital in the East End of London cheered the 1,000 or so crowd, organised by the ELFS and escorted by mounted police, who marched to Victoria Park in Hackney, with the words 'SPRING AND PEACE MUST COME TOGETHER' on their first banner. A crowd of 50,000 awaited them in the park but unfortunately the platform had been hijacked by about 500 opponents. Sylvia Pankhurst and Charlotte Despard spoke to the people standing at the base of the railings: 'We don't want the German terms: we want out terms!' yelled some men to Despard.

'You will have neither the German terms nor your own terms; you will have God's terms!' she retorted and then, after a few minutes silence, someone shouted, 'You'd better get out of this before you get hurt.'

'I'm not afraid of Englishmen,' she said. 'None of you will hurt me.'[17]

Catherine Marshall took on yet more work by helping to form a Committee for Anglo-Russian Co-operation which organised the first mass public welcome of the revolution with a meeting in the 12,000-seat Albert Hall on March 31st, from which at least 5,000 were turned away. And then there was the Leeds Convention on June 3rd, called by ILP and trade union activists to celebrate what had happened in Russia. Out of about 800 delegates, fifty-four were from women's organisations:[18] Ethel Snowden, Mary Macarthur, Emmeline Pethick-Lawrence, Sylvia Pankhurst and Charlotte Despard were there. For many it was a time of great optimism and euphoria, but not for Helena Swanwick:

> I find some people extraordinarily hopeful but I'm not. The Russians are likely to have a long time of muddle and disorder and though I think they have done wonders and all my sympathy goes out to them I don't believe they are going to be formidable as enemies or helpful as friends. A separate peace seems a strong likelihood and then – God knows how long a war till America comes to full strength.

and later she wrote,

> I think no real *building* can come out of revolutions which make a dust and a mess and bitterness and reaction. They put a premium on violence and spoil *thinking* and all these industrial questions need very hard thinking.[19]

Mary Sheepshanks had her doubts too. Anything, she thought, could happen in Russia. The abdication of the Russian Tsar did not seem to have dampened the desire for a 'knock-out blow' in Aberdeen, where the Pethick-Lawrences fought a by-election.

They stood on the issue of peace by negotiation, and were pelted with coal and pushed from platforms for their pains, collecting only a few votes. WIL supported Peace by Negotiations candidates at two by-elections. A Mr Taylor did better at Rossendale, with nearly 2,000.

Public attitudes seemed to have changed little in the Colne Valley. 'There was no evidence of the new spirit, of which I had heard so much at my meetings,' recalled Florence Lockwood, who had by now joined both WIL and the UDC.

> None of the revolt of the modern mind against war; no sign that we were not all bowing down to the fetish of war. So I thought I would awake the village to realise the movement and, at the close of a particularly jingo song I hissed instead of clapping. No-one understood why! The curate looked around in amazement. The concert party was perturbed . . . and Josiah gave me a good wigging on the way home in the cab.[20]

Predictably, WIL opposed the Pankhurst Russian visit: Swanwick wrote to Marshall,

> You know Pankie has been given a passport to Russia. We have on foot a scheme to ask for passports for three or four of our section: Mrs Snowden, Mrs Lawrence, Miss Bondfield, and perhaps Mrs Despard. . . . I don't for a moment expect that we shall get passports but we felt that we must ask for them and make a fuss and a manifesto if we don't. . . .
>
> It is nauseating to read Mrs Pankhurst. I heard today that Christabel is always going to Walton Heath [Lloyd George's country house] and behaves there as if she were at home. She drives down from town in her motor. . . . I happened to allude to him [Lloyd George] in speaking to Mrs Fawcett as 'that little blackguard' & she said 'Oh you mustn't call him that. He's going to give us the vote.' She was only half serious, but it is the cynical view in politics.[21]

WIL did not get its passports. It was not very likely that the British government, alarmed by French mutinees, would allow women who wanted to stop the war into Russia. Recording the refusal of passports in the 1917-18 WIL Annual Report, it was stated somewhat snootily, 'It is not yet known why exception was made in the case of Mrs Pankhurst but it can be guessed.'

She represented the British War Cabinet and not British women, they said, and had run the WSPU autocratically when the freedom of women was 'bound up with the defeat of militarism and the attainment of democracy'.

Making do with 'An Open Letter to Russian Women', to be carried by four visiting Russian men, Despard wrote, 'My sisters, I cannot use the ordinary commonplaces. To say that I congratulate you would be out of place. Rather – I am with you – we are one.'[22]

On July 8th, the Women's Peace Crusade in Glasgow organised a demonstration of 12,000. Two separate marches with banners and music converged on Glasgow Green and unanimously passed the following resolution: 'This mass meeting of Glasgow citizens, summoned by the Women's Peace Crusade, sends to the Russian Revolutionary Government warm sympathy and congratulations.' Clydeside was as radical as ever. Since the previous summer, Crawfurd and friends had been active in the city, organising public and street corner meetings, plays, children's demonstrations with banners like 'I WANT MY DADDY' and heckling Emmeline Pankhurst. Their Women's Peace Crusade badges sold well: the design was blue and white with an Angel of Peace protecting children.[23]

By July 28th, Patrick Dollan was writing in the *Daily Herald*,

Reports coming in from comrades who have been spending their holidays in doing propaganda all over Scotland reveal in a striking manner the change that is coming over public opinion. . . .

Peace crusaders in Glasgow . . . are most gratified to see how the work is being taken up in other places. From their experience they know that what the people are waiting for is a strong lead, and surely it is women's solemn duty to give that lead – now and without delay.[24]

Throughout the summer, Women's Peace Crusade demonstrations were held in the northern towns of Manchester, Bradford, Leeds and Nelson, and in the Midlands, in Birmingham, where 12,000 people gave their support.[25] The Nelson organising group formed itself three days after the Glasgow demonstration. On August 11th, the day of their march, they were so unpopular that no band would agree to play for them. Holding banners: 'WE DEMAND A PEOPLE'S PEACE' and 'LONG LIVE THE INTERNATIONAL', with the local ILP Girls' Guild, dressed in white with green shoulder sashes with the word PEACE written on them, and each carrying a wreath of leaves, the brave women walked amidst jeering onlookers until they reached the local recreation ground. There, to their horror, was a hostile crowd, 15,000 strong. Clumps of earth were thrown at the speakers and violent renderings of 'Britons never, never, never shall be slaves' drowned out any hope of peace propaganda. 'You are all slaves!' one of the women cried back from the platform.

Selina Cooper was one of those leading the procession. She was an active working-class suffragist, well known in the local Co-operative Guild and cotton weavers' trade union. Much of her time during the war was spent setting up maternity and child care centres. Despite having always been a keen internationalist, she retained her membership of the NUWSS of which she was a paid employee. No doubt being far away from the leadership debates in London allowed for greater psychological and physical freedom and she did not feel compelled to resign. Loyalty to the Union bit deep and it seemed folly to resign after half a century of struggle, when women's suffrage was at last in sight.[26] She was shaken by the hostility to the women's peace demonstration on August 11th. It was much worse than anything she had experienced in suffrage campaigns (soon her house was to be searched). But Cooper and other local feminists worked on with their peace propaganda, keeping in touch with the network of Women's Peace Crusade groups around the country which was gradually building up.

All the radical suffragists who had been associated with the Lancashire cotton industry, one of the few adequately paid and unionised industries for women before the war, and who were in the vanguard of the suffrage movement amongst working-class women, wanted an early, negotiated peace. One of them, Ada Nïeld Chew, scornfully dismissed many of her former suffrage sisters in the *Cotton Factory Times*:

> The militant section of the movement . . . would without doubt place itself in the trenches quite cheerfully, if allowed. It is now . . . demanding, with all its usual pomp and circumstance of banner and procession, its share in the war. This is an entirely logical attitude and strictly in line with its attitude before the war. It always glorified the power of the primitive knock on the nose in preference to the more

humane appeal to reason. . . . What of the others? . . . The non-militants – so-called – though bitterly repudiating militancy for women, are as ardent in their support of militancy for men as their more consistent and logical militant sisters.[27]

Ellen Wilkinson, many years later to become famous for leading the Jarrow March of hungry unemployed shipbuilders as MP for that town, was 23 at the outbreak of the 1914-18 war. Her father was an insurance agent, the family neither rich nor poor. Teaching (which she hated) had seemed to be the only occupation open to a young woman like her but then she became the NUWSS organiser for Manchester and was able to revel in noisy open-air meetings, when crowds of men in caps called her 'Carrots' and told her to 'go home and darn the stockings'. With her sister Annie, she soon became active in Manchester WIL. The group found it difficult to gain permission to use public halls, and except for the *Manchester Guardian* had a rough ride in the local press.

Esther Roper and Eva Gore-Booth, past mentors of Christabel Pankhurst, joined the Women's Peace Crusade and travelled the country on speaking tours. They also did relief work amongst German prisoners of war and worked for Catherine Marshall at the NCF, attending tribunals and recording what happened to individual conscientious objectors, or 'conchies' as they were known by then. These two women had a long history of organising working-class women, believing passionately in their right to earn their own living. Barmaids, hotel attendants, female gymnasts, circus performers and flower girls, whose jobs had all been threatened under the pretence of a 'moral spring-clean', were helped by Gore-Booth and Roper.

Meanwhile, in London, the East London Federation of Suffragettes, which had changed its name to the Workers Suffrage Federation was organising a 'Big Push Campaign' with regular pickets outside the House of Commons. 'NEGOTIATE FOR PEACE ON THE RUSSIAN TERMS: NO ANNEXATIONS: NO INDEMNITIES' said their banner. Sylvia Pankhurst remembered one exchange with a passing clergyman: 'You ought to be ashamed of yourself,' he said. To which came the reply, 'I think the boot is on the other foot. I read in my Bible "Thou shalt not kill!" What do you read there?'

In the September 21st copy of the *Daily Herald*, Sylvia Pankhurst reported that they needed new banners to replace those that had been 'captured by the enemy or destroyed by the rain'. They were also picketing outside the Labour conference. 'The principal reproach now hurled at the picketers is that they are mostly working women. Perhaps they will soon be told that some of them are related to soldiers!' she added sardonically.[28]

The previous month, the Executive Committee of the Irish Women's Franchise League passed a resolution supporting the Pope's plea to end the war and to say that they 'desired to associate themselves with the good work being done by the Irishwomen's International League for Permanent Peace and also the courageous activities of the Women's Peace Crusade of Great Britain.'[29]

There were many women and men in Ireland who asked why they should fight for the rights of small countries like Belgium and Serbia, when Britain was not willing to give them their own independence. That June, Constance Markievicz, Eva Gore-Booth's sister, had returned home to Dublin to a heroine's welcome, after being imprisoned in Aylesbury Prison for her part in the Easter 1916 Irish uprising. Most of the men had been shot but she had escaped execution because of her sex.

News of all this women's peace campaigning was given at a conference organised by WIL headquarters on October 15th in Central Hall, Westminster. Delegates made the long journey to London to tell their stories. There were rumours that 'a band of stalwarts, 100 strong' had been organised to break up the meeting but there were no interruptions. Margaret Haley, the Birmingham delegate, revealed that she was also preparing a local campaign in Newcastle. And the Crusade had reached the South-West; a Miss Tothill described the work she was doing in Bristol. Altogether thirty-three groups had sprung up around the country.

Resolutions don't make exciting reading but it is worth quoting one from the conference at length, because it gives an idea of WIL and WPC's thinking on the war at this time. Isabella Ford (who was secretary of the WPC in Leeds) and Margaret Haley moved the following, which was passed:

'This meeting declares that the political situation in

Germany, rightly handled, gives opportunity for a democratic peace. It deplores the incessant shifting of ground by the various exponents of the Western Powers, and in particular repudiates the view put forward by Mr Churchill on October 9 . . . that the fate of Alsace and Lorraine should be decided as a "symbol of victory". Believing that the only guarantees for a lasting peace are the satisfaction of the peoples and the establishment of a League of Nations, making disarmament possible, this meeting declares that negotiations should now be begun to those ends, and that such a policy would be approved by the great mass of the people of this country, who are sick of the slaughter and starvation of millions, not only on the battlefields but in the homes of Europe.'[30]

Between August and November 1917, 250,000 British and 200,000 German troops died fighting at Passchendaele in France. General Haig wanted to break through to the Belgian ports Ostende and Zeebrugge, which were harbouring German submarines, but instead they advanced eleven kilometres over a nightmare landscape of water-filled shell holes, dead trees and acres and acres of knee-deep mud. On the eastern front, the Russians were pulling out. The Bolsheviks had seized power in the October Revolution and surrendered to the Germans but nearly two million Russians had already died fighting, and many thousands from starvation.

Austria-Hungary and Germany could not feed their people either. In Germany alone, 380,000 – mainly children and the elderly – had died by the end of 1917. They lived mainly on turnips; there was no butter, eggs, milk or fat and the bread ration was two and a half ounces a day. In winter women would go walking the snow-covered streets hoping to meet a coal lorry, there was no fuel for light or heat.

The fourth and final year of the war opened with two events which gave women pacifists in Britain some hope. On January 4th, an invitation to the Allies from Russia and the Central Powers to take part in the Brest-Litovsk negotiations appeared in the British press. These negotiations were to decide peace terms between Germany and Bolshevik Russia. In effect they were saying, 'come and make peace too.' The Allies had to answer by a certain date. Unfortunately, the British censor only allowed publication on that date so no public pressure could be brought on the government. WIL sent a cable to Leon Trotsky, which 'heartily supported' the Russian policy of public negotiations and claimed that 'people's representatives must take part . . . if people's peace is to be secured'. The Bolsheviks had published details of the Secret Treaties between Russia, Britain, France and Italy which had been drawn up before the war. Since they showed that Britain was committed to join France in any war against Germany, the claim that Britain entered the war to liberate 'little Belgium' began to look less plausible. Meanwhile, President Wilson, despite having brought America into the war, had still not given up trying to get 'Peace Without Victory'. On January 8th, he issued his 'Fourteen Points for Peace' as a formula for how the war should end – which were remarkably like the resolutions passed at the Women's International Congress at the Hague in 1915.

By the beginning of 1918, Charlotte Despard was beginning to feel that after three and a half years of military fighting and rampant zenophobia, European civilisation would be crushed for ever. Like Sylvia Pankhurst, she had worked throughout the war to ameliorate conditions for poor, working-class women and children, which were never good at the best of times. Her views were far more pacifist than the official policy of the Women's Freedom League but she remained President, and worked with the League's Women's Suffrage National Aid Corps. The Corps distributed cheap clothes made in its own workshops in Glasgow and Birmingham, opened vegetarian restaurants in London and the provinces, with meals for as little as half a penny, and set up milk depots, maternity clinics and a hostel where children could stay for up to three months while their mothers were recovering from illness or childbirth. She personally raised funds to run the fifty-bed hospital for women and children, which was converted from the home of a League member, and she opened The Despard Arms in the Hampstead Road, a kind of 'alternative pub' where non-alcoholic drinks and food were served to both women and men, from 10 in the morning until 10 at night.

But in the last year of the war, Despard gave up all her other work to devote herself to the Women's Peace Crusade. She toured Scotland, Wales and the Midlands twice, Yorkshire and Lancashire three times. She wanted a federated Europe, if possible a federated world. How else were wars between countries to cease? More than a 100,000 people bought her pamphlet *An Appeal to Women*, which was the Crusade's best-selling piece of literature. Reading the entries in her diary for January, we can imagine the reception she received:

January 6th: Keighley, Yorkshire. I delight in the family with whom I am staying. Morning and afternoon went with them to the Baptist Mission Service: afternoon held our Crusade meeting in a large dingy hall – packed! At first there were signs of disturbance, but it passed and I had a very attentive meeting.

January 7th: Stayed with another Yorkshire family, father a railway worker, all keen ILPers, much enthusiasm for peace. Hall not so large, but well-filled with a most sympathetic audience.

January 8th: To Blackburn. Almost all women in the 'Friends' meeting house – rapt attention. A fine young factory girl was in the chair – her sweetheart is in prison. I am finding a fine, spirited audience in these women of the north.

January 9th: To Bolton. Met by WPC secretary, an eager-eyed girl, one of her brothers is a Conscientious Objector in Wakefield prison. Atmosphere of enthusiasm and determination at the meeting which helped me.

January 10th: To Nelson. The Great Hall held a large and very enthusiastic crowd – the Peace resolution was passed by acclamation. Stayed in a worker's pleasant little home; his son is a CO in Dartmoor.

January 11th: Snow falling persistently and I bought a pair of man's galoshes to put over my sandals – these make me impervious to weather.

January 13th: To Accrington. Heavy snow blocked the tramlines. Earnest little crowd in the ILP rooms – many women; they flocked around me after it broke up to ask what they could do. A meeting is to be held to start a Crusade here.[31]

Helena Swanwick spoke for the Women's Peace Crusade too. She wrote to Catherine Marshall, 'I am stomping the country again quite a lot for the UDC ILP WIL WPC (Do you know your alphabet?)'[32]

Travelling in wartime was not easy. The transportation of

troops and supplies took priority over everything else and trains were often three hours late. Swanwick remembered being stranded on one station platform, shivering with flu and going to the address of an old suffrage colleague – only to have the door slammed in her face. Accommodation was usually in the homes of working-class supporters:

> in one place 15° below zero in my bedroom & only 1 blanket – the rest cotton quilts! However, I arrived & made some good friends. I sometimes wonder whether we Bourgeois will all have to take refuge with these kind folk when our Bolsheviks make their revolution![33]

she confided to Marshall,

> I pin my hopes to nothing and no one. One just has to go on; do what one can, till one dies. The whole world is going to be different. I feel as if I were living at a time of cosmic upheaval & floating on a stream of tendencies so huge that individuals cannot be counted.[34]

A wave of depression seems to have hit many of the women in WIL and the WPC. How much longer would the slaughter go on? How much longer would casualty lists appear in local newspapers and shop windows? Would there be anything worth fighting for at the end of it? Ethel Snowden wrote afterwards,

> For months before the sudden end of war, acute sadness and cruel pessimism had possessed us all. Ten, twenty, thirty years, the best that life held, had been devoted by one or the other to the building of a better humanity and this destruction of everything we had worked for, this swift rattling back to the beginning of things, and to worse than the beginning in some ways, was at times too tragic to be borne.[35]

In the midst of such gloom came votes for women. By 1916, the parliamentary register had become desperately out of date because of the mobilisation of the war and it was necessary to compile a new one. This led to widespread speculation that the franchise would be extended. The existing householder or 'occupancy' franchise, which dated from 1885, gave the vote to only three adult males out of five and to no women at all. Emmeline Pankhurst and Millicent Fawcett publicly declared they would not want women 'to presume' over the soldiers in the trenches as far as votes were concerned. WIL, the Women's Freedom League and the East London Federation of Suffragettes declared that their desire was for complete adult suffrage and Catherine Marshall was told privately that the government was coming under pressure to disenfranchise conscientious objectors. A great deal of lobbying went on.

The Representation of the People Act (1918) was passed in the House of Commons on December 1917 and, after a delay in the Lords, was made law the following June. It gave votes to women over 30 years old who had 'occupancy' (which could be derived from the husband) and to all men over 21 with six months' residence in the same place. There was little parliamentary opposition to the principle of votes for women but it was thought necessary to impose the 30 age limit otherwise women voters would outnumber men. Even the fiercest anti-suffrage male parliamentarians, apparently bowled over by female wizardry at issuing tram tickets and delivering explosives, overcame their prejudices, and in October 1918 the Commons also voted by 274 votes to 25 to allow women to become MPs.

It is often said, rather dismissively, that British women won the vote because of their war work, as if to negate the pre-war women's suffrage movement. But would women have got the franchise if they had not been demanding it for the previous half a century? Is there sufficient evidence to show that female suffrage *would not* have come if war had not broken out? French women, who were as active in war work but less militant for their own rights, did not receive the vote until 1945. And America granted the vote to women in eleven states before that country entered the war.

Whatever the official reason, at last women were politically represented. Differences between suffragists were at least temporarily overruled in the celebrations. Catherine Marshall wrote to Millicent Fawcett,

It was not possible, in view of what you felt at the time when I and others left the Executive Committee of the NU, to say then, in any way that would have been acceptable to you, what most of us – certainly Kathleen & I – felt about the years during which we had worked with you as our 'Chief'. . . .

But believe me, nothing that happened then, or that has happened since, has altered our feeling in any way. . . .
Those years are a *fact* in our lives. Nothing can make them as if they had not been.[36]

At an International Suffrage Rally in the Kingsway Hall on March 9th, a message of congratulations was read out from Marie Stritt, President of the German Union for Women's Suffrage in Dresden. The reader will remember that she had written to *Jus* in 1914 upon the outbreak of war, saying that nationalism had to come before international feminism. It was quite the Hague spirit, with speakers from Russia, Belgium, Poland and from as far away as India and China. Pethick-Lawrence, Ashton, Despard, Ford, Macmillan, and Eleanor Barton were all on the platform, as well as Evelyn Sharp, the journalist who had written the witty prose about the press coverage of the 1915 Congress, and May Whitty, representing the Actresses' Franchise League. What light relief it must have been.[37]

There were exciting plans, too, to organise another unofficial peace initiative, similar to the one in 1915. It emanated not from British women but from French. As early as August 1916, some French women pacifists had tried to contact Rosika Schwimmer by wiring to Budapest from neutral Switzerland. But Schwimmer was not in Hungary and by the time the telegram reached her in Bergen, Norway, where she was waiting to set off on a third trip to America, the French women had had to return home. A year later, they telegraphed her at The Hague and after a two-month delay in getting a transit visa to cross Germany (she could not have travelled through France because she was an 'enemy alien') she met up with one French woman, who had been allowed to stay. Together with the Swiss IWCPP committee, they planned an international women's conference for February 1918, with visits to European politicians to follow. Initially, all the German, Hungarian and Austrian delegates to the planned conference received an encouraging response from their governments regarding the granting of passports. But then, for some unknown reason, the Swiss committee had to postpone the conference until March. Suddenly, all the belligerent governments decided to 'batten down the hatches'. Each with an eye on what the others were doing with 'their women', the

German, Hungarian, Austrian, French and British authorities all refused passports. In Britain both *The Times* and the *Daily News* reported that there were to be no British delegates because various women who were invited had 'refused to attend'! In the event, the Second Women's International Conference on April 15th, 1918, at Berne was attended by 70 French, Russian, German, Austrian, Italian, Polish and Belgian feminists, despite passport difficulties. It issued an 'Appeal to the Peoples of all Countries', urging women to abstain from giving any sort of physical or intellectual support to the war. But the original plan to take action was abandoned.[38]

Almost certainly the real reason why women did not get their passports was because of the sensitive military situation. On March 21st, the Germans had begun a ferocious attack in what was to be a final all-out effort to win the war. Transferring their troops from the eastern front, they were able to outnumber the Allied forces for a short time before the full flow of American troops arrived in Europe. By May, under General Ludendorff, hero of the victories against the Russians in 1914, they were within forty miles of Paris.

British Cabinet ministers were forced to tour the country in an effort to maintain the will to fight. These were some of the tensest months of the war for the British War Cabinet. More men were conscripted into the army, more women into war work; there was a renewed hostility towards 'enemy aliens' and conscientious objectors. Little wonder that Margaret Haley's Women's Peace Crusade meetings in Birmingham were prohibited and Margaret Ashton was threatened with prosecution for advising the citizens of Warrington not to buy War Bonds. And in tune with the new mood of repression a mammoth WIL and WPC demonstration planned for July, in Hyde Park, was banned at the last minute. Questions in the House of Commons demanding the prohibition of the demonstration gave WIL more publicity (albeit unfavourable) than it had ever had in its short existence.[39]

But German military success did not last long. By August 8th, the Allies were fighting back and Ludendorff called it 'the black day of the German army'. Contrary to common belief, the collapse in morale in the German interior during the summer of 1918 was caused more by soldiers writing angry letters home and circulating dissent when on leave than by the food shortage. The 'stab-in-the-back' legend appears to have been invented to save the honour of the German army.[40]

Earlier, the Brest-Litovsk settlement and the temporary advance on the western front had raised the spirits of German civilians, worn down as they were with deprivation, but the new stories from the troops made them long for peace at any price; who cared if they became English or French, as long as they had enough to eat? German women doing heavy industrial work were starving themselves to feed their children, although now, with even less food, even the children were suffering from malnutrition. Mothers watched them become skin and bone and take on their own unhealthy, yellow pallor on the ever decreasing rations of bread and turnips. There was no transport, no medicines, and rampant inflation. Clothes and shoes cost ten times more than they had before the war. Women even had to queue for hours to get a bit of sewing cotton. Yet the black market still operated for the rich. Women must have listened in horror when their husbands and lovers reported the hopeless military situation; how the troops hated the officers and how the men were now refusing to obey orders. On no account, the men urged, must the women support the ninth war loan.

By September, the British and French armies had advanced all along the western front and Germany's allies in the East began to crumble: Bulgaria admitted defeat on September 29th. Ludendorff asked the German government to seek an armistice with President Wilson at once so that the army had a breathing space, but while talks went on, Turkey surrendered on October 30th and Austria-Hungary four days later. At the same time, not wishing to lose their lives in a war which was already lost, German sailors and soldiers mutinied at Wilhelmshafen and Kiel and the unrest quickly spread to other ports and cities. By November 9th there was a general strike in Berlin and the Kaiser had abdicated, fleeing to Holland. The armistice was signed at 5 a.m. on November 11th and came into force at 11 a.m.

When news of peace negotiations first filtered through to Britain in October, Charlotte Despard could physically feel the relief flow through her. 'I had not realised,' she said, 'the weight, the awful tension that had been upon us.'[41]

On the day before the armistice was signed, Florence Lockwood was speaking at her first Women's Peace Crusade meeting. It was a dismal room and only twelve women came:

> Nothing could have been more disheartening; we few
> women assembled on this dark Saturday afternoon with my
> poor stumbling utterances. . . . Once I was nearly out-voiced
> by a drum-and-fife band with soldiers passing in the street,
> which seemed emblematic of what we were up against.[42]

On her way home, Lockwood saw a man reading a newspaper
on the tram, with the headline 'ABDICATION OF THE
KAISER.'

Catherine Marshall, who had had a nervous breakdown in
September 1917 because of her despair at the war and the
strain of working long hours for the NCF, was in Edinburgh
having treatment when peace came. She walked into the empty
cathedral and stood on the step of the chancel, singing
Schubert's *Litanei*, with the words 'Alle Seelen ruh'n Frieden'
('All souls rest in peace').

On November 11th, Helena Swanwick was in the middle of
a speaking tour in Scotland and since a considerable number of
the British people were still abusing the Germans even though
the guns had stopped, she just carried on. She was too weary
and sickened to feel elation. 'I seemed still to be crying all the
time inside and I had to hold myself tight,' she remembered.[43]

Meanwhile, as the bells struck 11, people in towns all over
the country left their work in offices, shops and factories to
celebrate. Often a din of car horns, police whistles and clanging
dustbin lids broke out. Buses were hijacked; there was kissing,
singing and dancing and great roars of cheers. It is said that
complete strangers had sex in doorways and in the road. A
huge bonfire, stacked up against Nelson's Column, blazed into
the night and the revelling went on in some places for three
days, until finally stopped by police. Five soldiers had died
every minute of the war, culminating in a total of ten million. A
further twenty million were injured. No one quite knows the
number of civilians who died from starvation.

CHAPTER 10

At the foot of the mountain

> When I hear that women are unfit to be diplomats, I wonder by what standards of duplicity and frivolity they could possibly prove themselves inferior to the men who represented the victors at Versailles.[1]

Helena Swanwick never forgave the Big Four – French Prime Minister Clemenceau, Lloyd George, President Wilson and the Italian Prime Minister Orlando, for the terms of the Treaty of Versailles. Neither did the other women in the British WIL, nor the other national sections of the ICWPP. Mary Sheepshanks remembered sitting in the Tuileries gardens in Paris, when she first heard the news, realising the meaning of the terms. The ICWPP Women's International Congress held in Switzerland at Zurich, between May 12th and 17th, issued the first public comment (carried by a unanimous vote) on the terms, and was strongly critical. They would, the Congress resolution stated,

> create all over Europe discords and animosities which can only lead to future wars . . . by the financial and economic proposals a hundred million people of this generation in the heart of Europe are condemned to poverty, disease and despair, which must result in the spread of hatred and anarchy within each nation.[2]

How depressingly right these prophesies were to turn out to be. Germany, already exhausted by the war, was unable to pay the compensation demanded of it by the victorious Allies and so French troops took over German coalfields and factories, and confiscated everything they produced as part payment. The German army was reduced from four million to 100,000 men, and the German air force and navy were handed over to the Allies. German land was lost both at home and abroad. The Germans needed little excuse to feel bitter and revengeful.

It was by coincidence that the peace terms were published on the first day of the Women's International Congress in Zurich. As we know, one of the ICWPP aims had been to hold a conference at the same time and place as the official one at the end of the war – and to try and influence its terms. Everyone had imagined that this official conference would take place in some neutral country, so that women from both defeated and 'victorious' nations would be able to attend the 'parallel' meeting, but the politicians chose Paris as their venue. Excluding Austrian, German and Hungarian women was out of the question and so the ICWPP Congress was held in Zurich. Jane Addams arrived from Paris with still scarce copies of the peace terms and a committee spent most of the first night studying them.

But if the women despaired at the misuse of power by male politicians, their reunion did not disappoint them. 'As you doubtless know, my going was an act of faith, not of conviction,' wrote Florence Kelley, an American friend of Jane Addams and founder of the National Consumers' League in the United States. Her letter back home continued,

> But next time I would go on my knees. It was unbelievably wonderful. There were twenty-five English women sitting with the Germans in front, and the Irish at one side, alike engrossed in the common effort. . . . Never have I seen so generous a spirit in any group of human beings.[3]

Lists can be boring but this one is surely celebratory: 147 women represented 15 of the 21 national sections of the ICWPP at the Congress: America sent 27, Australia 3, Austria 4, Britain 26, Denmark 6, France 4, Germany 25, Holland 5, Hungary 2, Ireland 3, Italy 1, Norway 6, Roumania 1, Sweden 11 and Switzerland 23.[4]

Besides harshly criticising the Treaty of Versailles (public opinion caught up with them about three years later), a whole host of radical resolutions and proposals for study were discussed.

One of the priorities was a demand for the Allies to lift the food blockade which was preventing food reaching Germany and Austria-Hungary. The blockade was still operating although it was six months since the war had ended. Emmeline Pethick-Lawrence moved this resolution and it was unanimously decided to cable it to Paris immediately. Later Jane Addams read out the telegram President Wilson sent in reply: 'Your message appeals both to my head and my heart, and I hope most sincerely that ways may be found, though the present outlook is extremely unpromising, because of infinite practical difficulties. . . .' Presumably 'difficulties' was a euphemism for 'fellow politicians'.[5]

The subjects of two other major resolutions were the planned League of Nations; and whether or not Congress should condone violence in social revolutions.

Some delegates thought the League was merely the means by which the iniquitous terms of the peace treaty were to be enforced and would make Europe less secure than ever; others thought it was at least a step in the right direction and did not want to damn it at birth. As a compromise, it was decided to list the Convenant's faults, such as its non-inclusion of Germany and lack of disarmament and arbitration proposals, and to recommend improvements. As for the place of violence in social revolutions, this also caused heated debate. Several of the German and Austrian delegates described how they had attempted to keep their revolutions peaceful and it was finally decided, by a majority of one vote, to support only peaceful methods of social change.

Above all, this was an international feminist conference – and it proposed that a Women's Charter be inserted into the peace treaty. This should state that member countries should hold 'that it is injurious to the community to restrict women to a position of dependence, to discourage their education or development, or to limit their opportunities'.[6]

Signatories to the peace treaty should also agree that 'the recognition of women's service to the world not only as wage earners but as mothers and home-makers is an essential factor in the building up of the world's peace'.[7]

The Congress wanted countries joining the League to agree to: women's suffrage; equal status with men on legislative and administrative bodies; the same protection as men in laws against slavery; full personal and civil rights for women upon marriage; equal rights for mothers with fathers over children; equal pay; education and training opportunities; and the right for a married woman to change or retain her nationality. And

At the 1919 Zurich Congress: from left to right: Anita Augspurg, Charlotte Despard, Lida Gustava Hermann, Rosa Genoni, Frau Kulka, Alice Hamilton. 'Only in freedom is permanent peace possible,' Catherine Marshall told the Congress, and they adopted the name Women's International League for Peace and Freedom. They also voted to support only peaceful methods of change.

they wanted 'adequate economic provision for the service of motherhood'.[8]

> What was surprising . . . was that we, who had not met since the spring of 1915, who had had to work without any direct communication and over whose heads four years of such tragic and embittered folly had passed, came together to find ourselves in accord, not only as to the war, but as to the peace: what we wanted it to be and how we would work for it.[9]

So wrote Helena Swanwick. But agreement amongst the delegates was also deliberately fostered by adopting particular methods of working. As in 1915, they laid upon themselves an embargo on discussions about who was responsible for the war. German, Austrian and Hungarian women deliberately kept silent about the cruelties of the Allies' food blockade, leaving it to delegates from the so-called victorious nations to protest. Conclusions were reached not by imposing the will of the majority or by evading the issues but by constantly trying to analyse the meaning of opposing arguments and synthesise the two views. Emily Greene Balch explained it thus:

> We try both to create agreement and to bring clear expression to all the agreement there is latent among us. We must all the time be trying as much to agree with others as trying to get others to agree with us. This is as new in debate as peaceful settlement of disputes is new in international politics.[10]

This time the British delegation were not prevented from attending, and amongst the twenty-six women were Margaret Ashton, Kathleen Courtney, Helen Crawfurd, Charlotte Despard, Isabella Ford, Emmeline Pethick-Lawrence, Emily Leaf, Chrystal Macmillan, Catherine Marshall, Mary Sheepshanks, Ethel Snowden, Helena Swanwick and Ellen Wilkinson – plus Louise Bennet from the Irish WIL.

Only a couple of problems snarled up the British travel arrangements: Swanwick missed all but the last two days of the Congress because the authorities would not give her a French visa, and the new British National WIL Secretary, Mrs Ayrton Gould, was unable to leave the country because she had an appointment in court. A WIL leaflet, distributed at a 20,000-strong Trafalgar Square demonstration and blaming the British government for the starvation of Austrian children, had her name on the bottom. Still, the demonstration was worth a prosecution, because as a result, WIL had managed to collect one million rubber teats to send to German mothers unable to nurse their babies because of their own malnutrition. Some milk supplies were getting through to Germany but they could not be used for infants because there were no feeding bottles.

Helen Crawfurd gave the report of the British WIL. She had travelled to Switzerland with Ellen Wilkinson and they were sharing accommodation at a nearby hotel in Zurich. Crawfurd recalled that her friend's speeches were full of 'revolutionary zeal' and received so much publicity in the Swiss press that Ethel Snowden asked her to tone them down. Crawfurd was delighted when Chairwoman Chrystal Macmillan – another Scot – upheld Wilkinson's right to talk as much as she liked about 'workers' control in Russia'.

Once again, the American delegates were brought safely across the Atlantic by the trusty *Noordam*. Before they had left, in fact just a few days after the armistice had been declared, Anita Augspurg and two other German women sent telegrams to Jane Addams and Clara Wilson (who was married to the President) pleading that they demand the lifting of the food blockade so that German women and children would not starve. However, Addams only heard of the cables through the press, whereupon she was instructed by the State Department not to answer.

Like the British public, many Americans were eager for vengeance and Addams was deluged with vitriolic letters demanding why she wanted to help 'the wives of Huns'. Upon discovering that a Women's International Congress was to be held in Zurich, the *New York Times* suddenly became unexpectedly concerned about possible damage to the women's movement. In an editorial, it argued that those who sought the vote for women believed that 'women were people', 'sharing the same rights and duties as men', but the Zurich Congress was being held on the grounds that

> women are not people; they are a class, a group, something apart, with class interests which require a congress of their own for definition; a class which apparently hates and distrusts men. . . . The millions of women who have worked and suffered to help win the war for democracy will hardly

relish the revival of sex-antagonism by women who insisted the war was wrong.[11]

Emily Greene Balch, Madeleine Doty, Lillian Wald and Alice Hamilton were some familiar names amongst the delegation – which, of course, included Jane Addams. Mary Church Terrell, a newcomer and the first women member of the Washington Board of Education, was the only black woman. Jeannette Rankin, the first woman member of Congress, whose vote against America joining the war was now world-famous, was there too. 'Crystal Eastman is here as Mrs Walter Fuller,' wrote Alice Hamilton to a friend at home. 'For once she has found husbands valuable.'[12]

This disapproval of Eastman's sex life, which was considered rather too casual for the time, was common amongst the leaders of the American group and she had not been chosen as an official delegate. Interestingly, she seems to have struck up a friendship with Helen Crawfurd, who took her back to Glasgow to report on the socialist movement there for *The Liberator*, the successor to *The Masses*.

The Scandinavian delegates had spent eight days travelling through Germany – normally a three-day journey – carrying their own food and sometimes waiting all night for trains. Clara Tybjerg, the International Secretary of the Danish Council of Women, was one of the Danes, and perhaps the most well-known names from Norway and Sweden were Emily Arnesen, who was interested in international education, and Elizabeth Waern-Bugge, a keen suffragist. Naturally, Aletta Jacobs was present from Holland. The Swiss, who had been absent at The Hague, were well represented on their home ground: Clara Ragaz was the President of the ICWPP section, and Marguerite Gobat, the daughter of Albert Gobat, the well-known Swiss pacifist who had won the Nobel Peace Prize in 1902, was there. Both were to play an active part in the international women's peace movement in the future.

Only three French women managed to attend because of passport difficulties but Gabrielle Dûchene (head of the national section), although not allowed to leave France, entertained the American delegation in Paris. Italian Rosa Genoni, who was a costume designer, managed to get a passport by saying she was going to research international fashion! Three Australian women travelled for two months to attend the Congress: they were Vida Goldstein, Cecilia John and Eleanor Moore, who had campaigned with Adela Pankhurst in the Women's Peace Army in their home country. The Belgians who had been to the Hague Congress were said to have been threatened with exile if they tried again and there were no official Belgian delegates. Nothing was heard of the Russian women; by March 1918, there had even been a clamp down on reports to *Jus Suffragii*.

'The radicalism of the newly enfranchised German and Austrian women is delicious. They scorn our snail-like Anglo-Saxon ways,' wrote an American delegate in a letter back home. 'Why not overthrow everything and start afresh as they have done (they say).'[13]

Most outstanding of the Germans were Anita Augspurg and Lida Gustava Heymann, who had been at The Hague. Ethel Snowden saw them thus:

> They live together in Munich, and were as inseparable at the Conference as the Siamese twins. Dr Augspurg suggests a Franciscan monk in appearance. She wears her grey hair short. Her strong pleasant face has the expression of the religious fanatic whose conviction is founded upon reason, she wears a severe and loose style of dress . . . she is kind austerity embodied simple and dignified.[14]

Heymann was more emotional, wrote Snowden, 'full of quick passion', with a voice of 'masculine timbre' and 'vigorous and compelling gestures'. They were both cynical of men and once declared that they would rather run over a man than a dog. 'If we did not have the one-sided rule of men which seeks conquest and profit, we would not need militarism' was their philosophy.[15]

As one might expect, the women from central Europe as well as the French, tended to be more in favour of revolutionary action than the Americans, Scandinavians, Swiss and British – although the British women nearly all made a point of stressing that they were socialists. The two Hungarians told of the revolutionary turmoil in their country. For the second time Rosika Schwimmer had not been permitted a passport, and could not attend the Congress, but her friend Vilma Glücklich was there. In November 1918, the Hungarian liberal Count Karolyi had established a democratic government in Hungary upon the collapse of the Austro-Hungarian Empire but this had been quickly followed by a Bolshevik takeover.

Under Karolyi, Schwimmer had been made Ambassador to Switzerland – the first woman Ambassador in history – and whilst working in Berne had helped organise an earlier, smaller ICWPP post-war conference in February 1919,[16] which had passed very similar resolutions to the one in Zurich in May. For those who are getting confused, Zurich was strictly speaking the fourth Women's International Congress, although the middle two were less representative: the first was at The Hague in April 1915, the second in Berne in April 1918, the third in Berne in February 1919 and the fourth in Zurich in May 1919. However, Schwimmer was recalled a few days before the communist coup and prevented from leaving the country again.

In the particular polarised way in which people responded to Schwimmer, some delegates missed her, others did not. Emily Greene Balch successfully moved a motion to send her a telegram saying, 'We recognise in you one of the most passionate champions of the cause of peace and join you in wishes for the better time we are all working for.'[17] Florence Holbrook, an American friend, wrote to her from Vienna, saying the Congress was like '*Hamlet* with *Hamlet out*' but went on to add,

> Dreadful things have been said of you – but never a
> *proof* – and we have tried to make them understand your
> position. The papers always ridicule the peace people, Ford,
> etc. all the time and class them with the foes of their country
> when all the time we are the truest patriots.[18]

Florence Kelley, Addams's friend, wrote that 'fourteen nations' were represented at the Congress when she left, 'and no one of the nature of Rosika or Frau Selenka', which was obviously meant as a derogatory comment.[19]

While the international delegates debated in beautiful Switzerland, with apple trees blossoming in the spring sunshine and snow-capped mountains glinting in the distance, the peoples of Austria, Germany and Hungary were starving. Helene Stöcker, from Berlin, estimated that half of the babies born in that city in 1918-19 had died, and those who had survived were fed with meal mixed with water, and sometimes a little milk. Frau Lehmann of Göttingen reported that tuberculosis had increased by leaps and bounds, but that what had distressed her country people the most was the death rate amongst 15- to 20-year-olds, from the influenza epidemic in 1918. They were so weakened by lack of food that all their resistance had vanished.

But it was Austria and Hungary who were suffering the most. Frau Kulka from Vienna read figures to the Congress showing the large number of children between 5 and 7 years old who were unable to walk because of malnutrition. The death rate amongst babies was so high that parents no longer held funerals but would wrap their little one's dead body in newspaper, and take it by train at night to the cemetery. Frau Kulka herself was much changed by the war. For her, the worst aspect of starvation was being so preoccupied with the search for food that one was unable to think about anything intellectual or political. Never again, she said, would she expect the poor to be interested in transforming the world.

Jane Addams had difficulty recognising Kulka when she first saw her in a Zurich street. She was so shrunken and changed from the beautiful woman she had been at The Hague:

> She was not only emaciated by a wasting illness, looking as if she needed immediate hospital care – she did in fact die three months after her return to Vienna – but her face and artist's hands were covered with rough red blotches due to the long use of soap substitutes, giving her a cruelly scalded appearance. My first reaction was one of over-whelming pity and alarm as I suddenly discovered my friend standing at the very gate of death.[20]

If Jane Addams had thought then of the letters she had received about 'Hun's wives', she surely would have felt ashamed. Austrian and Hungarian delegates dared not eat the good food spread before them, for fear that their digestion would not cope with it. Bars of scented soap were the greatest luxury their 'victorious' sisters could give them.

One day, remembered Ethel Snowden, 'tender-hearted Isabella Ford' came to her in tears because the daugher of one of the German delegates had died of tuberculosis. The girl had been treated in a hospital where there was no linen. ' "She is heart-broken," said Ford of the mother. "She was an only child and it was through hunger that the decline set in. She cannot speak to us this morning. And I do not wonder." '[21]

The German-speaking delegates showed their mental as well as physical fatigue by being slow to follow the Congress proceedings. Instead of leading the debate, as they had done at The Hague, Jane Addams, who was in the Chair most of the time, had to delay discussions whilst some point was translated over and over again for them. Their moods seemed to swing from high to low: one German woman was the life and soul of a mountain-side picnic they had one afternoon, laughing at her son's excitement at finding some bread by his plate a few days before. She good-naturedly told the British women, 'It is you who are starved with your ban on German music, not we!' But later, on the journey home, as the bus bumped down the mountain road, she sat with tears streaming down her face.[22]

'Only in freedom is permanent peace possible,' urged Catherine Marshall, who proposed that a permanent organisation be formed out of the International Committee of Women for Permanent Peace, to be called the Women's International League for Peace and Freedom. Nearly all the delegates had worked for women's freedom – in suffrage and other campaigns – and many had worked for economic and personal freedom, for women and men, through trade unions and socialist parties. They did not want a peace that depended on oppression and adopted the name enthusiastically.

Jane Addams was elected President, Lida Gustava Heymann and Helena Swanwick Vice-Presidents. The German delegation never forgot their intense gratitude at being equally represented, when the rest of the world seemed to be in a permanent fit of 'Hun' hatred and Germany had been excluded from the League of Nations. But, of course, there was no question of it being otherwise in the WILPF.

Emily Greene Balch received a cable while she was in Zurich, telling her that the Board of Trustees at Wellesley College had decided not to re-appoint her, as they said she had been employed 'to teach economics not pacifism'. She 'celebrated' by smoking a cigarette (strictly forbidden at Wellesley) with Emmeline Pethick-Lawrence and Madeleine Doty and, much to her delight, was nominated first International Secretary and Treasurer of the League. She would work in Geneva.

On the last morning of the Congress, Jane Addams announced quietly that a fourth Frenchwoman had arrived. Her name was Jeanne Mélin and she had come from the devastated area of Carignan in the Ardennes. As she approached the platform, Heymann, who had just finished making a speech, leapt to her feet, clasped Mélin's hand and presented her with a bunch of roses, saying,

> 'A German woman gives her hand to a French woman, and
> says in the name of the German delegation, that we hope we
> women can build a bridge from Germany to France and
> from France to Germany, and that in the future we may be
> able to make good the wrong-doing of men.'[23]

Mélin replied with a stirring speech against the male
politicians at Versailles and urged women everywhere to be 'les
forces de demain' and to struggle for a just and peaceful
society. Emily Greene Balch got to her feet and, raising her
hand in the air, cried out, 'I dedicate my life to the cause of
Peace!' Everyone rose and a great shout went out in several
different languages: 'We dedicate our lives to Peace!' Helena
Swanwick wrote, 'I have never witnessed or imagined so
remarkable an affirmation. Such scenes can, of course, be
staged, but only intense feeling can cause them to occur
spontaneously, as this did.'[24]

For the next two decades (and still today) the Women's
International League for Peace and Freedom continued to lobby
governments along the principles of peace, freedom, and justice
for women laid down at the Hague and Zurich Congresses.[25]
For many years its headquarters was an old, creeper-covered
house built on a hill in Geneva and nicknamed the Maison
Internationale. It had a library for lectures, conferences and
receptions, a dining-room and bedrooms for visiting members
from all over the world. At the back, there was a little garden
with roses and a fountain. In the summer, women would eat
there, under a linden tree.

As first International Secretary, Emily Greene Balch remembered the excitement of being at the centre of a world women's
organisation. In the early days, she had letters from Iceland,
South Africa, the Fiji Islands; and one from an American
woman, who said she had first worked to abolish slavery, then
for women's suffrage, and now she wanted to work for world
peace. Balch edited the League's magazine *Pax International*
and was able to employ two full-time secretaries, one for
French, the other for German.

The WILPF resisted the temptation to become a relief agency
but tried to concentrate instead on analysing the causes of war
and attempting preventative action. It never aimed to be a mass
movement, more a well-informed lobbying group. It worked

closely with League of Nations officials and delegates, launched its own investigations into conditions in political 'hot spots' and, fifty years before Amnesty International, pledged to work for all political prisoners who were not terrorists and campaigned for those imprisoned for their political beliefs.

In 1920, Catherine Marshall was the first person to study the rules of procedure for the League's first Assembly (no one else had bothered to ask). She found them thoroughly undemocratic and at her suggestion they were modified. In 1921, members took their own food and typewriters to WILPF's third Congress in still starving Vienna. In 1924, the venue of the fourth conference was Washington, where war-engendered paranoia still reigned, and their *Pax Special* railway coach was attacked by the Daughters of the American Revolution who thought they were spies. In 1926, WILPF sent a delegation to Haiti, which had been occupied by US marines since 1915. Their report recommended complete withdrawal, which eventually was achieved.

By 1930, the then Secretary, Mary Sheepshanks, and many others had already diagnosed the conditions for fascism. An urgent message had come from persecuted Jews in Bucharest to WILPF headquarters, pleading for help. Rosika Schwimmer, who was Jewish herself and had been refused American citizenship because of her pacifism, suggested a conference to take action on statelessness which WILPF organised in Geneva in 1930. In 1929, prominent scientists, including Albert Einstein, backed their conference on 'Modern Methods of Warfare', which demanded that the public be informed of the dangers of the future.

This was the decade which saw the failure of the 1932-7 Disarmament Conference (WILPF collected six million signatures for the mammoth international petition presented there), Mussolini's invasion of Ethiopia, the Spanish Civil War, the Japanese military intervention in China, Hitler's persecution of the Jews, the absorption of Austria by Germany and the swallowing up of Czechoslovakia. Peace and freedom were in short supply.

Jane Addams spent much of her time outside America in the 1920s, travelling on behalf of the WILPF and chairing international conferences as its President. This was a relief, as the 'Red Scare' at home was depressing and she and Emily Greene Balch headed the 1919 Military Intelligence Bureau list of *Who's Who of Pacifists and Radicals* (albeit for alphabetical reasons). As someone with 'dangerous, destructive and anarchistic sentiments' she was under government surveillance and followed by detectives. Travelling to the Far East and round the world in 1928, she chaired a conference in Honolulu as President of the Pan-Pacific Women's Union but resigned as active WILPF President the next year at the Prague Congress. She continued in an honorary capacity until her death – from cancer – in May 1935, having won the Nobel Peace Prize in 1931.[26]

Catherine Marshall continued to work with the League of Nations, through WILPF. Considering her public stand for the conscientious objectors during the war, it was ironic that in the 1920s Lloyd George should invite her to Downing Street and Chequers. Between bouts of illness, she also worked for the Labour Party but refused to stand as an MP when she was asked.[27] Other ex-NUWSS members Chrystal Macmillan and Kathleen Courtney were also active in WILPF. Macmillan (who died in 1937, the same year as Margaret Ashton) specialised in the subject of nationality laws for married women. After the war, she was able to practise as a barrister. Courtney sat on the League of Nations Union.

Charlotte Despard and Sylvia Pankhurst did not remain active WILPF members. The former thought the League of Nations was a 'capitalist fraud' and, at the age of 74, returned to her native Ireland to work for Sinn Fein. Twenty-one years later, she died at the age of 95, still considered a danger to the State. Sylvia Pankhurst had never really got over her distaste for the 'cautious and moderate' ex-Fawcett followers and had not gone to the Zurich Congress. By May 1919, she was far too busy helping to set up the British Communist Party. In 1928, she shocked her mother once more, by having a baby at 46 and not marrying the father. In the late 1930s she was active in Women Against War and Fascism, an organisation which was backed by the Communist Party. Charlotte Despard and Selina Cooper were other leading members. The exotic ending to Sylvia Pankhurst's life was played out in Ethiopia, where she worked for the Emperor Haile Selassie and championed the right of African countries to rule themselves. In 1960, she died of a heart attack in Addis Ababa – a long way from the Old Ford Road. She was aged 78.

Crystal Eastman was another woman who believed that

liberty and capitalism were incompatible. After her visit to Glasgow with Helen Crawfurd, she travelled to Hungary and Russia doing investigative reporting for *The Liberator*, which she co-owned with her brother Max. It was the only magazine in America to report on worldwide socialist movements of the time, and had published John Reed's famous account of the 1917 Bolshevik Revolution. She was not active in WILPF. The 1920s were not a good time for American progressives: the blacklisted Eastman, a self-confessed workaholic, could not find employment between 1922 and 1928, either in Britain or the United States, and lived off the income from two houses she owned. In 1928, she died of kidney disease, unhappy and frustrated, aged only 46.[28]

But not all the revolutionaries were outside the WILPF. In an age when the example of the Russians was still seen as the hope of the world by many, it would be surprising if this were not the case. The French and German section leaders were particularly sympathetic to this line of thinking. Lida Gustava Heymann and Anita Augspurg, two such examples, continued to play a prominent part in WILPF until 1933, when they fled to Switzerland. In that year Hitler came to power and threatened all pacifists, socialists and Jews with persecution and imprisonment. At Heymann's last peace meeting in Munich she stood guard at the door herself to keep a look out for Nazis. She was 65.

Once in Zurich, Heymann and Augspurg carried on their work from an attic and refused to acknowledge that either of them was living 'in exile', since the 'whole world was their country'. When Heymann died in 1943, aged 75, and Augspurg, who was eleven years older, followed a few months later, their ashes were buried in the garden of the Maison Internationale in Geneva.

Helena Swanwick was sent to Geneva as part of the British delegation to the League of Nations in both 1924 and 1929, during which time she tried to open up the committees to more women. As editor of the journal *Foreign Affairs*, she grew increasingly disturbed by world events. In her book *Roots of Peace*, published in 1938, when she was 74, she wrote,

in a *Times* leader of January 12, 1938, it is blandly
explained that 'the object of the bomber is not to defeat the
rival air force, but to terrify into submission populations

whose women, children and homes are attacked and destroyed by fire, explosives and gas.'

To this pass have we been brought by men's double infatuation with machines and domination. . . . Blind men of science provide the engines wherewith gallant youths, equally blind, will at the command of helpless politicians, blindest of all, destroy alike men, women and children.[29]

Swanwick spent much of her last years trying to escape from distressing international affairs by working in her beloved garden at her home near the river at Maidenhead. She dreaded the aerial bombardment she knew another war would bring, and yet Hitlerism was as repugnant to her as anyone. In November 1939, three months after war was declared, she died.[30]

Many WILPF women lost their pacifism in the Second World War. Fascism was seen as a greater evil.[31] One British WILPF member visited Munich in 1934 and 'from the moment' of her arrival, fear never left her. Her German man-friend, whom she had gone to visit, waxed lyrical about the new regime and the 'new sense of being a man given to every German'.

We were bound sooner or later to have a row. It came, suddenly, about the position of women. He, and his wife, insisted fervently that of a woman all that should be asked was charm; that 'masculine' (i.e. intellectual) pursuits should be deprived her; she had a higher function. In the new Germany, things were being rightly organised. . . . Resistance to Hitler from the 'better element' was not to be expected. The ideological web had got the intelligent flies helplessly caught.[32]

Catherine Marshall gave asylum to German and Austrian Jews at 'Hawse End'. So did Mary Sheepshanks in her home – and had hostile slogans painted on her wall as a result. Emily Greene Balch applied for the much coveted affidavits required for entry into America on behalf of desperate refugees, many of whom she knew from her days in Europe. She wrote to all her American friends asking for money, work and homes for the homeless. At 72, she was still a tireless worker.

During the Second World War, most WILPF members lived through Nazi persecution, occupation, or blitz. Dutch Rosa Manus, colleague of Aletta Jacobs[33] and pictured with her on the stage at The Hague in 1915, died in a German concentration camp. The Hungarian WILPF section disappeared. Eugenie Miskolczy Meller, who led the organisation after Vilma Glücklich died, was murdered in Auschwitz, as were many others of the leadership group. Czech members were also brutally murdered; the groups in Austria, Holland, Poland and Yugoslavia vanished too. WILPF members in France and Norway were active in the Resistance.

Rosika Schwimmer had sought asylum in America twenty years earlier. Under Bela Kun's 1919 communist regime, she nearly starved because she could not get work as a 'bourgeois feminist', but it was during the 'White Terror' that her life was in danger. Admiral Horthy's fascist dictatorship used terror squads to torture and kill Jews and suspected Bolsheviks: on house-to-house searches they would point at her photograph and say, 'We'll get that bitch next.' With the help of foreign friends, she was smuggled out of Hungary to Vienna, from where she travelled to America. But upon her arrival in 1921, she was accused of being a German spy, who had prevented 'military preparedness' in America and kept the country out of the war for two years. She, too, was blacklisted in the 1920s and 1930s and depended entirely on her sister, Franciska, who had also emigrated, and her close friend, Lola Maverick Lloyd, for emotional and financial support. In a series of controversial court cases, she was denied American citizenship on the grounds that she 'refused to bear arms', and she died, stateless, in 1948, at the age of 71. The Feminist Association in Budapest, which was also the Hungarian WILPF section, had been revived by the surviving leader, Irma Szirmai, at the end of the Second World War, and in October 1948 they organised an impressive memorial service for Schwimmer.

With the dropping of the first atomic bomb on Hiroshima in 1945, Schwimmer's Campaign for World Government, which she had founded with Lola Maverick Lloyd in 1937, had received a sudden rush of support. Other founder members of WILPF lived long enough to watch the subsequent nuclear arms race, which today threatens to destroy the world: Mary Sheepshanks, aged 86, took her own life in 1958; Catherine Marshall, 81, and Emily Greene Balch, 94, died in 1961 and Kathleen Courtney, aged 96, in 1974.

In 1948, Rosika Schwimmer was nominated for the Nobel Peace Prize by members of Parliament in Britain, Hungary,

Sweden, France and Italy, but she died before the award could be made. No prize was given that year. A month before her death from bronchial pneumonia, she sent a message to the Seneca Falls Centennial Celebration of the 1848 Women's Rights Convention. She wanted, she wrote, to remember the radical suffragists' pledge to abolish war if granted political power.

> I really believed in this pledge of ours, not because I thought that women were superior to men but because having been isolated from public affairs, I believed we were less conditioned to corruption, less perverted by narrow nationalism and protected from the militarisation to which men were subjected.
>
> [But] from our objective of women working to abolish war, we descended to the women's auxiliary, aiding the war effort in the First World War, then to the Women's Army and Navy Corps in the Second World War. . . .
>
> I hope that on this centennial, which falls in the third year of the atomic era, women will retrace their steps from the many paths and blind alleys to which they have strayed in imitation of the social, political and economic morass of what we once called the 'man-made world', and that they will remember that we sought equality for our half of the human race, not at the lowest, but at the highest level of human aspirations.[34]

APPENDIX 1

The manifesto of the Woman's Peace Party

The initial manifesto

WE, WOMEN OF THE UNITED STATES, assembled in behalf of World Peace, grateful for the security of our own country, but sorrowing for the misery of all involved in the present struggle among warring nations, do hereby band ourselves together to demand that war be abolished.

Equally with men pacifists, we understand that planned-for, legalized, wholesale, human slaughter is today the sum of all villainies.

As women, we feel a peculiar moral passion of revolt against both the cruelty and the waste of war.

As women, we are especially the custodian of the life of the ages. We will not longer consent to its reckless destruction.

As women, we are particularly charged with the future of childhood and with the care of the helpless and the unfortunate. We will not longer endure without protest that added burden of maimed and invalid men and poverty-stricken widows and orphans which war places upon us.

As women, we have builded by the patient drudgery of the past the basic foundation of the home and of peaceful industry. We will not longer endure without a protest that must be heard and heeded by men, that hoary evil which in an hour destroys the social structure that centuries of toil have reared.

As women, we are called upon to start each generation onward toward a better humanity. We will not longer tolerate without determined opposition that denial of the sovereignty of reason and justice by which war and all that makes for war today render impotent the idealism of the race.

Therefore, as human beings and the mother half of

humanity, we demand that our right to be consulted in the settlement of questions concerning not alone the life of individuals but of nations be recognized and respected.

We demand that women be given a share in deciding between war and peace in all the courts of high debate – within the home, the school, the church, the industrial order, and the state.

So protesting, and so demanding, we hereby form ourselves into a national organization to be called the Woman's Peace Party.

We hereby adopt the following as our platform of principles, some of the items of which have been accepted by a majority vote, and more of which have been the unanimous choice of those attending the conference that initiated the formation of this organization. We have sunk all differences of opinion on minor matters and given freedom of expression to a wide divergence of opinion in the details of our platform and in our statement of explanation and information, in a common desire to make our woman's protest against war and all that makes for war, vocal, commanding and effective. We welcome to our membership all who are in substantial sympathy with that fundamental purpose of our organization, whether or not they can accept in full our detailed statement of principles.

Platform

THE PURPOSE of this Organization is to enlist all American women in arousing the nations to respect the sacredness of human life and to abolish war. The following is adopted as our platform:

1. The immediate calling of a convention of neutral nations in the interest of early peace.

2. Limitation of armaments and the nationalization of their manufacture.

3. Organized opposition to militarism in our own country.

4. Education of youth in the ideals of peace.

5. Democratic control of foreign policies.

6. The further humanizing of governments by the extension of the franchise to women.

7. 'Concert of Nations' to supersede 'Balance of Power'.

8. Action toward the gradual organization of the world to substitute Law for War.

9. The substitution of an international police for rival

armies and navies.

10.Removal of the economic causes of war.

The later, more detailed plan

Program for constructive peace

I. *To secure the cessation of hostilities:*
1. We urge our government to call a conference of representative delegates from the neutral nations to discuss possible measures to lessen their own injuries, to hasten the cessation of hostilities, and to prevent warfare in the future.
2. In case an official conference of the kind named above proves impossible or impracticable, we pledge ourselves to work toward the summoning of an unofficial conference of the pacifists of the world to consider points named.

II. *To insure such terms of settlement as will prevent this war from being but the prelude to new wars:*
1. No province should be transferred as a result of conquest from one government to another against the will of the people. Whenever possible, the desire of a province for autonomy should be respected.
2. No war indemnities should be assessed save when recognized international law has been violated.
3. No treaty alliance or other international arrangement should be entered upon by any nation unless ratified by the representatives of the people. Adequate measures for assuring democratic control of foreign policy should be adopted by all nations.

III. *To place the future peace of the world upon securer foundations:*
1. Foreign policies of nations should not be aimed at creating alliances for the purpose of maintaining the '*balance of power*', but should be directed to the establishment of a '*Concert of Nations*', with
   (a) A *court, or courts*, for the settlement of all disputes between nations;
   (b) An *international congress*, with legislative and administrative powers over international affairs, and with permanent committees in place of present secret diplomacy;
   (c) An *international police force*.

2. As an immediate step in this direction, a permanent League of Neutral Nations ('League of Peace') should be formed, whose members should bind themselves to settle all difficulties arising between them by arbitration, judicial, or legislative procedure, and who should create an international police force for mutual protection against attack.

3. *National disarmament* should be effected in the following manner: It should be contingent upon the adoption of this peace program by a sufficient number of nations, or by nations of sufficient power to insure protection to those disarmed. It should be graduated in each nation to the degree of disarmament effected in the other nations, and progressively reduced until finally complete.

4. Pending general disarmament, all manufactories of arms, ammunitions and munitions for use in war should hereafter be national property.

5. The *protection of private property at sea*, of neutral commerce and of communications should be secured by the *neutralization of the seas* and of such maritime trade routes as the British Channel, the Dardanelles, Panama, Suez, the Straits of Gibraltar, etc.

6. National and international action should be secured to remove the *economic causes of war*.

7. The democracies of the world should be extended and reinforced by general application of the principle of self-government, including the extension of *suffrage to women*.

IV. *Immediate national program for the United States:*

1. We approve the Peace Commission Treaties which our country has negotiated with thirty nations, stipulating delay and investigation for the period of a year before any declaration of war can take place. We express the hope that all other countries will be included.

2. We protest against the increase of armaments by the United States. We insist that the increase of the army and navy at this time, so far from being in the interest of peace, is a direct threat to the well-being of other nations with whom we have dealings, an imputation of doubt of their good faith, and calculated to compel them in turn to increase their armies, and in consequence to involve us in an ever-intensifying race for military supremacy.

3. We recommend to the President and Government of the United States that a commission of men and women be created, with an adequate appropriation, whose duty shall be to work for the prevention of war and the formulation of the most compelling and practical methods of world organization.

Source: From Woman's Peace Party 'Program for Constructive Peace, January 10, 1915', from *History of the Woman's Peace Party* by Marie Louise Degen.

APPENDIX 2

IWSA voting on whether or not to hold an international conference to discuss the war

Officers: Mrs Fawcett, Mme Schlumberger, Mrs Cormick, Miss Furuhjelm, Mme Brigode:
   No   5
   Miss Macmillan, Mrs Coit:
   Yes   2
   Mrs Lindemann, Mrs Stritt, Miss Bergmann
   Not heard from

Auxiliaries: Great Britain, Holland, Denmark (one society), Hungary (through Schwimmer):
   Yes   4
   France, Norway, S. Africa, Canada, Finland, United States:
   No   6

(Canada said a conference might be possible in the United States but not anywhere else.)

Source: From minutes of NUWSS executive meeting, March 4th, 1915.

APPENDIX 3

Speech made by the Prime Minister, Herbert Asquith, in Dublin on 26 September 1914

'I should like, beyond this enquiry into causes and motives, to ask your attention and that of my fellow-countrymen to the end which in this war we ought to keep in view. Forty-four years ago, at the time of the war of 1870, Mr Gladstone used these words: "The greatest triumph of our time will be the enthronement of the idea of public right as the governing idea of European politics."

Nearly fifty years have passed. Little progress, it seems, has as yet been made towards that good and beneficent change: but it seems to me to be now at this moment as good a definition as we can have of our European policy – the idea of public right. What does it mean when translated into concrete terms? It means first and foremost the clearing of the ground by a definite repudiation of militarism as the governing factor in the relation of States and of the future moulding of the European world.

It means next that room must be found and kept for the independent existence and free development of the smaller nationalities, each with a corporate consciousness of its own. Belgium, Holland and Switzerland and Scandinavian countries, Greece and the Balkan States – they must be recognised as having exactly as good a title as their more powerful neighbours, more powerful in strength and in wealth, to a place in the sun.

And it means, finally, or it ought to mean perhaps, by a slow and gradual process, the substitution for force, for the clash of competing ambitions, for groupings and alliances and a precarious equipoise, of a *real European partnership based on the recognition of equal right and established and enforced by a common will.*

A year ago this would have sounded like a Utopian idea. It is probably one that may not or will not be realized either today or tomorrow. If and when this war is decided in favour of the Allies it will at once come within the range and before long within the grasp of European statesmanship.' (author's emphasis)

NOTES

Introduction

1 WIL yearly report, October 1915-October 1916, British Library of Political and Economic Science, London. WIL was formed on Sept 30th/Oct 1st, 1915.

2 Ethel Snowden, *A Political Pilgrim in Europe*, Cassell & Co, 1921, pp. 81-2. See also H. Swanwick, *I Have Been Young*, Gollancz, 1938.

3 See the Margaret Ashton Memorial Lecture for 1948, in Lady Simon of Wythensawe, *Margaret Ashton and Her Times*, Manchester University Press.

4 For more details on Catherine Marshall, see Jo Vellacott-Newberry, *Anti-War Suffragists*, an offprint from *History*, vol. 62, no. 206, October 1977, in the Fawcett Library, London. Jo Newberry is writing a biography of Catherine Marshall and has sorted the Marshall papers at the Cumbria County Record Office, Carlisle.

5 See obituaries, *The Times*, July 31st, 1956, and *Manchester Guardian*, July 31st, 1956, at the Fawcett Library.

6 See article by Mary Stott in the *Manchester Guardian*, 1967, Fawcett Library.

7 See obituaries in *The Times*, *International Women's News* and *Women's Bulletin* at the Fawcett Library, and *A Biographical Sketch* published by the Middle Temple for the Chrystal Macmillan Memorial Prize.

8 See E. Pethick-Lawrence, *My Part in a Changing World*, Gollancz, 1938.

9 H. Crawfurd's unpublished autobiography is in the Marx Memorial Library, London.

10 See article in *The Times* by Jill Craigie, May 1st, 1982;

S. Pankhurst, *The Home Front*, Hutchinson, 1932; Richard Pankhurst, *Sylvia Pankhurst, Artist and Crusader*, Paddington Press, 1979.

11 See *An Unhusbanded Life, Charlotte Despard: Suffragette, Socialist and Sinn Feiner*, Hutchinson, 1980, and Snowden, *A Political Pilgrim in Europe*, op. cit., pp. 83-5.

Chapter one: A Hungarian in London

1 Whether or not the militant campaign was 'disastrous for the campaign' at this stage (it was in its arson phase) is open to debate, but the IWSA suffragists thought it was. Catherine Marshall thought they would kill someone soon. This does not mean, however, that they did not admire the Pankhursts in many ways.

2 The day-to-day suffrage activities and the life of Rosika Schwimmer in Chapters One and Two are based on an incomplete, unpublished manuscript by her, written in 1922, as well as on diary notes and notes which were intended to be included in the MS. Any direct speech in the text is taken directly from this MS, to be found in Box B20, and various boxes in General Correspondence, 1914, Schwimmer/Lloyd Collection, New York Public Library.

3 Ethel Snowden, *A Political Pilgrim in Europe*, Cassell & Co., 1921, p. 42.

4 Schwimmer speech on board *Oscar II*, December 6th, 1915, Ford Expedition, Schwimmer/Lloyd Collection, op. cit., Box E4.

5 Snowden, *A Political Pilgrim in Europe*, op. cit., p. 42.

6 A. Johnson (ed.), *The Dictionary of American Biography*, Section 4, Scribners, 1945, gives further details of Schwimmer's biography.

7 Biographical details of Emily Leaf from Records and Election Addresses of candidates for election to the WIL executive, no date, presumably during the war. Fawcett Library, London. Details of Mary Sheepshanks from Sybil Oldfield, *Spinsters of this Parish: The Life and Times of F.M. Mayor and Mary Sheepshanks*, Virago, 1984.

8 Thanks to Edith Wynner for telling me this.

9 The pre-First World War Austro-Hungarian Empire included the modern cities of Prague, Vienna and Budapest. After the war, Czechoslovakia and Yugoslavia were created. Poland, formerly part of both Germany and Russia, was

also constituted as an independent country.

10 David Lloyd George, *War Memoirs*, vol. 1, chapter 2, p. 50. Also Rosika Schwimmer, unpublished MS, op. cit. A letter from Mrs Lola Lloyd to Schwimmer on December 19th, 1926 from Geneva, Switzerland, said, 'She [Catherine Marshall] sends you pleasant messages, and told me about your prophecies of war at the breakfast with Lloyd George in 1914. Later she had to see him – during the War – and he recalled them and said you knew more of European Affairs than any of them!' General Correspondence, Schwimmer/Lloyd Collection, op. cit.

11 The final wording was as follows:

In this dread hour when the fate of Europe depends on decisions which women have no power to shape, we, realising our responsibility as mothers of the race, cannot stand passively by. Powerless though we be politically, we call upon the governments of our several countries to avert the threatened and unparalleled disaster. Women see all they most reverence and treasure, the home, the family, the race, subjected to certain damage which they are powerless to avert or assuage. Whatever its result, the conflict will leave mankind the poorer, will set back civilisation, check the amelioration in the condition of the masses on which the welfare of nations depends. We, women of 26 countries in the International Woman Suffrage Alliance, appeal to you to leave untried no method of conciliation or arbitration which may avert deluging half the civilised world in blood.

12 Schwimmer, unpublished MS, op. cit. For criticism of Rosika Schwimmer see letter to Chrystal Macmillan, probably from Kathleen Courtney, June 15th, 1915, File D/Mar/4/1, Marshall papers, Cumbria Record Office, Carlisle. See also Barbara Kraft, *The Ford Peace Ship*, Macmillan, 1978; Snowden, *A Political Pilgrim in Europe*, op. cit.; and Jane Addams, *Peace and Bread in Time of War*, Macmillan, 1922.

13 Letter quoted in Ray Strachey, *Millicent Garrett Fawcett*, John Murray, 1931, p. 301. Ann Oakley analyses the NUWSS President's character in *Feminist Theorists*, ed. Dale Spender, The Women's Press, 1983, p. 184.

14 Minutes of NUWSS executive meeting end July/beginning August 1914, show that the Union only agreed to co-

operate on condition that '(1) nothing in the resolution involved support of any particular policy in relation to the war (2) that it was made clear that each speaker spoke only for herself or the organisation which she represented'. In other words, it was careful not to commit itself to opposing any policy the British government might decide, war or no war.

15 See Ruth First and Ann Scott, *Olive Schreiner*, Andre Deutsch, 1980, and John Fisher, *That Miss Hobhouse*, Secker & Warburg, 1971.

16 Some historians put more emphasis on European competition for the world market – especially between Germany's burgeoning colonies and Britain's established but threatened ones – as a cause for the war than others. Professor Fritz Fischer in *Germany's Aims in the First World War* (Chatto & Windus, 1967), argues that Germany had a long-term plan for war, whereas A.J.P. Taylor in *English History 1914-45* (Oxford University Press, 1965) describes the chain reaction of hostilities as almost accidental. See also *Britain and the Origins of the First World War* by Zara S. Steiner (St Martin's Press, 1977).

17 F.L. Carsten, *War Against War*, Batsford, 1982, p. 25.

18 Schwimmer, unpublished MS, op. cit., Box B20.

19 Quoted in Carsten, *War Against War*, op. cit., p. 24.

20 Schwimmer, unpublished MS, op. cit.

21 Ibid.

22 Ibid.

23 Ibid.

24 Ibid.

Chapter two: Enemy alien

1 Leaflet, *Britain's Stand for Peace: The Woman's Voice*, Box A39, General Correspondence 1914, Schwimmer/Lloyd Collection, New York Public Library; Rosika Schwimmer, unpublished, unfinished MS, Box B20, New York Public Library; Helena Swanwick, *I Have Been Young*, Gollancz, 1935.

2 Ray Strachey, *Millicent Garrett Fawcett*, John Murray, 1931, pp. 274-5.

3 Ibid.

4 Box A39, General Correspondence 1914, Schwimmer/Lloyd Collection, op. cit.

5 Schwimmer, unpublished MS, op. cit.

6 Schwimmer to Fawcett (copy), August 5th, 1914; General Correspondence 1914, Schwimmer/Lloyd Collection, op. cit.

7 Jo Vellacott-Newberry, *Anti-War Suffragists*, offprint from *History*, vol. 62, no. 206, October 1977, in the Fawcett Library, London, p. 416, n. 20.

8 *Common Cause*, August 14th, 1914, Fawcett Library.

9 NUWSS Report entitled *Suffragists and The War, What The National Union is Doing*, c. January 1915, D/Mar/3/43, Catherine Marshall papers, Cumbria County Record Office, Carlisle.

10 Swanwick's suggestion: Minutes of NUWSS Executive Meeting, October 15th, 1914, D/Mar/3/37, *ibid.*; The Union of Democratic Control was formed in August 1914 by Philip Morrel (Liberal MP), Ramsay MacDonald; Bertrand Russell, Arnold Rowntree, Charles Trevelyan, Arthur Ponsonby, Norman Angell and E.D. Morel. It was not a 'stop-the-war-movement' but was anxious that the eventual peace terms should ensure that a world war could not happen again. It wanted: terms which would not humiliate the defeated countries nor create borders which would cause future conflict; the end of the 'balance of power' defence policy; nationalisation of defence industries; disarmament; democratisation of foreign policy. At its inaugral meeting the UDC had 5,000 individual members; by autumn 1915, it claimed an *affiliated* membership of 300,000. See F.L. Carsten, *War Against War*, Batsford, 1982.

11 Letter from Schwimmer to Mrs Illingworth (copy), August 18th, 1914, Box A39, Schwimmer/Lloyd Collection, op. cit.

12 Rosika Schwimmer, 'To foreign women resident in Great Britain' (copy), Box A39, Schwimmer/Lloyd Collection, op. cit.

13 We only have Schwimmer's account of this incident which makes Mary Sheepshanks seem timid and conservative, which she was not, although she did have an abrasive temper and a sharp tongue. The British suffragists, having lived through the Boer War, knew all too well the excesses of the jingo mob spirit. Sheepshanks was no doubt afraid *of* Schwimmer and *for* her. However, Schwimmer never let Sheepshanks into her confidence again.

14 Fawcett to Schwimmer, August 9th, 1914, Box A37, Schwimmer/Lloyd Collection, op. cit. On August 24th, Chrystal Macmillan wrote to Rosika Schwimmer,

I was also asked to let you know from the Committee that although Mrs Fawcett's letter accepting your resignation had meant the resignation to take effect from the date of the letter, it had not meant to exclude you from the office. The Committee at its previous meeting had had under discussion whether it was possible for you to do work at the office and the decision was pending when the meeting was interrupted. When you decided to go to America, the Committee did not think it necessary to discuss the question further. (General Correspondence 1914, Schwimmer/Lloyd Collection, op. cit.)

15 Box A38, General Correspondence 1914, Schwimmer/Lloyd Collection, op. cit.

16 In his book *History of England 1914-45*, A.J.P. Taylor comments on how atrocity stories were widely believed in the First World War, although not true, while the reverse happened in the Second World War.

17 Letter from Mrs Illingworth to Schwimmer, c. August 1914, Box A39, Schwimmer/Lloyd Collection, op. cit.

18 Schwimmer, unpublished MS, op. cit.

19 Schwimmer to Illingworth (copy), c. August 25th, 1914, Box A39, Schwimmer/Lloyd Collection, op. cit.

20 Hardie to Schwimmer (then in New York), undated, Box A39, Schwimmer/Lloyd Collection, op. cit.

21 Schwimmer, unpublished MS, op. cit.

22 *The Autobiography of Bertrand Russell* (1975), quoted in Carsten, *War Against War*, op. cit., p. 32.

23 See Carsten, *War Against War*, op. cit., chapter 1.

24 Dame Christabel Pankhurst, *Unshackled: The Story of How We Won The Vote*, ed. by Rt. Hon. Lord Pethick-Lawrence of Peaslake, Hutchinson, 1959, p. 288.

25 *The Suffragette*, 19th June 1914, vol. 3, no. 88, p. 163, Fawcett Library, London.

26 Ibid., August 7th, 1914.

27 Quoted in Rupert Butler, *As They Saw Her: Emmeline Pankhurst*, Harrap, 1970, pp. 100-1.

28 Pankhurst, *Unshackled*, op. cit., p. 288.

29 Women's Suffrage Collection, London Museum, folder, *Demonstrations and Political Action*, E. Pankhurst, 13th

August, 1914, quoted in Andrew Rosen, *Rise Up Women!*, Routledge & Kegan Paul, 1974, p. 248.

30 K. Marion, unpublished MS, London Museum, 50.82/1124, quoted in Rosen, *Rise Up Women!*, op. cit., p. 252.

31 Annie Bell incident, in David Mitchell, *Women on the Warpath*, Cape, 1966, p. 50; protest meetings, in Rosen, *Rise Up Women!*, op. cit., pp. 252-3.

32 Sylvia Pankhurst, *The Home Front*, Hutchinson, 1932, p. 66.

33 *Manchester Guardian*, September 9th, 1914, quoted in Rosen, *Rise Up Women!*, op. cit., p. 250.

34 Quoted in Butler, *As They Saw Her*, op. cit., p. 103.

35 Swanwick, *I Have Been Young*, op. cit., p. 187-8; *Britannia*, March 17th, 1916, Fawcett Library, London; Mitchell, *Women on the Warpath*, op. cit., p. 45.

36 Interview with *Weekly Dispatch* quoted in Butler, *As They Saw Her*, op. cit., p. 113.

37 Christabel Pankhurst speech at Carnegie Hall, New York, 24th October, 1914 and Emmeline Pankhurst interview, 'Why women should be mobilized', *Sketch*, March 23rd, 1915, quoted in Rosen, *Rise Up Women!*, op. cit., p. 251.

38 Pankhurst, *The Home Front*, op. cit., p. 66.

39 Adela Pankhurst was five years younger than Christabel; three years younger than Sylvia. A teacher, she emigrated to Australia and joined a Women's Peace Crusade there. She was sentenced to nine months' imprisonment with another ex-WSPU organiser, Jennie Baines, for marching on the Australia Parliament to demand a more equitable rationing system.

Chapter three: American incredulity

1 *New York Times*, September 19th, 1914.

2 Quoted in Marie Louise Degen, *The History of the Woman's Peace Party* (1939), New York Public Library.

3 *Jus Suffragii*, September 1914, Fawcett Library, London.

4 Mia Leche, *Den Kinesiska Muren*, Stockholm, 1917, pp. 82-9, quoted in 'Out of the trenches by Christmas' (p. 32), an article by Edith Wynner published in *The Progressive*, 1965; see also *Jus Suffragii*, June 1st, 1915, p. 300.

5 Barbara Kraft, *The Ford Peace Ship*, Macmillan, 1978, p. 13; Box E4, Schwimmer/Lloyd Collection, New York Public Library, Rosika Schwimmer speech on Ford Peace Ship.

6 Winston Churchill, *World Crisis*, vol. 1, ch. 2, quoted in Kraft, *The Ford Peace Ship*, op. cit., p. 12.

7 Allen F. Davis, *American Heroine: The Life and Legend of Jane Addams*, Oxford University Press, 1973. Rosika Schwimmer was one of the few to criticise Jane Addams; she disliked visiting Hull House because it reminded her of her old convent school. Carrie Chapman Catt called Addams 'slippery Jane'. Edith Wynner, research notes.

8 Jane Addams, *Peace and Bread in Time of War*, Macmillan, 1932.

9 Ibid.

10 See Blanche Wiesen Cook (ed.), *Crystal Eastman: On Women & Revolution*, Oxford University Press, 1978.

11 Quoted in Degen, *The History of the Women's Peace Party*, op. cit.

12 Jane Addams to Rosika Schwimmer, Dec. 11th, 1914, General Correspondence 1914, Schwimmer/Lloyd Collection, op. cit.

13 Emmeline Pethick-Lawrence to Jane Addams, December 1st, 1915, Addams papers, Swarthmore College Peace Collection, Swarthmore, Pennsylvania. Quoted in Kraft, *The Ford Peace Ship*, op. cit., p. 10.

14 Thanks to Edith Wynner for pointing this out to me.

15 Helena Swanwick, *I Have Been Young*, Gollancz, 1935.

16 Quoted in Degen, *The History of the Woman's Peace Party*, op. cit.

17 Ibid.

18 Ibid.

19 Addams, *Peace and Bread*, op. cit.

Chapter four: Bitter divide

1 *Jus Suffragii*, November 1st, 1914, p. 184, Fawcett Library, London.

2 Ibid., p. 188.

3 *Jus Suffragii*, December 1st, 1914, p. 207.

4 John Williams, *The Home Fronts, 1914-18*, Constable, 1972, p. 28.

5 The Irish Women's Franchise League took a somewhat different line and publicly declared that war was a 'negation of the women's movement'.

6 *Jus Suffragii*, November 1st, 1914, front page; *Jus Suffragii*, December 1st, 1914, p. 200.

7 Ibid. and *Jus Suffragii*, January 1st, 1915, p. 228.
8 January/February 1915, Rosika Schwimmer General Correspondence, Schwimmer/Lloyd Collection, New York Public Library.
9 *Jus Suffragii*, December 1st, 1914, p. 200.
10 *Labour Leader* (the ILP newspaper), *The Tribunal* (the No Conscription Fellowship newspaper) and the *Daily Herald* were the only newspapers to oppose the war.
11 Typescript by Mary Sheepshanks by kind permission of Sybil Oldfield, who has written a biography of her entitled *Spinsters of This Parish* (Virago, 1984).
12 Union of Democratic Control in Britain, Bund Neues Vaterland in Germany and Anti-Oorlog Raad in Holland.
13 Box E40, Schwimmer/Lloyd Collection, op. cit.
14 John Fisher, *That Miss Hobhouse*, Secker & Warburg, 1971, pp. 234-7.
15 *Labour Leader* also published greetings from Karl Liebknecht, Rosa Luxemburg, Clara Zetkin and Franz Mehring, the four most prominent German radical left leaders and virtually the only German socialists openly criticising the war at this time.
16 General Correspondence 1914, Schwimmer/Lloyd Collection, op. cit.
17 Eugenie Hamer and Marguerite Sarter were two of the Belgians and Dr Mia Boissevain and Rosa Manus were active in leading the Dutch group along with Aletta Jacobs.
18 Isabella Ford to Catherine Marshall, October 25th, 1914, File D/Mar/4/1, Catherine Marshall papers, Cumbria County Record Office, Carlisle. (Isabella Ford was not Catherine Marshall's real aunt.) *Anti-war Suffragists* by Jo Vellacott-Newberry, an offprint from *History*, vol. 62, no. 206, October 1977, in the Fawcett Library, London, gives an account of the NUWSS split.
19 Alice Clark to Catherine Marshall, November 15th, 1914, File D/Mar/4/1, Marshall papers, op. cit. Alice Clark was formerly Assistant Secretary to the NUWSS Election Fighting Fund. During the war she was a research student at the London School of Economics. She had also lived with Mary Sheepshanks at Barton Street.
20 Minutes of NUWSS executive meeting on November 4th, 1914, File D/Mar/3/39, Marshall papers, op. cit.
21 See Minutes of Provincial Council, November 12th, 1914,

Marshall papers, op. cit.

22 Minutes of NUWSS executive committee meeting on November 4th, 1914, p. 4, File D/Mar/3/39, Marshall papers, op. cit.

23 Catherine Marshall to Millicent Fawcett (copy), November 28th, 1914, File D/Mar/3/39, Marshall papers, op. cit.

24 The phrase 'right instead of might' was used frequently in the arguments of the internationalists, for example in Catherine Marshall's plans for a Women's Independent Party, File D/Mar/3/45 (copy), Marshall papers, op. cit.; thanks to Jo Vellacott for her comments here.

25 Minutes of NUWSS executive meeting on November 14th, 1914, p. 1.

26 Notes for speech to North-Eastern Federation of NUWSS, January 26th, 1915.

27 Eleanor Rathbone to Catherine Marshall, November 14th, 1914, File D/Mar/3/39, Marshall papers, op. cit.

28 Catherine Marshall to Millicent Fawcett (copy), November 28th, 1914, File D/M/3/39, Marshall papers, op. cit.

29 Minutes of NUWSS executive meeting on December 3rd, 1914, Fawcett Library, London.

30 Printed in Ray Strachey, *Millicent Garrett Fawcett*, John Murray, 1931, pp. 283-4.

31 Millicent Fawcett did not write about the NUWSS split in her autobiography and the only account of her views and feelings, besides a few letters, is in Ray Strachey's biography, *Millicent Garrett Fawcett*, op. cit. Strachey was a friend of Fawcett's and 'on her side' over the war issue.

32 *Jus Suffragii*, March 1st, 1915, p. 250.

33 See Agenda for Annual Council with Catherine Marshall's pencilled comments, Marshall papers, op. cit.

34 Catherine Marshall to Millicent Fawcett (copy), March 3rd, 1915, File D/Mar/3/45, Marshall papers, op. cit.

35 Strachey, *Millicent Garrett Fawcett*, op. cit., p. 289.

36 Catherine Marshall to unknown correspondent (draft), undated, File D/Mar/3/43, Marshall papers, op. cit.

37 Minutes of NUWSS executive meeting on March 6th, 1915, p. 3, Fawcett Library, London.

38 Caroline Marshall to Catherine Marshall, undated, File D/Mar/3/43, Marshall papers, op. cit.

39 Correspondence between Mrs Fawcett and Miss Marshall circulated to the executive committee on March 3rd, 1915,

File D/Mar/3/45, Marshall papers, op. cit.

40 Draft outline for Women's Independent Party, File D/Mar/3/45, Marshall papers, op. cit.

41 Helena Swanwick to Catherine Marshall, 5th April, 1915, File D/Mar/3/45, Marshall papers, op. cit.

42 'Correspondence between Mrs Fawcett and Miss Marshall circulated to the Executive Committee', March 3rd, 1915, File D/Mar/3/45, Marshall papers, op. cit.

43 See Minutes of NUWSS executive meeting on March 4th, 1915, Fawcett Library, London. Marshall and Courtney were not mentioned in the official NUWSS history, and a year later, Fawcett refused to even see Courtney (thanks to Jo Vellacott for pointing this out to me).

44 According to a list compiled by Catherine Marshall at a meeting of the internationalists on May 9th, 1915 (File D/Mar/3/46, Marshall papers) those who strongly opposed talk of peace were Millicent Fawcett, Lady Frances Balfour, Ray Strachey, Miss Palliser, Mrs Auerbach and Miss Atkinson. The resigning members were Margaret Ashton, Isabella Ford, Alice Clark, Kathleen Courtney, Cary Schuster, Mrs Harley, Catherine Marshall, Emily Leaf, Helena Swanwick, Maude Royden, Miss Tanner and Mrs Stanbury. The members of the executive on May 9th who were progressive, or at least not obstructive, were Chrystal Macmillan, Mrs Rackham, Mrs V. Jones, Miss Fry, Miss Tuke and Mrs Osler (but Catherine Marshall put question marks after all but the first two).

45 Helena Swanwick to Catherine Marshall, March 22nd and 23rd, 1915, File D/Mar/3/45, Marshall papers, op. cit.

46 Catherine Marshall to Millicent Fawcett (copy), March 26th, 1915, File D/Mar/3/44, Marshall papers, op. cit.

47 Kathleen Courtney to Catherine Marshall, April 6th, 1915, ibid.

48 Alice Clark to Catherine Marshall, March 29th, 1915, ibid.

49 Emily Leaf to Catherine Marshall, April 5th, 1915, ibid.

50 Minutes of NUWSS executive committee meeting, April 15th, 1915, p. 8, Fawcett Library, London.

51 Ibid.

52 Millicent Fawcett to Miss Atkinson, February 19th, 1916, Fawcett Library, London.

53 Minutes of NUWSS executive committee meeting April 15th, 1915; Cary Schuster to Catherine Marshall (c. May

9th, 1915); Cary Schuster says she had to resign from the Chair of her local committee in Berkshire because the committee passed a resolution expressing complete confidence in Mrs Fawcett's leadership and it was made clear to her she was not wanted as an officer. 'I believe roughly speaking, the NU is divided geographically – the North are anti-militarist and the South pro-war.' Bristol and Weston-super-Mare appear to be the only southern societies protesting about not being able to attend the Hague Congress. The first mention of the peace question in the NUWSS appears to have been raised by Ethel Williams from Newcastle on October 6th, 1914, writing to say that prominent NU members in that area wanted to set up a UDC branch if they could guarantee equal treatment for women and men (File D/Mar/3/37). See also Minutes of NUWSS executive committee, May 6th, 1915 for letters supporting Millicent Fawcett.

54 Catherine Marshall to Millicent Fawcett (copy), March 26th, 1915, File D/Mar/3/44, Marshall papers, op. cit.

55 *Questions to Be Addressed to Candidates For Election to the National Union Executive Committee*, February 1915, sent to Catherine Marshall by Ray Strachey on December 31st, 1914, Marshall papers, op. cit.

56 Notes for speech to North-Eastern Federation of Women's Suffrage Societies, January 26th, 1915, Marshall papers, op. cit.

57 Minutes of informal meeting of ex-executive members at Sesame Club, May 9th, 1915, File D/Mar/3/46, Marshall papers, op. cit.; see also Catherine Marshall's notes on proposing to *formally* split the Union.

58 Alice Clark to Catherine Marshall, undated, File D/Mar/3/46, Marshall papers, op. cit.

59 The only source I have been able to trace on this is the account in Ray Strachey's *Millicent Garrett Fawcett*, op. cit. The records of the NUWSS for the June 1915 Council Meeting have been destroyed.

60 Kathleen Courtney to Chrystal Macmillan (copy), June 15th, 1915, Marshall papers, op. cit.

61 M.A. Marshall to C. Marshall, June 29th, 1915, Marshall papers, op. cit.

Chapter five: Meeting across enemy lines

1 *The Suffragette*, April 16th, 1915, editorial under the subheading 'Our country is our temple'. Fawcett Library, London.

2 Ibid., April 23rd, 1915 issue, p. 26. Fawcett Library, London.

3 Sylvia Pankhurst, *The Home Front*, Hutchinson, 1932, p. 150.

4 British Committee of the Women's International Congress, *Towards Permanent Peace: A Record of the Women's International Congress*, p. 5. Fawcett Library, London.

5 *Daily Express*, April 24th, 1915.

6 Pankhurst, *The Home Front*, op. cit., p. 152.

7 Jane Addams quoted in *Chicago Record Herald*, April 13, 1915, printed in M. Randall, *Improper Bostonian: Emily Greene Balch*, Twayne Publishers, 1964, p. 144.

8 Quoted from the *Boston Herald* by the *New York Times* on April 29th, 1915 and reprinted from Marie Louise Degen, *The History of the Woman's Peace Party*, New York Public Library, 1939.

9 Box A60, Frida Perlen to Rosika Schwimmer, March 2nd, 1915, Schwimmer/Lloyd Collection, New York Public Library.

10 Carrie Chapman Catt to Aletta Jacobs, March 2nd, 1915, ibid.

11 See Evelyn Sharp's summary of the Congress and the British press in BCWIC, *Towards Permanent Peace*, op. cit., p. 20.

12 *Daily Express*, April 27th, 1915.

13 Ibid., April 30th, 1915.

14 Ibid., April 28th, 1915.

15 *Jus Suffragii*, June 1st, 1915, p. 300.

16 Box 0-112, Lola Maverick Lloyd Diary, Schwimmer/Lloyd Collection, op. cit.

17 See the statement issued by the British Committee on April 26th and reprinted the next day, in full, by the *Manchester Guardian*.

18 BCWIC, *Towards Permanent Peace*, op. cit., p. 10. There is also a report of the Hague Congress in the June 1st issue of *Jus Suffragii*: on pp. 301-2 the full list of resolutions can be found.

19 Alice Hamilton to Mary R. Smith, May 5th, 1915, Jane Addams papers, Swarthmore College Peace Collection,

Swarthmore, USA. From Edith Wynner research notes. I am uncertain whether the pamphlet entitled *International Plan for Continuous Mediation without Armistice* in the British Foreign Office files of 1915 is the article referred to here or whether the pamphlet was written later.

20 Impromptu speech by Rosika Schwimmer in the dining-room on board *Oscar II*, the boat hired for the Henry Ford Peace Expedition, on December 6th, 1915. Box E4, Schwimmer/Lloyd Collection, op. cit.

21 BCWIC, *Towards Permanent Peace*, op. cit., p. 15.

22 Jane Addams, Emily Balch and Alice Hamilton, *Women At The Hague*, Macmillan, 1915, p. 16.

23 *Report of the International Congress of Women* (The Hague, 1915), Fawcett Library, London, p. 314.

24 BCWIC, *Towards Permanent Peace*, op. cit., p. 3.

25 Schwimmer speech December 6th, 1915, op. cit.

26 BCWIC, *Towards Permanent Peace*, op. cit., p. 20.

27 Box 0-112, Lola Maverick Lloyd Diary, Schwimmer/Lloyd Collection, op. cit.

28 *Report of the International Congress of Women*, op. cit., p. 173.

29 Ibid.

30 Ibid.

31 Box 0-112, Lola Maverick Lloyd Diary, Schwimmer/Lloyd Collection, op. cit.

Chapter six: To the rulers of Europe

1 Impromptu speech by Rosika Schwimmer in the dining-room on board *Oscar II*, the boat hired for the Henry Ford Peace Expedition, on December 6th, 1915. Box E4, Schwimmer/Lloyd Collection, New York Public Library.

2 Quoted in William B. Lloyd, Jr., *Peace Requires Peacemakers*, p. 16, one of a series of papers on peace published with the assistance of the Laucks Fund by the Center for the Study of Democratic Institutions, Santa Barbara, California. Thanks to Edith Wynner for sending me this.

3 Schwimmer speech December 6th, 1915, op. cit.

4 Catherine Marshall to Jane Addams, May 1915, Jane Addams papers, Swarthmore College Peace Collection, Swarthmore, USA. From Edith Wynner research notes.

5 Kate Courtney, *Extracts from a War Diary*, privately

published, 1927, p. 35, entry for May 18th, 1915.

6 *Proposal for a Conference of Neutral Governments*: extracts from the report of the delegates' interviews with the governments put together by Schwimmer and Macmillan for Knut Wallenberg, the Swedish Foreign Minister, on August 2nd, 1915, Schwimmer/Lloyd Collection, op. cit., from Edith Wynner research notes.

7 Princess Blücher, *An English Wife in Berlin*, 1920, p. 100, quoted in John Williams, *The Home Fronts 1914-18*, Constable, 1972, p. 94.

8 Courtney, *Extracts*, op. cit., pp. 42-3, entry for June 23rd, 1915.

9 Alice Hamilton to Family, May 31st, 1915 from Berne. Lillian Wald Papers, Manuscript Division, New York Public Library. Edith Wynner research notes.

10 Reprinted from Allen F. Davis, *American Heroine, The Life and Legend of Jane Addams*, Oxford University Press, 1973, p. 221.

11 *New York Times Magazine*, July 11th, 1915, interview with Jane Addams. Thanks to Edith Wynner for this.

12 Schwimmer speech December 6th, 1915, op. cit.

13 Ibid.

14 Emily Balch to Jane Addams, June 8th, 1915, en route from Stockholm to Petrograd, Jane Addams papers, Swarthmore College Peace Collection, Swarthmore, USA.

15 Jane Addams, Emily Balch and Alice Hamilton, *Women at The Hague*, Macmillan, 1915, p. 30.

16 Jane Addams in *New York Times Magazine*, July 11th, 1915.

17 Emily Balch to Jane Addams, June 8th, 1915, op. cit., a 'p.s.' by Chrystal Macmillan.

18 Telegram from Schwimmer to Hohmeyer for Lloyd, July 2nd, 1915, Box A65, Schwimmer/Lloyd Collection, op. cit.

19 *Proposal for a Conference of Neutral Governments*, August 2nd, 1915, op. cit.

20 Schwimmer/Lloyd Collection, op. cit.

21 Rosika Schwimmer Diary notes, July 30th, 1915, describing interview with Wallenberg on Wednesday, July 28th at 4:15, Edith Wynner research notes.

22 Ibid.

23 *Proposal for a Conference of Neutral Governments*, op. cit.

24 Ibid.

25 Rosika Schwimmer to Vilma Glücklich (copy), August 25th, 1915, Schwimmer/Lloyd Collection, op. cit., from Edith Wynner research notes, translated from the Hungarian by her.
26 Interview with Jane Addams in *New York Tribune*, July 6th, 1915.
27 The only complete version of the speech, which was transcribed in shorthand, is in an article entitled 'The revolt against war', in *Survey*, vol. 24, July 17th, 1915, pp. 355-9. Part is reprinted in *American Heroine*, op. cit., p. 226.
28 *New York Topics*, July 15th, 1915.
29 *New York Times*, July 13th, 1915; *Rochester Herald* (New York), July 15th, 1915.
30 Charles Seymour, *The Intimate Papers of Colonel House*, Boston, 1926-8, vol. 2, p. 22.
31 Box A77, Schwimmer/Lloyd Collection, op. cit.
32 See the very detailed *Wilson – Confusions and Crises 1915-1916* by Arthur S. Link, 1964. Also *Wilson – Campaigns for Progressivism and Peace 1916-1917*, by the same author, 1965, both published by Princeton University Press.

Chapter seven: Most dangerous pacifists

1 Internal Circular Letter, ICWPP. Thanks to Edith Wynner for sending me this. Box A66, Schwimmer/Lloyd Collection, New York Public Library.
2 Julian Bell (ed.), *We Did Not Fight: 1914-18*, Cobden-Sanderson, 1935.
3 There was repression in other German towns. Frida Perlen in Stuttgart and Marie Wegner in Breslaw had their local meetings broken up by police and were personally harassed. Writing of her German sisters after the war, Jane Addams said that Hague Congress delegates from one northern city were put in prison when they returned home from Holland.
4 Thanks to Edith Wynner for sending me her translation of Marguerite Gobat's report of the International Women's Conference in Berne on February 13th, 1919, in which German and Hungarian women outline their pacifist activities. See also *The Feminist Movement in Germany 1894-1933* by Richard J. Evans and *Rosa Luxemburg* by Peter Nettl. For German readers there is *Frauen gegen den Krieg* published by Fischer Taschenbuch Verlag and L. Heymann's *Erlebtes, Erschautes*, Anton Hain, 1978. For

details of the Italian and Scandinavian activities see *Towards Peace and Freedom*, the British report of the Zurich Congress in 1919, p. 4, in the Fawcett Library and Crystal Eastman's interview with Aletta Jacobs in *On Women and Revolution*, Oxford University Press, p. 239. Hopefully, feminist historians are working on the stories of their own national WILPFs, which will one day be translated into English. The International WILPF papers are at the University of Colorado Library, Western Historical Collections, Denver, Colorado.

5 Reference to West Lancashire: Captain B.S. Townroe to Kitchener, *Anti-Recruiting and Peace Propaganda 1914-19*, HO 10742/263275/61, Public Record office, London; Ethel Snowden, *A Political Pilgrim in Europe*, Cassell & Co., 1921, p. 2; Sylvia Pankhurst, *The Home Front*, Hutchinson, 1932, p. 369.

6 WIL yearly report October 1917 to October 1918; UDC affiliated membership, A. Linklater, *An Unhusbanded Life*, Hutchinson, 1980, p. 179; see also F.L. Carsten, *War Against War*, Batsford, 1982, p. 32. In July 1915, the number of *individual* members was 6,000; by the autumn of 1915, the associated membership was claimed as 300,000.

7 WIL Executive Committee: from yearly report October 1915 to October 1916; executive members besides those mentioned were 'Mrs Barton, Miss M. Bondfield, Lady Courtney of Penwith, Miss Marian E. Ellis, Miss I.O. Ford, Mrs Bruce Glasier, Miss M.H. Huntsman, Miss Eva Macnaghten, The Hon. Mrs Rollo Russell, Mrs Alfred Salter, Miss Sophy Sanger, Mrs Ethel Snowden, Mrs Mason Thompson, Mrs C.P. Trevelyan, Miss Helen Ward, Miss Th. Wilson Wilson'.

8 Thanks to Jo Vellacott for sending me her introduction to Irene Cooper-Willis's *England's Holy War*, republished by Garland Publishing, which has biographical details of Cooper-Willis.

9 Pankhurst, *The Home Front*, op. cit., p. 153.

10 Helen Crawfurd's unpublished autobiography, Marx Memorial Library, London.

11 Florence E. Lockwood, *An Ordinary Life 1861-1924*, British Library.

12 Jane Addams, *Peace and Bread in Time of War*, Macmillan, 1922, p. 147.

13 Helena Swanwick, *I Have Been Young*, Gollancz, 1935, p. 286.
14 *Daily Express*, November 25th-29th, 1915.
15 Swanwick, *I Have Been Young*, op. cit., p. 287.
16 HO 45/10814 312987, *Pacifist Activities of Mrs and Mrs Philip Snowden 1916-18*.
17 Swanwick, *I Have Been Young*, op. cit., p. 285.
18 HO 45/10743 263275/293.
19 WIL yearly report 1916-17.
20 Pankhurst, *The Home Front*, op. cit., p. 329.
21 David Mitchell, *Women on the Warpath*, Cape, 1966, pp. 64, 339-40.
22 Pankhurst, *The Home Front*, op. cit., p. 64.
23 *Labour Leader*, January 27th, 1916, p. 9; *The Guild in War and Peace. 3. The Road to Peace* (thanks to David Thomas of Coventry Polytechnic for sending this to me); *Labour Leader*, July 9th, 1916, p. 5. Labour Party archives, Walworth Road, London SE17. As yet there is no comprehensive study of how these working-class organisations responded to the war.
24 Carsten, *War Against War*, op. cit., pp. 67-9; the NCF started when Fenner Brockway wrote to the *Labour Leader* suggesting such an organisation (at Lilla Brockway's suggestion). For a while the organisation was run from their Derbyshire cottage with Lilla as secretary but response was so great that it moved to London.
25 Pankhurst, *The Home Front*, op. cit., p. 331.
26 Ibid., pp. 304-6.
27 C. Allen to H. Bryan, 10th August 1916, quoted in Carsten, *War Against War*, op. cit., p. 67.
28 C. Marshall to H. Swanwick, 7th September 1916, quoted in Thomas Kennedy, *Hounds of Conscience*, University of Arkansas Press, 1981, p. 148. Friends House, London.
29 See Jo Vellacott, *Bertrand Russell and the Pacifists in the First World War*, and her article 'Anti-War Suffragists', in *History*, vol. 62, no. 206, October 1977, Fawcett Library.
30 Jo Vellacott, *Bertrand Russell*, op. cit.
31 See Mitchell, *Women on the Warpath*, op. cit., pp. 331-46.
32 Helena Swanwick to Catherine Marshall, 5th August, 1916, D/Mar/4/78, Marshall papers.
33 Margaret Hills to Catherine Marshall, November 3rd, 1917, D/Mar/2/35, ibid. Margaret Hills was Margaret

Robertson before she married. She was a paid NUWSS organiser, and member of the ILP. The *Labour Leader* editor, Fenner Brockway, thought she would end up leader of the party. For more see Jill Liddington, *The Life and Times of a Respectable Rebel*, Virago, 1984.

34 Helena Swanwick to Catherine Marshall, September 9th, 1916, ibid.

35 *Labour Leader*, June 8th, 1916.

36 Helen Crawfurd's unpublished autobiography, Marx Memorial Library, London.

37 Ibid.

38 Ibid.

39 Ibid.

40 *The Woman's Dreadnought*, July 29th, 1916.

41 Ibid.

42 *The Woman's Dreadnought*, June 10th, 1916.

43 Figures from A.J.P. Taylor, *English History 1914-45*, Oxford University Press, 1965, p. 60 and Craig Mair, *Britain At War 1914-1919*, Murray, 1982, pp. 50-1.

Chapter eight: Keep America out!

1 Blanche Wiesen Cook (ed.), *Crystal Eastman On Women and Revolution*, Oxford University Press, 1978, p. 17.

2 Ibid., p. 14.

3 Chrystal Macmillan to Jane Addams, January 14th, 1916, Addams Papers, Swarthmore Peace Collection, Swarthmore, Pennsylvania. Thanks to Edith Wynner for pointing this out to me.

4 Jane Addams, *Peace and Bread in Time of War*, Macmillàn, 1922, p. 34.

5 Ibid., p. 38.

6 In *Peace and Bread* Addams writes that she had three years of semi-invalidism from pleuro-pneumonia from late 1915.

7 Ford to Wales, November 25th, 1915, Wales Papers, State Historical Society of Wisconsin, quoted in Barbara S. Kraft, *The Peace Ship*, Macmillan, 1978, p. 71.

8 Interview with Edith Wynner, February 1983 and letter to the author, November 12th, 1983. However, by mid-June, Schwimmer was well enough to join with other former members of the Neutral Conference to form the International Committee for Immediate Mediation, which

carried out confidential mediating missions.

9 Addams Papers, Swarthmore Peace Collection, Swarthmore, Pennsylvania, from Edith Wynner research notes.

10 Undated letter, Catherine Marshall papers, Cumbria County Record Office, Carlisle.

11 See Chrystal Macmillan to Jane Addams, January 14th, 1916, Swarthmore, from Edith Wynner research notes, and Allen F. Davis, *American Heroine: The Life and Legend of Jane Addams*, Oxford University Press, 1973.

12 Edith Wynner, 'Out of the trenches by Christmas', *The Progressive*, 1965, p. 33.

13 Julian Bell (ed.), *We Did Not Fight: 1914-18*, Cobden-Sanderson, 1935; see the chapter 'The Ford Peace Ship and after' by Lella Secor Florence.

14 Ibid., p. 112.

15 Ibid., pp. 112-13.

16 Ibid., p. 116.

17 Published in Mercedes M. Randall, *Improper Bostonian: Emily Greene Balch*, Twayne Publishers, 1964, pp. 217-18. No original source given. However, Emily Greene Balch did not side with Rosika Schwimmer when she visited the Ford Neutral Conference after Schwimmer had resigned, according to Edith Wynner.

18 Bell (ed.), *We Did Not Fight*, op. cit., p. 117. The letter was smuggled out of Britain and into America by Katherine Dudley; see Jo Vellacott, *Bertrand Russell and the Pacifists in the First World War*, Harvester, 1980, p. 149.

19 *Ogden Examiner*, January 15th, 1916, quoted in Davis, *American Heroine*, op. cit., p. 240.

20 Eastman, *On Women and Revolution*, op. cit., p. 13.

21 Ibid., p. 20.

22 Arthur Link, *Wilson – Campaigns for Progressivism and Peace 1916-1917*, Princeton University Press, 1965.

23 Quoted in Randall, *Improper Bostonian*, op. cit., p. 227.

24 Bell (ed.), *We Did Not Fight*, op. cit., p. 119.

25 Randall, *Improper Bostonian*, op. cit., p. 219.

26 Link, *Wilson*, op. cit., p. 305.

27 Bell (ed.), *We Did Not Fight*, op. cit., p. 120.

28 Addams, *Peace and Bread*, op. cit., p. 64.

29 Mary Gray Peck, *Carrie Chapman Catt*, H.W. Wilson Co., 1944, pp. 267-71. Catt co-operated with the government

throughout the war but seems to have exploited war propaganda for suffrage purposes, by arguing that the President said the US was fighting for democracy, so perhaps it should start at home. The National Woman's Party, however, refused all co-operation with the government, picketing the White House throughout the war and displaying banners comparing Wilson with the Kaiser when representatives from the Allied countries visited Washington. They were often imprisoned.

30 Chrystal Eastman, 'War and Peace', *The Survey*, December 30th, 1916, reprinted in Eastman, *On Women and Revolution*, op. cit., p. 253.
31 Randall, *Improper Bostonian*, op. cit., pp. 233-4.
32 John L. Heaton, *Cobb of 'The World'*, New York, 1924, pp. 267 ff, quoted in Randall, *Improper Bostonian*, op. cit., p. 232.
33 Addams, *Peace and Bread*, op. cit., p. 55.
34 Quoted in Eastman, *On Women and Revolution*, op. cit., p. 19.
35 *Four Lights* was banned under the American Espionage Act in May 1918.

Chapter nine: Hail the Revolution
1 *Yashka: Maria Botchkareva: My Life As Peasant, Exile and Soldier* as set down by Isaac Don Levine, Constable, 1919.
2 See report in November 1st issue of *Jus Suffragii*, pointed out in Sybil Oldfield, *Spinsters of this Parish*, Virago, 1984 (this book contains a biography of Mary Sheepshanks).
3 Jessie and Annie Kenney were sisters from Lancashire, who worked closely with the Pankhursts in the WSPU and during the war. For more on their trip to Russia see David Mitchell, *Women on the Warpath*, Cape, 1966, p. 65.
4 *Yashka*, op. cit., pp. 170-1.
5 Ibid.
6 *Programme for Women's Great Patriotic Procession*, July 17th, 1915, Fawcett Library, London.
7 *Labour Leader*, September 12th, 1916. Australian *Worker* quoted in *Labour Leader*.
8 Figures from 'Women At War 1914-18', a poster published by the Imperial War Museum; J. Bruce Glasier, *The Meaning of Socialism*, 1919, 6th impression 1939, quoted in Sheila Rowbotham, *Hidden from History*, Pluto Press,

1973, p. 110; Mitchell, *Women on the Warpath*, op. cit., pp. 197, 261, 267.

9 Rowbotham, *Hidden from History*, op. cit., p. 110.

10 Mitchell, *Women on the Warpath*, op. cit., pp. 261-2.

11 E. Royston Pike, *Human Documents of the Lloyd George Era*, Allen & Unwin, 1972, p. 182. This collection of documents gives a vivid picture of life for women during the war.

12 Ibid.

13 Quoted in Rowbotham, *Hidden from History*, op. cit., p. 119.

14 Catherine Marshall to Russell, undated [March 1917], Bertrand Russell Archives, Ontario, quoted in T. Kennedy, *Hounds of Conscience*, University of Arkansas Press, 1981, pp. 226-7, Friends House, London.

15 Rationing was not introduced on a national scale until April 1918.

16 WIL yearly report 1916-17, British Library of Political and Economic Science, London; *Jus Suffragii* quoted in Oldfield, *Spinsters of this Parish*, op. cit.

17 Sylvia Pankhurst, *The Home Front*, Hutchinson, 1932.

18 Jo Vellacott, *Bertrand Russell and the Pacifists in the First World War*, Harvester, 1980, p. 157.

19 Swanwick to Marshall, June 10th, 1917 and October 11th, 1917, File D/Mar/4/79, Marshall papers, Cumbria County Record Office, Carlisle.

20 Florence E. Lockwood, *An Ordinary life 1861-1924*, published privately, 1932, p. 210.

21 Swanwick to Marshall, June 10th, 1917, File D/Mar/4/79, Marshall papers, op. cit.

22 Quoted in A. Linklater, *An Unhusbanded Life: Charlotte Despard*, Hutchinson, 1980, p. 193.

23 In her unpublished autobiography, Helen Crawfurd wrote that the Crusade owed a great deal to Mrs McCree, 'a brilliant clever woman with great dramatic and artistic gifts', and two 'dramatic, spectacular tableaux' were organised. On one occasion, Crawfurd went with Agnes Dollan into the Glasgow Council Chambers whilst the town council was in session and showered leaflets on the councillors, shouting out demands for peace. Meanwhile, their supporters, who were standing outside with banners, were being jeered at by a jingo group called the 'Economic

League'. Manuscript in Marx Memorial Library, London.

24 *Daily Herald*, July 28th, 1917, Labour Party archives, London.

25 Birmingham demo reported in *Daily Herald*, July 14th, 1917.

26 Selina Cooper's Crusade activities are described in Jill Liddington, *The Life and Times of a Respectable Rebel*, Virago, 1984, p. 277; thanks to Jill Liddington for sending me proof copies of the book and for informing me of Cooper's attitude to the NUWSS during the war.

27 Quoted in Jill Liddington and Jill Norris, *One Hand Tied Behind Us*, Virago, 1979, p. 257.

28 *Daily Herald*, August 25th, 1917, p. 14; ibid., September 21st, 1917. (On October 6th, Sylvia's *Dreadnought* advocated a referendum on ending the war amongst troops at all fronts, which prompted a series of three police raids.)

29 *Daily Herald*, September 8th, 1917.

30 WIL yearly report, 1917-18, p. 15.

31 Quoted in Linklater, *An Unhusbanded Life*, op. cit., p. 197.

32 Swanwick to Marshall, February 5th, 1918, Marshall papers.

33 Ibid.

34 Swanwick to Marshall, March 4th, 1918, ibid.

35 Ethel Snowden, *A Political Pilgrim in Europe*, Cassell & Co., 1921, p. 3.

36 Marshall to Fawcett, February 7th, 1918, Fawcett Library, London.

37 WIL yearly report 1917-18, p. 15.

38 Thanks to Edith Wynner for sending me her translation of a report in *A Nö*, the Hungarian feminist pacifist journal, October 22nd, 1918 issue, pp. 129-30; see also British WIL yearly report 1917-18, p. 23. Helen Crawfurd and Emmeline Pethick-Lawrence had applied for passports, see letter from Swanwick to Marshall, March 4th, 1918, File D/Mar/4/80, Marshall papers, op. cit.

39 It's interesting to note the support WIL had for this demonstration from other organisations. On a national basis: National Amalgamated Furnishing Trades Association; Free Church League for Women's Suffrage; Christian Peace Crusade; plus various London branches of: The Women's Co-operative Guild; National Union of Railworkers; Society of Amalgamated Toolmakers; UDC;

ILP; Amalgamated Instruments Makers Society; London Jewish Trades Council.
40 See F.L. Carsten, *War Against War*, Batsford, 1982, pp. 181-7. This book uncovered new German archival material.
41 Linklater, *An Unhusbanded Life*, op. cit., p. 199.
42 Lockwood, *An Ordinary Life*, op. cit., p. 215.
43 Helena Swanwick, *I Have Been Young*, Gollancz, 1935, p. 307.

Chapter ten: At the foot of the mountain

 1 Helena Swanwick, *I Have Been Young*, Gollancz, 1935, p. 323.
 2 *Towards Peace and Freedom: Report of International Congress of Women, Zurich 1919*, Fawcett Library, London, p. 18; C. Despard, R. Genoni, J. Addams, C. Macmillan, C. Ragaz and G. Dûchene formed a delegation to take the resolutions to Paris.
 3 Florence Kelley to M.R. Smith, May 22nd, 1919, Swarthmore Peace Collection, Pennsylvania, quoted in Mercedes Randall, *Improper Bostonian*, Twayne Publishers, 1964, p. 264.
 4 *Towards Peace and Freedom*, op. cit., p. 19; in 'The Women at Zurich', an article published in *Survey*, June 14th, 1919 (thanks to Edith Wynner for sending me this) Mary Chamberlain, the writer, says there was a delegate from Argentina.
 5 Wilson's reply in *Towards Peace and Freedom*, op. cit., p. 162, quoted in Randall, *Improper Bostonian*, op. cit., p. 267.
 6 Ibid., pp. 246-8.
 7 Ibid.
 8 *Towards Peace and Freedom*, op. cit. Thanks to Edith Wynner for sending me this. During the Congress Aletta Jacobs was delighted to hear that Dutch women had been granted the vote. Suffrage victories could now be listed as Denmark (1915), Iceland (1915), Canada (1917), Britain (1918), Ireland (1918), Germany, Austria and Hungary (1918), and Poland (1919).
 9 Swanwick, *I Have Been Young*, op. cit., p. 319.
10 Emily Greene Balch, undated leaflet, no title (c. 1926) quoted in Randall, *Improper Bostonian*, op. cit., p. 273.

11 *New York Times*, November 30th, 1918 quoted in Allen F. Davis, *American Heroine: The Life and Legend of Jane Addams*, Oxford University Press, 1973, p. 255.

12 Alice Hamilton to M. Smith, May 12th, 1919, Addams papers, from Edith Wynner research notes.

13 Ibid.

14 Ethel Snowden, *A Political Pilgrim in Europe*, Cassell & Co., 1921, p. 83.

15 From a Report of the Berne Conference in February 1919 by M. Gobat. Thanks to Edith Wynner for her translation from the German.

16 I have not been able to trace exactly how many women were at this conference but there were delegates from Austria, Alsace, Britain, France, Hungary, Germany and Lithuania. Ethel Snowden and Margaret Bondfield were British delegates; A. Augspurg and L. Gustava Heymann came from Germany. In December 1916, there was also a conference among the Scandinavian Sections at Stockholm – see *Towards Peace and Freedom*, op. cit., pp. 433 and 437.

17 Randall, *Improper Bostonian*, op. cit., pp. 274-5.

18 Florence Holbrook to Rosika Schwimmer, June 6th, 1919, Box A149, Schwimmer/Lloyd Collection, New York Public Library, from Edith Wynner research notes.

19 Florence Kelley to Mary R. Smith, May 22nd, 1919, Addams papers, Swarthmore Peace Collection, Swarthmore, Pennsylvania, from Edith Wynner research notes.

20 Jane Addams, *Peace and Bread in Time of War*, Macmillan, 1922, p. 159.

21 Snowden, *A Political Pilgrim*, op. cit., p. 82.

22 M. Chamberlain, 'The women at Zurich', op. cit.

23 Randall, *Improper Bostonian*, op. cit., pp. 275-6.

24 Swanwick, *I Have Been Young*, op. cit., p. 318.

25 For a detailed history of the WILPF see Gertrude Bussey and Margaret Tims, *Pioneers for Peace*, first published in 1965 by Allen & Unwin, re-issued in 1980 by WILPF; see also Randall, *Improper Bostonian*, op. cit. and Sybil Oldfield, *Spinsters of this Parish: The Life and Times of F.M. Mayor and Mary Sheepshanks*, Virago, 1984. The International Secretaries based in Geneva were:
Emily Greene Balch   1919-1922
Vilma Glücklich   1922-1925
Madeleine Doty   1925-1927

Mary Sheepshanks	1927-1930	
Camille Drevet	1930-1934	
Emily Greene Balch	1934-1936	(on an unpaid basis because of lack of funds)
Lotti Birch	1936-1939	(when the Second World War stopped internatiol work)

For more information see *Pioneers for Peace*.

26 See Davis, *American Heroine*, op. cit. Emily Greene Balch took over from Jane Addams as President; Balch was also awarded the Nobel Peace Prize in 1946.

27 Thanks to Jo Vellacott for telling me this.

28 See Linklater, *An Unhusbanded Life*, op. cit.; article by Jill Craigie on Sylvia Pankhurst in *The Times*, May 1st, 1982; Blanche Wiesen Cook (ed.), *Crystal Eastman on Women and Revolution*, Oxford University Press, 1978.

29 Helena Swanwick, *Roots of Peace*, Cape, 1938, p. 181.

30 In Vera Brittan's *Testament of Experience*, the author states that Swanwick committed suicide but there is no other evidence for this.

31 Many were not 'absolute' pacifists in any case (see Introduction). When the British Quaker Edith Pye said what was 'going on in Germany and Austria' was worse than war, another British Quaker, Barbara Duncan Harris, replied that 'it wasn't worse than war, it *was* war'. See Chapters 14, 15 and 16 in Bussey and Tims, *Pioneers for Peace*, op. cit.

32 Mary Agnes Hamilton, *Remembering My Good Friends*, Cape, 1944, pp. 216-18.

33 Aletta Jacobs died in 1929.

34 Schwimmer's last speech reported in *Peace News*, July 23rd, 1948, Box 172.4(06), Fawcett Library, London. For biography see *Rosika Schwimmer World Patriot*, Fawcett Library; Schwimmer-Lloyd papers open for research, two articles in *World Peace News*, February and March 1974; 'Rosika Schwimmer' entry in *The Dictionary of American Biography*, Supplement 4. The Hungarian WILPF and Feminist Association was forced to dissolve in 1949 by the Soviet Hungarian Government. Eugenie Meller, who died at Auschwitz, was posthumously decorated for heroism by the short-lived, post-Second World War Hungarian Republic.

BIBLIOGRAPHY

Books

Jane Addams, *Peace and Bread in Time of War*, Macmillan, New York, 1922.

Jane Addams, Emily Balch and Alice Hamilton, *Women at The Hague*, Macmillan, New York, 1915.

Paul Adelman, *The Rise of the Labour Party 1880-1945*, Seminar Studies in History, Longmans, London, 1972.

Julian Bell (ed.), *We Did Not Fight: 1914–18: Experiences of War Resisters*, Cobden-Sanderson, London, 1935.

Maria Botchkareva, *Yashka: My Life as Peasant, Exile and Soldier*, Constable, London, 1919.

Gertrude Bussey and Margaret Tims, *Pioneers for Peace: Women's International League for Peace and Freedom 1915–1965*, first published by Allen & Unwin, London, 1965, re-issued by WILPF, 1980.

Rupert Butler, *As They Saw Her: Emmeline Pankhurst*, George Harrap, London, 1970.

F.L. Carsten, *War Against War*, Batsford, London, 1982.

Doris Nield Chew (ed.), *Ada Nield Chew: The Life and Writings of a Working Woman*, Virago, London, 1982.

Roger Chickering, *Imperial Germany and a World Without War: The Peace Movement and German Society, 1892-1914*, Princeton University Press, New Jersey, 1975.

Blanche Wiesen Cook (ed.), *Crystal Eastman on Women and Revolution*, Oxford University Press, 1978.

Kate Courtney, *Extracts from a War Diary*, for private circulation, 1927.

Allen F. Davis, *American Heroine: The Life and Legend of Jane Addams*, Oxford University Press, 1973.

Bibliography

Marie Louise Degen, *The History of the Woman's Peace Party*, Maryland College for Women, 1939.

Richard Evans, *The Feminist Movement in Germany, 1894-1933*, Sage Publications, London, 1976.

Fritz Fischer, *Germany's Aims in the First World War*, Chatto & Windus, London, 1967.

Wilfred Fest, *Peace or Partition: The Habsburg Monarchy and British Policy 1914–18*, St Martin's Press, New York, 1978.

John Fisher, *That Miss Hobhouse*, Secker & Warburg, London, 1971.

Frauen gegen den Krieg, Fischer Taschenbuch Verlag, Frankfurt am Main, 1980.

Mary Agnes Hamilton, *Remembering My Good Friends*, Cape, London, 1944.

Cate Haste, *Keep The Home Fires Burning, Propaganda in the First World War*, Allen Lane, London, 1977.

Leslie Parker Hume, *The National Union of Women's Suffrage Societies 1897-1914*, Garland Publishing, New York and London, 1982.

Alan Johnson (ed.), *Dictionary of American Biology*, Scriber Press, New York, 1945.

T. Kennedy, *Hounds of Conscience*, University of Arkansas Press, 1981.

Barbara Kraft, *The Ford Peace Ship*, Macmillan, New York, 1978.

Jill Liddington, *The Life and Times of a Respectable Rebel: Selina Cooper, 1864-1946*, Virago, London, 1984.

Jill Liddington and Jill Norris, *One Hand Tied Behind Us: The Rise of the Women's Suffrage Movement*, Virago, London, 1978.

Arthur S. Link, *Confusions and Crises, 1915–1916*, Princeton University Press, New Jersey, 1964.

Arthur S. Link, *Wilson: Campaigns for Progressivism and Peace 1916–1917*, Princeton University Press, New Jersey, 1965.

A. Linklater, *An Unhusbanded Life: Charlotte Despard: Suffragette, Socialist and Sinn Feiner*, Hutchinson, London, 1980.

Florence E. Lockwood, *An Ordinary Life, 1861-1924*, published privately, 1932.

Craig Muir, *Britain at War 1914–1919*, Murray, London, 1982.

Bibliography

A.J. Anthony Morris, *Radicalism Against War 1906–1914*, Longmans, London, 1972.

David Mitchell, *Women on the Warpath*, Cape, London, 1966.

Peter Nettl, *Rosa Luxemburg*, Oxford University Press, 1966.

Sybil Oldfield, *Spinsters of This Parish: The Life and Times of F.M. Mayor and Mary Sheepshanks*, Virago, 1984.

Christabel Pankhurst, *Unshackled: The Story of How We Won the Vote*, ed. Lord Pethick-Lawrence of Peaslake, Hutchinson, London, 1959.

R. Pankhurst, *Sylvia Pankhurst: Artist and Crusader*, Paddington Press, 1979.

Sylvia Pankhurst, *The Home Front*, Hutchinson, London, 1932.

Mary Gray Peck, *Carrie Chapman Catt*, H.W. Wilson Co., New York, 1944.

Emmeline Pethick-Lawrence, *My Part in a Changing World*, Gollancz, 1938.

E. Royston Pike (ed.), *Human Documents of the Lloyd George Era*, Allen & Unwin, London, 1972.

Mercedes Randall, *Improper Bostonian: Emily Greene Balch*, Twayne Publishers, New York, 1964.

E. Roper, *The Poems of Eva Gore-Booth*, Longmans, London, 1929.

Andrew Rosen, *Rise Up Women!*, Routledge & Kegan Paul, London, 1974.

Sheila Rowbotham, *Hidden from History: 30 Years of Women's Oppression and the Fight Against It*, Pluto Press, London, 1973.

Ethel Snowden, *Through Bolshevik Russia*, Cassell, London, 1920.

Ethel Snowden, *A Political Pilgrim in Europe*, Cassell, London, 1921.

Dale Spender (ed.), *Feminist Theorists: Three Centuries of Women's Intellectual Traditions*, Women's Press, London, 1983.

Ray Strachey, *The Cause*, first published by G. Bell & Sons, London, 1928, republished by Virago, London, 1978.

Zara S. Steiner, *Britain and the Origins of the First World War*, St Martin's Press, New York, 1977.

H. Swanwick, *I Have Been Young*, Gollancz, London, 1935.

H. Swanwick, *Roots of Peace*, Cape, London, 1938.

A.J.P. Taylor, *English History 1914-1945*, Oxford University

Press, 1965.

A.J.P. Taylor, *Picture History of the First World War*, Hamish Hamilton, London. 1963

D. Thompson (ed.), *Over Our Dead Bodies: Women Against the Bomb*, Virago, London, 1983.

Jo Vellacott, *Bertrand Russell and the Pacifists in the First World War*, Harvester, Hassocks, Sussex, 1980.

A. Whittick, *Woman Into Citizen*, Athenaeum, New York, with Frederick Muller, London, 1979.

J. Williams, *The Home Fronts 1914–1918*, Constable, London, 1972.

Articles and pamphlets

Jo Vellacott-Newberry, 'Anti-war Suffragists', *History*, October 1977, vol. 62.

Helen Ward, *A Venture in Goodwill, Being the Story of the Women's International League 1915–1929*, Women's International League, London, 1929.

Edith Wynner, 'Out of the trenches by Christmas', *The Progressive*, 1965.

Edith Wynner, 'Thirty-fifth anniversary of Hague Congress of Women', press release issued May 1950.

Edith Wynner, *Scholarship? Trivialization, Slander: A Critical Analysis of Barbara S. Kraft's History of the Ford Peace Ship*, unpublished, restricted circulation, December 12th, 1978.

INDEX

Index

Index

259

Index

Marshall, Caroline, 4, 73
Matters, Muriel, 151
Mead, Lucia Ames, 54
mediation, R. Schwimmer's open
    letter, 25; from individual
    countries, 111, 168, 169;
    Stockholm unofficial conference,
    158, 162
Mélin, Jeanne, 210
Meller, Eugenie Miskolczy, 216
Men's Political Union for Women's
    Enfranchisement, 39
Milholland, Inez, 154, 158
militancy, 1, 38, 178–9
Military Service Act, January 1916,
    142
Moore, Eleanor, 207
Morgan, Angela, 157
Morning Post, 59, 84
Morrel, Lady Ottoline, 83
Mott, Lucretia, 43
Munch, Elna, 20, 43, 58–9
Mygatt, Tracy, 175

National American Woman Suffrage
    Alliance, 46, 53
National Council of French Women,
    97
National Federation of Women
    Workers, 22, 83
National Peace Congress, 48
National Union of Suffrage Societies,
    2; mass resignations, 72, 77;
    members' reaction to split, 78–80;
    reaction to war, 22, 27, 28, 63,
    65–7, 70–2
New Statesman, 127
New York Times, 43, 170, 173
Newer Ideal of Peace, 48
No Conscription Fellowship, 131,
    141, 142, 145–6
Noordam, 86, 88
North Eastern Federation (NUWSS)
    65, 79
Norway, envoy visits, 110
Norwegian National Council of
    Women, 129
Norwegian women, 129, 206

Orlando, Italian Prime Minister, 200
Oscar II, Peace Ship, 158

pacifism, definition, 109; Anti-Orloog
    Raad (Dutch), 61, 117; Bund
    Neues Vaterland (German) 61,
    109, 117; criticism of, 32, 33, 47;
    general, 33, 139; Union of
    Democratic Control (British), 28,
    51, 77, 131
Page, Walter Hines, 88
Palmstierna, E., 113
Palthe, Wilhelmina van Wulfften, 116
Pankhurst, Adela, 42, 207
Pankhurst, Christabel, 1, 34; attitude
    to war, 36, 38, 39, 40; denounces
    pacifists, 179, 180; opposes
    Women's International Congress,
    83; works with Lloyd George, 186
Pankhurst, Emmeline, 1, 35; attitude
    to war, 36, 39, 40, 45, 180;
    criticised by WIL, 187; denounces
    Sylvia, 144; opposes Women's
    International Congress, 83, 139;
    visits Russia, 177–8, 179; women's
    suffrage, 194
Pankhurst, Dr Richard, 40
Pankhurst, Sylvia, 5, 6; criticises WIL,
    133, 134, 137; demonstrates
    against conscription, 142–3;
    demonstrates for equal pay, 182,
    184, 185, 190, 213; loses support
    for ELFS, 83, 84; reaction to war,
    42; resolutions to Women's
    International Congress, 85, 130;
    split with Christabel, 41
Park, Alice, 160
Passchendaele, 191
Pax International, WILPF journal,
    211
Peace Memorial, 138
Peace Negotiations Committee, 138
People's Council of America, 175
Perlen, Frida, 20, 63, 91
Pethick-Lawrence, Emmeline, 5;
    fights by-election, 185–6, 196; goes
    to US, 49, 51, 52, 83; in WIL, 131,
    185; at Women's International
    Congress, 96; at Zurich, 204, 210
Phillips, Marion, 22
Poincaré, French President, 35
Prisoners Temporary Discharge for
    Ill-Health Act 1913 (Cat and
    Mouse Act), 35

Index

195; worked with ILP, UDC, 131
Women's Labour League, 16, 22, 140, 195
Women's Peace Crusade, formation, 148, 151; philosophy, 151–2, 184, 187, 190
Women's Peace Meeting, August 4th, 1914, 22
Women's Peace Party (US): formation, 43–55; influences Wilson's policy, 54, 168, 175
Women's Political Union (US), 45, 53
Women's Social and Political Union, 5, 34; activities suspended, 37; attitude to war, 36–7; dissatisfaction from members, 38; pro-war demonstrations, 180
Women's Suffrage League (German), 128
Women's Suffrage National Aid Corps, 192

Women's war work (in Britain): conditions, 182; demonstrations, 180; Government appeal, 28; munition workers, 182; in NUWSS, 27; statistics, 181
Workers Suffrage Federation, 189
working-class women, 188, 189, 190, 193, 194
world government, Sylvia Pankhurst's views, 86; Rosika Schwimmer and, 216; in Women's International Congress 1915, resolutions (point six), 94

Yonker, Ralph, 158

Zampetti, Anita Dobelli, 21
Zetkin, Clara, 128, 140
Zietz, Luise, 57
Zimmerman telegram, 172–3

PANDORA

an imprint of Routledge and Kegan Paul

For further information about Pandora Press books, please write to the Mailing List Dept at Pandora Press, 39 Store Street, London WC1E 7DD; or in the USA at 9, Park Street, Boston, Mass. 02108; or in Australia at 464 St. Kilda Road, Melbourne, Victoria 3004, Australia.

ALL THE BRAVE PROMISES

memories of aircraftwomen 2nd Class 2146391

Mary Lee Settle

Mary Lee Settle was a young American woman living a comfortable life in Washington D.C. when the Second World War broke out. In 1942 she boarded a train, carrying 'a last bottle of champagne and an armful of roses', and left for England to join the WAAF. She witnessed the horror of war – the bombing raids, the planes lost in fog, the children evacuated, a blacked-out Britain of austerity and strain. She also witnessed the women, her fellow recruits, as they struggled to adapt to their new identities and new lives at the bottom of the uniformed pile. Dedicated 'to the wartime other ranks of the Women's Auxiliary Air Force – below the rank of Sergeant', this rare book captures women's wartime experience; a remarkable and important story by one of America's prizewinning novelists.

'One of the most moving accounts of war experience ever encountered' *Library Journal*

0-86358-033-5 General/Autobiography 160 pp 198 × 129 mm paperback

not for sale in the U.S.A. or Canada

DISCOVERING WOMEN'S HISTORY

a practical manual

Deirdre Beddoe

Rainy Sunday afternoons, long winter evenings: why not set yourself a research project, either on your own or in a group or classroom? This is the message from Deirdre Beddoe, an historian who tears away the mystique of her own profession in this step-by-step guide to researching the lives of ordinary women in Britain from 1800 to 1945. *Discovering Women's History* tells you how to get started on the detective trail of history and how to stalk your quarry through attics and art galleries, museums and old newspapers, church archives and the Public Records Office – and how to publish your findings once you have completed your project.

'an invaluable and fascinating guide to the raw material for anyone approaching this unexplored territory' *The Sunday Times*

'Thrilling and rewarding and jolly good fun' *South Wales Argus*

0-86358-008-4 Hobbies/Social History 232pp 198 × 129 mm illustrated

THE DORA RUSSELL READER

57 years of writing and journalism 1925-1982

Dora Russell

Dora Russell is one of the most remarkable women of this century. Her extraordinary life and work can now be appreciated in this, the first collection of her writings and journalism.

Dora Russell has campaigned tirelessly for peace since the First World War. In the 1950s she took the women's Caravan of Peace into Eastern Europe. In the 1980s she is as active as ever, as her passionate 1982 article on *The Challenge of Humanism in the Nuclear Age* demonstrates.

This book introduces a new generation to the powerful mix of intellect and compassion in the work of this courageous woman.

0-86358-020-3 Politics/Feminism 242pp paperback

MY COUNTRY IS THE WHOLE WORLD

an anthology of women's work on peace and war

Cambridge Women's Peace Collective (eds)

Women's struggle for peace is no recent phenomenon. In this book, the work of women for peace from 600 BC to the present is documented in a unique collection of extracts from songs, poems, diaries, letters, petitions, pictures, photographs and pamphlets through the ages. A book to give as a gift, to read aloud from, to research from, to teach from, *My Country is the Whole World* is both a resource and an inspiration for all who work for peace today.

'an historic document . . . readers will be amazed at the extent of the collection' *Labour Herald*

'a beautifully presented and illustrated book which makes for accessible and enlightening reading' *Morning Star*

0-86358-004-1 Social Questions/History 306pp A5 illustrated throughout paperback

TIME AND TIDE WAIT FOR NO MAN

the story of a feminist political weekly in the 1920s

Dale Spender

The magazine *Time and Tide* was founded as a feminist political weekly in 1920 by women who had been active in the battle for women's suffrage. It was to be a magazine run by women, for women, which would keep a sharp eye out for national and international developments as they affected women.

Its founders and contributors included Rebecca West and her sister Laetitia Fairfield, Cicely Hamilton, Emma Goldman, Vera Brittain, Winifred Holtby and Crystal Eastman.

Dale Spender takes us on a narrated journey through selections from the first fifteen years of *Time and Tide*.

0-86358-024-6   Social   History/Women's   Studies   287pp paperback